PREACHING
THE
GOSPEL
FROM THE
GOSPELS

PREACHING
THE
GOSPEL
FROM THE
GOSPELS

GEORGE R. BEASLEY-MURRAY

Preaching the Gospel from the Gospels was originally published by Epworth Press, London. The present edition is a complete reworking and expansion of that volume.

Copyright © 1996 by Hendrickson Publishers, Inc.
P. O. Box 3473
Peabody, Massachusetts 01961–3473
All rights reserved
Printed in the United States of America

ISBN 1–56563–166–8

First Printing — October 1996

Library of Congress Cataloging-in-Publication Data

Beasley-Murray, George Raymond, 1916–
    Preaching the gospel from the gospels / George R.
Beasley-Murray. — Rev. ed.
    Includes bibliographical references and index.
    ISBN 1–56563–166–8 (paper)
    1. Bible. N.T. Gospels.—Sermons. 2. Sermons, English.
I. Title
BS2555.4.B43   1996
251—dc20   96–10720
                                                  CIP

Unless otherwise indicated, all Scripture quotations are the author's own translation.

TABLE OF CONTENTS

Introduction   1

1   Preaching and the Writing of the Gospels   6

2   The Gospel in the Life of Jesus   30

3   The Gospel in the Miracles of Jesus   67

4   The Gospel in the Teaching of Jesus   106

5   The Gospel in the Parables of Jesus   167

Postscript   261

Bibliography   263

Index of Modern Authors   271

Index of Ancient Sources   274

INTRODUCTION

In the year 1954 I was invited by Baptist and Congregational lay preachers of London to deliver lectures on the theme "Preaching the Gospel from the Gospels." It was an exceptionally busy time for me then, but I was so intrigued with the title that I gladly agreed to prepare the lectures. The outcome of that was their publication in 1956. The book went through two editions, was translated into German, and finally was laid to rest.

In the early 1950s form criticism was still a dominant feature of Gospel criticism, and I had endeavored to exploit that discipline in a simple manner in the interest of preaching the gospel, i.e., the kerygma which lay at the heart of the Gospels. At that time redaction criticism was not on the horizon in Britain. When in later years I was urged to have the book reissued it was all too plain that it required to be revised and updated, and I was too preoccupied with other concerns to do the necessary revision. At length, however, Derek Tidball, then the secretary for evangelism of the Baptist Union of Britain, asked me to rewrite the book, and if other tasks precluded me from doing so he would arrange for a group to work on the theme and produce a symposium on it. Faced with such a request I felt compelled to embark on the former alternative. In the event I took the opportunity not only to enlarge the book considerably but also to widen its scope and make it of use to preachers generally.

Curiously, when undertaking the rewriting of the original book I found myself in the midst of yet another fresh development of Gospel studies. A major revival of interest in the historical Jesus was under way, resulting in a flood of publications on the subject. One was reminded how, in the early part of the twentieth century, Albert Schweitzer wrote a monumental work which in English bore the title *The Quest of the Historical Jesus*.[1] It was a devastating review of lives of Jesus that had appeared in the previous century, which he exposed as all too subjective. His attempt, however, to demonstrate the major mistake of the authors of those works on the life and teaching of Jesus was only partially successful. Whereas they had underestimated the significance of eschatology to Jesus, in his endeavor to correct their misunderstanding he actually distorted the teaching of Jesus on the kingdom of God and its effect on his ministry. Ironically, therefore, although Schweitzer had an immense influence on his contemporaries regarding the importance of eschatology he unwittingly led a whole generation astray on the authentic teaching of Jesus about the kingdom of God.

In the mid-twentieth century a new departure in gospel studies occurred. Ernst Käsemann challenged the belief that had arisen, doubtless influenced by form criticism, that it was no longer possible to recover a clear picture of the life and teaching of Jesus owing to the effect of Easter on the early church. Käsemann urged that a fresh inquiry should be made as to the significance of the historical Jesus for faith, for "only the proclamation of Jesus can enable us to encounter the historical Jesus and to comprehend his history."[2] An immediate response to this plea was made, and so arose a second quest of the historical Jesus.[3] That so-called second quest in fact was short lived, but what is now taking place is claimed to be a third quest, in which the variety of approaches to the life and teaching of Jesus formulated in recent years is being exploited to the full. Works, for example, utilizing literary approaches to the Gospels, notably structuralism, rhetorical criticism, reader-response criticism, and narrative criticism are being

---

[1]A. Schweitzer, *The Quest of the Historical Jesus: A Critical Study of Its Progress from Reimarus to Wrede* (2d ed.; London: A. & C. Black, 1911).

[2]E. Käsemann, "New Testament Problems Today," in *New Testament Questions of Today* (Philadelphia: Fortress, 1967) 9.

[3]See especially James H. Robinson, *A New Quest of the Historical Jesus* (London: SCM 1959).

enthusiastically applied to the Gospels, and commentaries from these angles are proliferating. Interest is increasing in the politics of Jesus and the social conditions of Jewish society in his time, the extent to which he involved himself in them, and the significance of this involvement for interpreting his teaching and his destiny.[4] Unprecedented attention is being given to non-canonical gospels, especially in the U.S.A., as sources for recovering the historical Jesus. To this end the Gospel of Thomas, Gospel of the Nazarenes, Gospel of Peter, and the Secret Gospel of Mark are being minutely examined. J. D. Crossan and H. Koester claim that many of the sayings of Jesus in these documents are not only independent of similar sayings in the Synoptic Gospels but even earlier and more authentic than they.[5] Understandably the substance of the teaching of Jesus is thereby considerably changed.

J. D. Crossan even maintains that he has isolated a source of the Gospel of Peter, which he names a Cross Gospel, and that it is a source of the passion narratives of all four canonical Gospels,[6] a position which is vigorously contested by a number of critics.[7]

Whereas since the mid-twentieth century a consensus of New Testament scholarship has maintained that the proclamation of Jesus centered on the kingdom of God, inaugurated in his ministry and coming in power in the future appearance of the Son of Man, debates about Jesus' teaching on the kingdom of God are setting aside established conclusions on very questionable grounds. B. L. Mack, for example, has set forth the proposition that Jesus distanced himself from the prophetic and apocalyptic tradition of the Jews, and holds that the impression that Jesus proclaimed the coming of the kingdom is due to Mark. In actuality, however, Jesus was a wandering Cynic sage who mocked and criticized the contemporary cultural views of his people.[8] Crossan adopted this position, and came to the conclusion that

---

[4]Note, e.g., Marcus J. Borg, "Jesus and Politics in Contemporary Scholarship" in *Jesus and Contemporary Scholarship* (Valley Forge, Penn.: Trinity Press, 1994) 97–126.

[5]H. Koester, "Apocryphal and Canonical Gospels," *HTR* 73 (1980) 105–30; J. D. Crossan, *Four Other Gospels: Shadows on the Contours of the Canon* (Minneapolis: Winston, 1985).

[6]J. D. Crossan, *The Cross That Spoke: The Origins of the Passion Narrative* (San Francisco: Harper & Row, 1988).

[7]See the discussion of Crossan's position in J. P. Meier, *A Marginal Jew: Rethinking the Historical Jesus* (New York: Doubleday, 1991) 1.116–18, 146–48.

[8]B. L. Mack, "The Kingdom Sayings in Mark," *Foundations and Facets*

> The Historical Jesus was . . . a peasant Jewish Cynic. His peasant village was close enough to a Greco-Roman city like Sepphoris that the sight and knowledge of Cynicism are neither inexplicable nor unlikely. But his work was among the farms and villages of Lower Galilee.[9]

There is, accordingly, some justification for seeing a parallel between the outcome of the first Quest of the Historical Jesus and much of the third one. When one surveys the varieties of interpretation that are on offer at the present time it is no exaggeration to describe the results thus far as leading to confusion, not to say chaos. J. P. Meier, in reviewing contemporary thought on the historical Jesus, affirms with his fellow critics the necessity of applying criteria of authenticity to the gospel records. His first such criterion is perhaps a surprising one, that of embarrassment, seen, e.g., in the baptism of Jesus by John the Baptist and Jesus' ignorance of the time of the end, Mark 13:32. In discussing this criterion Meier uses strong language.

> An intriguing corollary arises from these cases of "embarrassment." All too often the oral tradition of the early Church is depicted as a game of "anything goes," with charismatic prophets uttering anything or everything as the words of the Lord Jesus and storytellers creating accounts of miracles and exorcisms according to Jewish and pagan models. The evangelists would simply have crowned this wildly creative process by molding the oral tradition according to their own redactional theology. One would get the impression that throughout the first Christian generation there were no eyewitnesses to act as a check on fertile imaginations, nor original-disciples-now-become-leaders who might exercise some control over the developing tradition, and no striking deeds and sayings of Jesus that stuck willy-nilly in people's memories. The fact that embarrassing material is found as late as the redaction of the Gospels reminds us that beside a creative thrust there was also a conservative force in the Gospel tradition.[10]

It would require a much weightier volume than the present one to deal with the issues briefly mentioned in this introduction. They would demand more technical discussion and many more pages than are available for this book, and more importantly they

---

Forum 3 (1987) 3–47, and idem, *A Myth of Innocence: Mark and Christian Origins* (Philadelphia: Fortress, 1988) 125.

[9] J. D. Crossan, *The Historical Jesus*, 421–22. Crossan's view in this work is described and thoroughly approved by M. J. Borg in *Jesus in Contemporary Scholarship*, 32–36.

[10] Meier, *A Marginal Jew*, 169–70.

would deflect from the purpose for which it was written. Fortunately the majority of New Testament scholars are not swayed by every wind of doctrine. A splendid survey of contemporary approaches to the study of the historical Jesus is given in John P. Meier's three-volume work, *A Marginal Jew: Rethinking the Historical Jesus* of which two volumes have appeared at the time of writing and a third is awaited. That work is recommended to readers interested in the problems mentioned above. It is hoped that those who read this one will be stimulated to proclaiming with greater enthusiasm and effect the good news of God in Christ, and that "in Spirit and in truth."

1

PREACHING AND THE

WRITING OF THE GOSPELS

The preaching of the cross is . . . *nonsense!*" So
Paul learned from his contemporaries. How
could it be otherwise in his world with the proclamation of
salvation for all humanity through a crucified Jewish peasant in
the turbulent, far-off land of Palestine? Since Paul's day many
have found a pastime in attempting to demonstrate the alleged
nonsense of the Christian faith. The first literary opponent of
Christianity, Celsus, in the second century of our era, spent a good
deal of energy on this endeavor. Christians (and Jews) reminded
him of a swarm of bats, or ants creeping out of their nests, or frogs
holding a symposium round a swamp, or worms in a conventicle
in a corner of the mud! In his estimate their idea of the Incarnation was particularly stupid. "The comic poet, to make merriment
in the theatre, describes how Zeus waked up and sent Hermes to
the Athenians and Lacedaemonians; do you not think that your
invention of God's Son being sent to the Jews is more laughable
still?" The Christians' talk about life through the cross was one
stage worse. "If he had chanced to be thrown down a precipice, or
pushed into a pit, or choked in a noose, or if he had been a

cobbler, or a stone-mason, or a blacksmith, there would have been above the heavens a precipice of life, or a pit of resurrection, or a rope of immortality, or a happy stone, or the iron of love, or the holy leather! What old woman would not be ashamed to utter such things in a whisper, even when making stories to lull an infant to sleep?"[1]

In true succession to Celsus various modern agnostics have expressed their contempt for Christianity. Julian Huxley, commenting on the decline of the Christian faith in modern times, wrote, "God is simply fading away as the devil has faded before him." Yet, "a faint trace of God, half metaphysical and half magic, still broods over the world, like the smile of a cosmic Cheshire cat."[2] J. B. S. Haldane asserted with regard to the Christian doctrine of redemption, "God's goodness as shown in the incarnation exactly neutralizes his wickedness in demanding such a sacrifice."[3] I recall as a child looking in the window of a Secular Society hall, opposite the school I attended in the center of Leicester, in which were displayed citations from Christians with comments designed to ridicule them. One such instance was the beatitude of Jesus, "Blessed are the poor in spirit, for theirs is the kingdom of heaven," followed by the remark, "A typical example of the Christian ideal of man without guts." It took me years to overcome the revulsion I then experienced over the Beatitudes in the Gospels!

The uncultured man commonly shows respect for religion, still more for Jesus. But the coarseness shown by the soldiers who put on him what purported to be a royal robe, and a wreath of thorns on his head (in imitation of the emperor's laurel wreath of victory), and mockingly paid homage to him as to a Caesar from heaven, is far from solitary. In such a spirit a crude cartoonist of the Palatine depicted a slave bowing down to a crucified figure with a donkey's head; beneath the picture it was written, "Alexamenos worships his god!" While traveling in a public vehicle some years ago I heard a workman abuse Christian preachers as men who "kid the public with yarns that

---

[1] Origen, *Contra Celsum,* translated with an introduction and notes by Henry Chadwick (Cambridge: Cambridge University Press, 1953) 6.34.

[2] J. Huxley, *The Uniqueness of Man* (London: Chatto & Windus, 1941) 282.

[3] J. B. S. Haldane, *Science and the Supernatural* (New York: Sheed and Ward, 1935). I owe these two references to R. E. D. Clark, *Scientific Rationalism and Christian Faith* (Chicago: InterVarsity, 1951) 9, 52.

they don't believe, nor no one else neither—then skin them of every penny they can lay 'ands on!"

The preaching of the cross, then, is "nonsense." But to whom? *"To the lost!"* This judgment on the good news is given by individuals who have taken the wrong path in life and misunderstood the right one. Some of them live long enough to discover that what they thought was nonsense is in fact "the power of God" (1 Corinthians 1:18). Despite all that is said in defamation of the gospel, its heralds still find that it pleases God, by the "sheer folly" of the preaching, to "save those who believe" (1 Corinthians 1:21). The first time that the gospel of the crucified and risen Christ was preached—on the day of Pentecost—is a signal illustration of that fact. Peter's explanation of the phenomenon of the Christians' experience of the Holy Spirit on that day was to cite Joel's promise of the outpouring of the Spirit on the people of God (Joel 2:28–32). He affirmed that it had now been fulfilled, and went on to explain why it had happened: the promise of the salvation of God through the Messiah had also been fulfilled in the ministry, death, and resurrection of Jesus. "You killed him through handing him over to men outside the law, but God raised him from death . . . and made him Lord and Messiah" (Acts 2:23–24, 36). No wonder those Jews were horrified at hearing that. They asked, "Brothers, what are we to do?" Peter replied, "Repent and be baptized every one of you in the name of Jesus the Messiah so that your sins may be forgiven, and you too will receive the gift of the Holy Spirit." To be baptized "in the name of Jesus the Messiah" among other things signified owning him as Lord and Messiah and becoming one of his people; and so they did—they turned to God in repentance for their part in the rejection of the Messiah and were baptized in the name of Jesus, three thousand of them! That was prophetic of the impact that the preaching of Jesus crucified and risen was to make on the world.

"It pleased God by the foolishness of the preaching to save people," said Paul. Our intention in this volume is to consider the further proposition that *it pleased God by the foolishness of the preaching to give the world the Gospels.* These four slender works are the foundation documents of the historic Christian faith and the fountainhead of all preaching of the gospel. Consequently our discussion is more than an issue of academic criticism. It is relevant to all who teach or preach the word of God. It will not necessarily remove the "foolishness" from the gospel for those who view it so, but to grasp what happened and its implications for the Bible and the church should enable those who make it known to do so with increased effectiveness.

It is universally acknowledged by scholars today that the term "preaching" *(kērygma)* in 1 Corinthians 1:18–25 means the message preached rather than the act of preaching. The word was used by the Greeks for the proclamation of a herald, but it could be stretched to cover the act of preaching also (cf. Luke 11:32). Our thesis holds good in both respects. The proclamation of the earliest preachers became the material out of which the Gospels were produced, and it was because these men preached that the stories about Jesus and the teaching of Jesus, the bricks out of which the Gospels were constructed, were preserved for the world. The Gospels are the heritage bequeathed to humanity by the labors of preachers.

It was Martin Dibelius who first emphasized this and epitomized it in the statement, "In the beginning was the sermon," a deliberate allusion to the first sentence of the Gospel of John, "In the beginning was the Word." He, however, was at pains to make it clear that such an affirmation entails taking a broad view of the significance of the term "sermon": it includes every aspect of making the good news known, i.e., proclamation to people who do not know it (what we call nowadays evangelism); preaching in the context of Christian worship; and engaging in the kind of controversies which inevitably arose in the spread of the gospel among Jews, as also among Gentiles, when the church's mission extended beyond Palestine.[4] In all these activities the preachers will naturally have taken the foremost part; apostles in the first instance, since they had been the associates of Jesus, chosen and trained by him for this role in the mission he himself was sent to initiate; then teachers, many of whom in the beginning will have seen and heard Jesus in his ministry, and whose knowledge of the instruction given by Jesus will have been extended by the apostles (cf. 2 Timothy 2:1–2). Later this kind of function, in the tasks both of instruction and of worship, will have been a prime responsibility of elders and others, notably prophets, endowed by the Spirit with gifts for the service of the churches. In this way people learned about the life and teaching of Jesus and what it means to live under the saving sovereignty of God.

---

[4]M. Dibelius, *From Tradition to Gospel* (ET; New York: Scribners, 1935) 102.

Here it is desirable to make it plain that if it is right to affirm, "In the beginning was the sermon," the content of the "sermon" was not the bright (or not so bright!) ideas of the apostles and their associates and successors, but the revelation of the supreme Preacher, Jesus the Lord and Messiah. The fountainhead of the Christian message was the proclamation of the saving sovereignty (i.e., kingdom) of God which Jesus made known to his nation. Standing in the prophetic succession, he declared a message beyond that of any of his predecessors in the Old Testament or apocalyptic literature, namely, that God's promised intervention for the salvation of the world was now being inaugurated by the authority of his word. The declaration of Isaiah 52:7:

> How beautiful upon the mountains
> are the feet of the messenger who announces peace,
> who brings good news,
> who announces salvation,
> who says to Zion, "Your God reigns." (NRSV)

is taken up in the summary of the message of Jesus in Mark 1:15:

> The time of waiting is over,
> the kingdom of God has come upon you.
> Repent, and believe the good news.

The description of the kingdom of God as the commencement of the great year of Jubilee (Isaiah 61:1ff.) is read by Jesus in the synagogue at Nazareth; his exposition of the passage is summarized by Luke in a single sentence: "Today this scripture has been fulfilled in your hearing" (Luke 4:21). The inquiry of John the Baptist whether he was "the Coming One" was answered by Jesus in terms of the miraculous acts of God in the day of the kingdom, described in Isaiah 35:5–6, as now taking place in his ministry (Matthew 11:5). The ministry of Jesus was nothing less than the inbreaking of the kingdom of God, a process which came to its climax in his death and resurrection. That was the startling news which the earliest Christian preachers had to proclaim.

The discerning reader, however, will have perceived that the definition of the good news has been lengthened: what Paul described as "the preaching of the cross" has come to be the preaching of Christ in his ministry climaxed by his death and resurrection. Here a marked difference between the standpoint of the German and Anglo-Saxon New Testament scholars is observable; to the former the kerygma means the death and resurrection of Jesus the Christ for the salvation of humanity, to the latter it signifies the total ministry of Jesus, including his baptism, his message of the kingdom of God revealed in his words and deeds, climaxed by his death and resurrection and the sending of the Holy Spirit. In no small measure this difference was a corollary of the typical belief of German scholars, represented notably by Rudolf Bultmann, that Jesus proclaimed the kingdom of God exclusively as coming in the near future, whereas British scholars, influenced above all by C. H. Dodd, have been convinced that Jesus proclaimed the kingdom as breaking into history in his ministry–death–resurrection, and pressing on to its consummation in his coming at the end of history. Martin Dibelius, a pioneer in the method of study known as form criticism, even proposed that the earliest Christians' urgent expectation of the coming kingdom of God led them to understand the death and resurrection of Jesus as the beginning of the end of the world; hence the deeds of Jesus had only "incidental and not essential significance" and did not belong to the heart of the kerygma.[5] As a consequence Dibelius accepted Martin Kähler's intriguing description of Gospels as "passion narratives with extended introductions,"[6] leading a multitude of his colleagues to do likewise. One thing, however, should be clear to students of the Gospels in the light of further Gospel research: the writers of the Gospels did not so view the nature of a Gospel, for if they had their works would have been composed in very different ways. On the contrary, a reading of the Gospels leads one to affirm that the fundamental idea of a Gospel is the presentation of the facts of the ministry, death, and resurrection of Jesus with their saving significance. Let it be granted that the supreme moment of the revelation and redemption of God in Christ was the crucifixion–resurrection of the Son of God. Nonetheless, the Lord did not descend from heaven straight to Golgotha to accomplish the salvation of the world. It required the whole "Christ event," as theologians now describe the life, death, and resurrection of Jesus, to achieve that revelation and redemption, which in the language of Jesus should be termed the inbreaking of the saving sovereignty or kingdom of God.[7] That was the

---

[5] Dibelius, *From Tradition to Gospel*, 100.

[6] M. Kähler, *The So-Called Historical Jesus and the Historic, Biblical Christ* (ET Philadelphia: Fortress, 1964) 86 n. 11.

[7] Even the term "inbreaking" is dominical! The difficult saying Matthew 11:12 appears to involve a play on the Aramaic verb p^eras. The Hebrew equivalent *paraṣ* has the root meaning "to break through," especially of invaders breaking

burden of the early Christian "sermon," though naturally expressed in simpler terms. It was necessary for people to know how
God worked through Jesus in saving power, alike in the works of
his ministry and in the laying down of his life. The earliest
preachers of the gospel eventually came to understand that the
whole work of Jesus was a revelation of the kingdom of God for
the salvation of the world, and that it will be consummated
through his final coming—one unbroken series of acts of God in
Christ! That was the gospel they preached.

Here it is desirable to state briefly the contribution of C. H.
Dodd to our understanding of the gospel as preached in the
earliest church.[8] Beginning with the generally acknowledged assumption that the first generation of the church's existence was
dominated by oral tradition Dodd examined the writings of the
New Testament to seek out the earliest traces of the gospel proclamation (the *kērygma*), which he distinguished from the teaching
(the *didachē*). He found a surprising number of citations of primitive gospel traditions in Paul; comparing them with the early
sermons in the book of Acts he found a great deal of commonality
in the two representations. Three points above all were emphasized in the common proclamation:

(i) The hour of God's promised salvation has struck and
the kingdom of God has been opened for the world.

(ii) The Savior-Messiah has come. He is Jesus of Nazareth,
attested both by John the Baptist, the forerunner, and by the acts
of power which God did through him. Crucified for the sins of
humankind, he has been raised from death and exalted as Lord
of the universe. He is to come again for the judgment of the world
and the victory of his kingdom.

(iii) In face of this accomplished redemption and the
coming judgment, the appeal is made to turn to God, believe in

---

through a city wall, hence of Yahweh's breaking out in violent action (in judgment) and the violent action of men. This fundamental meaning continues to
appear in later Talmudic Hebrew and in Aramaic. It would appear accordingly
that Matthew 11:12 should be rendered: "From the days of John the Baptist until
now the kingdom of heaven is powerfully breaking into (the world), and powerful men are exercising force against it." See G. R. Beasley-Murray, *Jesus and his
Kingdom* (Grand Rapids: Eerdmans, 1986) 191–96.

[8]Dodd's views are set out in *The Apostolic Preaching and its Developments*
(London: Hodder & Stoughton, 1936). The book is very brief, consisting mainly
of three lectures delivered in King's College, London, in 1935, but it has exercised
enormous influence.

the Christ, be baptized for the forgiveness of sins, and receive the Holy Spirit, who is the Spirit of the kingdom of God (cf. Joel 2:28–32 with Acts 2:17ff.) and God's pledge of participation in the new creation (Ephesians 1:14).

This summary of the kerygma is most briefly stated by Paul in 1 Corinthians 15:3–4 (supplemented by other citations):

> I handed on to you as of first importance what I in turn had received: that Christ died for our sins in accordance with the scriptures, and that he was buried, and that he was raised on the third day in accordance with the scriptures. (NRSV)

Paul will presumably have "received" that formulation when he became a Christian in Damascus, but he will have had it confirmed—and a great deal more!—during the two weeks when he stayed with Peter in Jerusalem for fifteen days (Galatians 1:18). It is to be remembered that the phrase "according to the scriptures" conveyed not only the notion of fulfillment of the scriptures, but also that the time had come when the saving sovereignty of God promised in the scriptures would take place through the Messiah. Dodd thought it quite possible that this brief statement, followed as it is by a list of resurrection appearances of Jesus, is the conclusion of a summary of the gospel which may have included some reference to the ministry.[9]

The clearest example of the embodiment of the kerygma in an apostolic sermon is the record of Peter's preaching to the household of Cornelius in Acts 10:36–43. We take leave to reproduce it in full:

> You know the message [God] sent to the people of Israel, preaching peace by Jesus Christ—he is Lord of all. That message spread throughout Judea, beginning in Galilee after the baptism that John announced: how God anointed Jesus of Nazareth with the Holy Spirit and with power; how he went about doing good and healing all who were oppressed by the devil, for God was with him. We are witnesses to all that he did both in Judea and in Jerusalem. They put him to death by hanging him on a tree; but God raised him on the third day and allowed him to appear, not to all the people but to us who were chosen by God as witnesses, and who ate and drank with him after he rose from the dead. He commanded us to preach to the people and to testify that he is the one ordained by God as judge of the living and the dead. All the prophets testify about him that everyone who believes in him receives forgiveness of sins through his name. (NRSV)

---

[9] Dodd, *Apostolic Preaching,* 29.

It will readily be perceived that all that is required for the writing of a Gospel is to fill out this pattern of the kerygma with details of the Lord's life and with examples of his teaching. That, in fact, is what happened. The first of our Gospels, written by Mark, is an expansion of the outline of the story of Jesus such as that reproduced in Acts 10. Mark used John the Baptist's appearance as the starting point for his account of the ministry of Jesus, suitably prefaced by an Old Testament scripture "fulfilled" by John's ministry. He expanded the "acts of power" section by giving a brief sketch of the ministry in Galilee, and followed it with a detailed narration of the circumstances that led to the crucifixion. Some see that as beginning with the account of Peter's confession of Jesus as Messiah, since it is from that time that Jesus began to warn the disciples of his impending death (Mark 8:27ff.).[10] Mark's selection of the teaching of Jesus primarily relates to our Lord's message of the kingdom of God and the terms on which it is entered. Matthew and Luke reproduce the teaching of Jesus at greater length (they both had access to a source consisting almost entirely of sayings of Jesus), and have fuller accounts of the ministry of John the Baptist. They both preface their records of our Lord's ministry with accounts of his birth and round off their Gospels with narratives of the resurrection of Jesus. (We have no idea whether Mark provided any such conclusion to his Gospel. It is often thought that he did, and that the original end was lost or destroyed, or that he died before he could complete the work, or that he planned a further volume, as Luke did after him). As to the Fourth Gospel, it was Dodd's view that the primitive preaching concerning the Messiah and his redemption enters the warp and woof of his Gospel more completely than it does any of the others, in a manner we shall discuss shortly.

The point to be observed is that expansion of the primitive gospel by our evangelists in the second Christian generation was already begun by the earliest preachers in the first generation. As with the four evangelists, the crux of their preaching was the advent of the kingdom of God through the redemption accomplished by the Messiah. But from the beginning they will have illustrated the fact and the nature of his redeeming action by adducing incidents from Jesus' life and sayings. The choice will

---

[10] See especially the article of Rudolf Pesch, "The Gospel in Jerusalem: Mark 14:12–26 as the Oldest Tradition of the Early Church" in *The Gospel and the Gospels* (ed. Peter Stuhlmacher; Grand Rapids: Eerdmans, 1991) 106–48.

have been determined by the aspect of the good news emphasized at any given time and by the suitability of an event or saying to illustrate the theme.

To understand this aright we must be clear on one point, obvious enough when stated, but not always taken into account. In the earliest period of the church's life the acts and sayings of Jesus were recounted as occasion demanded. When we ponder the matter we realize that the situation could hardly have been otherwise. Whereas we are informed in the book of Acts that the Jerusalem Christians frequently met in the temple and heard the apostles, we can scarcely imagine that they listened to series of lectures on the life of Christ that provided day-to-day accounts, in precise historical order, of what Jesus had said and done. The apostles and other Christian preachers announced the good news to all kinds of hearers (even in the temple! Note the different groups addressed by the apostles in Acts 3–4). Much of the proclamation will have taken place in the open, as was the case with Jesus. Often it could have been for hours at a time, as open-air meetings are still prone to be prolonged by question and answer. Theirs will have been a spontaneous type of preaching, far removed from the reading of lectures. They had a wonderful theme, God's saving intervention in the midst of and for his people. For that topic they had dozens of illustrations from the life of their Lord. They poured them out in profusion as they declared what great things the Lord had done. There was no reason for excluding their own part in the incidents they narrated. Quite certainly they would frequently have told how they fitted into the picture, both for the sake of the added interest that a personal touch supplies and to ensure that their hearers knew that God had worked in their own lives as well as in those of others. What a story of this order Peter had to tell! Who of the apostles would have described his shameful denial of the Lord other than he himself? The story of his confession of Jesus as Messiah at Caesarea Philippi, with its utter misunderstanding of what the Messiah should accomplish, the account of his base denial of Jesus at the trial, followed by his restoration after the resurrection that humbled him to the dust, will have been told by the apostle time and again as he sought to make plain the reality of the Lordship of Jesus, the necessity of his sufferings precisely because he was the Messiah, the power of his risen life, and the completeness of his forgiveness.

For a modern preacher it is of importance that this process of the compilation of the Gospels be grasped, for it will determine his use of them. In a nutshell it is this: the works of Jesus in his ministry, leading to his death and resurrection and the glory to come at the final advent, are the acts of God for the redemption of the world; the words of Jesus in his ministry reveal the nature of God's redeeming kingdom, and the works of Jesus manifest that kingdom and show how it works itself out in people's lives.

Think for a moment from this point of view on the miracle stories of the Gospels. We shall deal with them in detail later, but the mention of some of them at this juncture will serve to make our point plain.

The whole group of stories in Mark 1:21–45 will first have been told to illustrate the power of Jesus to save, in the fullest sense of that ambiguous term. A demoniac is healed by a command from Jesus; the astonished onlookers cry, "What is this? A new teaching with authority! He commands even the unclean spirits and they obey him!" Peter's mother-in-law is stricken with fever; the Lord takes her by the hand and raises her, so that she is able to resume a normal life. In the evening, after the Sabbath has ended, crowds throng the door of the house where he is staying; he heals them all. A leper in his uncleanness accosts Jesus; the Lord rids him of his dread malady and the man has a new life. One needs little imagination to see how narratives of this kind were used to show what Jesus does for people, and what an impression they must have made when recounted by eyewitnesses in the first person. Let us think how Peter would have related them.

"There he stood in the synagogue, in the grip of an unclean power! He shrieked in terror before the holiness of the Lord. We were breathless as Jesus faced him. He used no magic. He performed no sorcery. He gave a command, and the demoniac was free. You should have seen his face and heard his shout when he realized what had happened! He was more than healed, he was a new creature! The crowd was filled with astonishment to witness such an act of power. But our Christ has done that to multitudes, and he's doing it still!

"Let me tell you about my wife's mother. On that very afternoon, when we reached home, we found her stricken with fever. My wife was apprehensive. The old lady could not stand many more of these attacks! But the Lord was with us. He had demonstrated what he could do for a person in the grip of an evil power; why should he not do the like for her in her physical weakness? I hurried out of her room to him. 'Teacher,' I said, 'she's very ill, but God is with you. You can help her, can't you?' He went to her bedside and looked at her. What followed was incredible but for seeing. He simply took my mother-in-law's hand and sat her up. 'God is good to you,' he said. 'You're well now.' And so she was! All trace of the fever had gone. 'Thank you, Rabbi,' she replied. 'Yes, I am well. God is good. And you are very kind.' Then she added, 'But I don't see the sense of sitting here. I feel as fit as a fiddle.' She got up, dressed herself, and prepared a meal for the whole company of us! That's the Jesus I preach to you! He sets a man or a woman free from the shackles of sin and makes them of use to God and man!"

Is this an unwarranted use of imagination? Surely not! The Gospel narratives were condensed to a minimum through the necessities of catechetical teaching and through lack of space in the papyrus rolls on which books were written. We were intended to read them in this way and to make explicit the motives that prompted their publication. Once we perceive their secret we find them yielding golden treasure.

What made a preacher first tell of the paralytic let down through the roof of a house where Jesus was teaching (Mark 2:1–12)? In the first place it was an illustration of our Lord's power to free a man from the crippling effects of the forces of decay and of death, linked perhaps in the case of the paralytic with a deeply rooted guilt complex. But it was more than physical or psychological. The saying of Jesus to the sick man had to do with his spiritual condition. "My son," he said to him, "Your sins are right now forgiven you" (the verb indicates a state begun at the moment of speaking). The lawyers in the congregation bristled. "What is the man saying?" they asked. "He talks blasphemy. Only God can forgive sins." That last statement accurately reflects Jewish beliefs; the notion that a man can pronounce forgiveness was alien to Jews. Jesus therefore replied, "Which is the easier thing to say? 'Your sins are forgiven,' or 'Get up and walk.' " The lawyers made no reply. To them the question was meaningless anyway, for both statements were futile. To declare that someone's sins were forgiven and to tell a paralytic to get up and walk were equally pointless. The former was easy enough to say, but it did no good. Who, however, would dare to order a paralyzed man to get up and walk? Not they, nor anyone else they knew! To tell such a man to walk, and see him lying helpless in spite of the command, would be thoroughly embarrassing! Jesus answers the silence of his opponents by doing both things: he pronounced the man to be forgiven, and he inspired him with power to walk. He said to the assembled group, "That you may know that the Son of Man has authority on earth to forgive sins"—then turned to the paralyzed man—"I tell you, stand up, pick up your mat, and go home!" And so he did!

Observe, however, the moral of the narrative. Its center of interest is not the healing as such, but the saying, "The Son of Man has power on earth to forgive sins." Contrary to the notions of any crass observers present, the greater act of power is not the healing of paralysis but the miracle of forgiveness. The divine prerogative of forgiveness is now seen to be given to the Man through whom the kingdom of God comes, for as the representative of the King he exercises kingdom authority. The reality of his commission from God is confirmed by the way God works through him for the healing of people in body and soul. The word by which he heals is the word by which he forgives. The preacher of this story would have gone on to declare that what Jesus did in the days of his flesh he does in the day of his resurrection. That is why the incident was first proclaimed to the world. And that is why it is written in the Gospels.

The considerations that led to the narration of Christ's acts of power in the lives of people who came to him also gave rise to the accounts of his own personal life. These we shall have to examine in detail later, but meanwhile we may affirm that it was important for the understanding of the gospel that people should know that Jesus had been baptized, and what happened when that event took place. It was similarly necessary that they should learn how the original disciples came to grasp the secret of his person at Caesarea Philippi—and of the transfiguration that followed; how he shrank from the burden of the cross in the agony of Gethsemane but overcame by prayer; with what humility and authority he faced his judges in his trial; his bitter distress in the darkness of his crucifixion, contrasting with the triumph and peace of his actual death; the power and glory of his resurrection, when he shared the joy of his victory with the disciples and commissioned them to go as his ambassadors to the world. These narratives are among the most powerful preaching material of the Bible in the service of the gospel. That's not surprising, for they are distilled from the preaching of men inspired by what they saw.

The teaching of Jesus stands on a different plane from the records of his deeds. Mark completes his introduction to the ministry of Jesus by a summary of the message of Jesus to his nation—and therefore to the world: it is an announcement that the time for the fulfillment of God's promise for the establishment of his kingdom of salvation had arrived (Mark 1:15). It is likely that that statement was composed in the earliest days of gospel proclamation to let people know exactly what the message of Jesus was and the response they should give to it. Naturally he himself could have used this form of words—they occur elsewhere in his teaching on the kingdom and exactly reflect its content, but it is hardly likely that he went about in Judea and Galilee endlessly repeating them. His followers who were responsible for bringing together the sayings of Jesus may well have put that statement at the head of their collection.

How early were such collections formed and written down? It is not possible to dogmatize about that issue. One thing, however, is crystal clear from the New Testament: from the beginning of the church's existence new believers were instructed as to the content of the faith they had embraced. This was distinct from the Christian preaching through which they were converted, and it was associated with baptism (in the earliest days, *after* baptism). Paul refers to it in the context of his discussion of baptism in Romans 6:17: "Thanks be to God that you, having been once slaves of sin, have become obedient from the heart to the form of teaching to which you were entrusted," (observe—not "which was entrusted to you"!). There are further references to this tradition in 1 Thessalonians 4:1–8 and 2 Thessalonians 3:6. A comparison of the letters in the New Testament as a whole has made it clear to contemporary scholars that this tradition forms the doctrinal and ethical substructure of them all.

It is altogether likely that this instruction included learning the cardinal sayings of Jesus. Increasingly it is being recognized that Jesus himself took pains to see that his disciples learned his teaching.[11] One simple fact appears to confirm that belief: many

---

[11] This view is especially associated with the Swedish scholar Harald Riesenfeld and his colleague Birger Gerhardsson. While acknowledging the value of form criticism for the classification of the material of the Gospels in their oral stage, Riesenfeld maintains that Jesus will have adapted the rabbinic custom of making students learn by heart the "holy" tradition, i.e., the interpretation and elaboration of the law, which was believed to have been derived from Moses and

of the sayings of Jesus are cast into poetic form. Two chief characteristics of Hebrew poetry are seen in the Old Testament, namely,
parallelism and rhythm. The former is evident in the Psalms, even
in translation, but the latter has been completely obscured
through translation, which makes the singing of the Psalms in
English an artificial accomplishment that requires a good deal of
practice.[12] It will be appreciated that when, as frequently in the
European tradition, poetry includes rhyme, its translation into
another language destroys its form and one has virtually to create
a new poem in the other language. Jesus spoke Aramaic, the
lingua franca of the Middle East in his day, but the Gospels were
composed in Greek; there is therefore little or no trace of rhythm
in the sayings of Jesus in the Gospels and no rhyme; consequently
people on the whole had no idea that the form of many of his
sayings is poetic. This knowledge was brought to light through the
labors of C. F. Burney in an illuminating book, *The Poetry of Our
Lord*.[13] Burney was an Old Testament scholar. It was already
evident to him that many of the sayings of Jesus in the Gospels
manifest the parallelism characteristic of Hebrew poetry. That led
him to translate such sayings of Jesus from Greek into Aramaic,
and he found that they frequently fell into one of the forms of
Hebrew rhythm. More astonishing still, whereas Hebrew poetry
does not normally include use of rhyme, a number of Jesus'
sayings do so. A notable instance of this is the prayer which Jesus
taught his disciples, the so-called Lord's prayer; Burney showed

---

was part and parcel of the revelation of God on Sinai. He wrote: "The words of
Jesus and the reports of his deeds and his life . . . were conceived from a very early
date to be the New Torah, and hence as the word of God of the new, eschatological
covenant," *The Gospel Tradition* (ET; Philadelphia: Fortress, 1970) 20. The opening
chapter sets forth Riesenfeld's views on the composition of the Gospels. Gerhardsson expands his comparable position in *The Origin of the Gospel Traditions*
(ET; Philadelphia: Fortress, 1979).

[12] It was an inspired idea that led the translators of *La Sainte Bible, traduite
en français sous la direction de l'Ecole biblique de Jérusalem* to ask a team of scholars
to render the Psalms in such a fashion as to reproduce the various rhythms of the
Hebrew original. The English version of that translation *(The Jerusalem Bible)* did
not attempt the like, but a group of Catholic scholars has provided an English
translation of the Psalms that preserves the original Hebrew rhythms: *The Psalms:
A New Translation from the Hebrew arranged for Singing to the Psalmody of Joseph
Gelineau* (New York: Paulist, 1983). It is a quite new experience to read—especially to read aloud—the Psalms in this way, and still more to sing them.

[13] Oxford: Oxford University Press, 1925. Burney wrote the introduction
to the book in December 1924 and died 15 April 1925.

that the version in Matthew has parallelism, rhythm, and rhyme.[14] There already existed in the day of Jesus an early form of the Jewish prayer known as the Eighteen Benedictions; this too exhibits rhyme, for not only was it included in every synagogue service, but it was expected to be used by every Jew three times a day, and the rhyme doubtless helped people to remember it. The same surely applies to the Lord's Prayer. Burney explicitly made that observation, but he went further with regard to the prayer and other sayings of Jesus cast in poetic form. He wrote:

> It is obvious that these traits must have been intended by our Lord as an aid to memory, and would have acted as such; hence it is scarcely to be overbold to believe that the Matthaean tradition represents the actual words of the prayer as they issued from his lips. So with other sayings which exhibit the formal characteristics of Hebrew poetry. Conformity to a certain type which can be abundantly exemplified—and that not only in one source, but in all the sources which go to form the Gospels—is surely a strong argument for substantial authenticity. For the alternative is that the different authors of the sources, if they possessed merely a vague recollection or tradition of the sayings, must have set themselves, one and all, to dress them in a parallelistic and rhythmical form; and that various writers, and in fact all writers to whom we owe records of our Lord's teaching, should have essayed independently to do the same thing, and so doing should have produced results which are essentially identical in form, is surely out of the question.[15]

That is a significant observation, and I'm not sure that it is taken into account by critics who assume that early Christian teachers and prophets speaking in the name of the Lord freely attributed sayings of their own to Jesus and that the evangelists did likewise in composing their Gospels. Naturally the apostles and other preachers of the gospel will often have cited sayings of Jesus in their public proclamation, but they will have done so out of a memory stamped by the recollection of Jesus' teaching.

Some of the earliest citations of our Lord's teaching in the Gospel records appear to have been recounted in an anecdotal form. That is to say, an important utterance of his was recalled in the circumstances which gave it birth. Our Gospels still reflect

---

[14] K. G. Kuhn in his monograph on the Lord's Prayer demonstrated that the version in Luke 11:2–4 also manifests the same poetic structure as Matthew's version; see *Achtzehngebet und Vaterunser und der Reim* (WUNT 1; Tübingen: Mohr, 1950) 30–40.

[15] Burney, *Poetry of Our Lord,* 6.

some of that preaching. The incident of the children being brought to Jesus for his blessing, which aroused the opposition of the disciples, was described that people might know how he said, "Let the children come to me and stop hindering them, for the kingdom of God belongs to such" (Mark 10:13–14). The famous saying about whether it was right to pay tribute to Caesar falls in the same category: "Give back to Caesar the things that are Caesar's, and to God the things that are God's" (Mark 12:17); the incident must have been unforgettable, but its significance centers in the principle enunciated, and to it everything is subordinated. That is typical of such "pronouncement-stories," as Vincent Taylor called them.[16] Many of our Lord's utterances will have circulated in episodes of this kind. In due time, however, the stories that gave their setting were forgotten. Accordingly it is not uncommon to find in our Gospels a series of quite unrelated sayings; they have been set by the evangelists in their present position simply because they did not know where to place them (see e.g., Luke 16:16–18). A consequence of this is that some sayings of Jesus have acquired a different significance through being placed in other contexts, as a comparison of Mark 4:21–25 with Matthew 5:15–16; 7:1–2, 25, 29 will illustrate. To make some of these unrelated sayings more easily remembered, they have been placed together through their common employment of a catchword (see, e.g., Mark 9:49–50). But this reflects a later stage when their original context was forgotten.

The parables of Jesus are in a class by themselves. They will have been repeated constantly by the apostles and other preachers and teachers. Some are short and some are long, but they virtually all embody aspects of the saving sovereignty of God. The fact that we find placed in one chapter the three parables of the Lost Sheep, the Lost Coin, and the Lost Son (Luke 15) may be due to a preacher who saw how powerfully they illustrate the seeking love of God and pressed them on his hearers that they, too, might be "found." It is unlikely that Jesus himself spoke those parables one after another in this manner, any more than he uttered at one time the seven parables of the kingdom which are recorded in Matthew 13. On the analogy of the latter, Luke himself could have brought together the three parables; their depiction of the joy of recovering

---

[16] V. Taylor, *The Formation of the Gospel Tradition* (London: Macmillan, 1933) 63–87.

something of great worth to very different kinds of persons eloquently sets forth the worth of the lost to God and his joy at their
restoration—a message close to the heart of Luke.

The more connected instruction of Jesus will probably have
been made known by the apostles in their function as teachers
rather than as preachers of the gospel. Most, however, of what is
presented in the Gospels as connected teaching is due to the
assembling of sayings of Jesus dealing with related themes in the
period of oral transmission. The outstanding example of this is
the Sermon on the Mount, Matthew 5–7. Joachim Jeremias made
the intriguing suggestion that the Sermon on the Mount represents the catechetical tradition of our Lord's teaching that was
prepared for Jewish converts, while Luke's related "Sermon on the
Plain" circulated among Gentile believers.[17] As various scholars
have perceived, the binding theme of the Sermon is life under the
saving sovereignty (i.e., kingdom) of God. It begins with a collection of beatitudes of the kingdom, which are really gospel, and
ends with the parable of the Two Houses, which is a parable of
judgment; the intermediate content sets forth the nature of the
Christian life, notably through the striking series of expositions
of the real intent of the law now that the time of salvation has
arrived (Matthew 5:21–48). The "Sermon" is thus a composite of
crucially important sayings of Jesus which set forth the essential
content of his message, directed to those who have responded to
his proclamation of the kingdom.

As I trust is evident, the foregoing has been concerned
entirely with the period prior to the composition of the four
Gospels. The sixty-four thousand dollar question is: How did
those Gospels come to be written? The chief cause may well be
the passing on of the primary eyewitnesses of the ministry, death,
and resurrection of Jesus. It was essential that their testimony be
preserved for the sake of the continuing mission of the church.
The majority of scholars (though by no means all) consider that
the first Gospel to be penned is that of Mark, an associate both of
Peter (1 Peter 5:13) and of Paul (Acts 12:25). Early traditions in
the church state that Mark wrote after the deaths of Peter and Paul.
From indications in chapter 13 of his Gospel it is likely that his
Gospel was written in the crucial period of the Roman-Jewish war,

---

[17] J. Jeremias, *The Sermon on the Mount* (Facet Books, Biblical Series 2;
Philadelphia: Fortress, 1963) 21–23.

perhaps A.D. 68, by which time Peter and Paul would have been martyred. Matthew and Luke appear to have used Mark plus an early collection of sayings of Jesus, which scholars have named Q (= *Quelle,* German for "source"), together with a collection of sayings known only to Matthew ("M") and one only to Luke ("L"). Since neither evangelist seems to have used the other's work, their Gospels must have been roughly contemporary, perhaps written about ten years or so after Mark. Self-evidently the sources available to Matthew and Luke were already in circulation among churches prior to their own writing; by the time that Matthew and Luke received them those sources will almost certainly have been committed to writing (note the implications of Luke 1:1–4).

It is understandable that investigators into the Gospels who had grasped the importance of the period when the sayings and deeds of Jesus were made known through preaching and teaching viewed the evangelists primarily as collectors and pre-servers of the churches' traditions about Jesus. In recent years it has been realized that such a view does not do justice to the work of the evangelists. These were not simply collectors of traditions; they were theologians who had particular insights into the work of Jesus, and their accounts of his life and death were written in the light of their understanding of him. From the second century onwards Christians have been aware that the four Gospels have special contributions to make to our knowledge of Jesus. That awareness came into its own, bringing with it a renewed interest in the theology of each Gospel, a process which is known as redaction criticism. The term "redaction" simply means the proc-ess of editing the evangelic material undertaken by the evangel-ists, with the presupposition that it is precisely in such editing of gospel materials that the interpretative work of the evangelists is revealed.

Perhaps the chief difference between this type of investiga-tion into the Gospels and the concentration on the period of oral tradition which preceded it is the issue of which situation deter-mined the nature and content of the Gospels. The earliest practi-tioners of form criticism were convinced that the situation of the first-generation church as a whole determined what went into the Gospels; there is truth in that, but the most influential propo-nents of this discipline did not take seriously enough the primary importance of the situation of Jesus himself. Redaction criticism seeks to redress this deficiency and distinguishes three different contexts, or "settings in life," to use the favorite expression of

German scholars: these are (i) the life setting of Jesus himself; (ii) that of the church, which preserved and circulated reports of the sayings and the deeds of Jesus; (iii) the situation of the evangelist and the church(es) for which he wrote. Clearly all three settings played their part in making the Gospels what they are, but the last of the three is the special concern of redaction criticism.

Of the legitimacy and importance of this branch of Gospel criticism there is no doubt, and it has led to an enthusiastic renewal of detailed investigations into the texts of the Gospels. As so often happens, however, this particular discipline has fostered some unwarranted scepticism, not at all integral to the method. For example Willi Marxsen, one of the initial exponents of redaction criticism, stated that the concern with the "third situation in life" excludes from the outset the question as to what really happened. "We enquire rather how the evangelists describe what happened. The question as to what really occurred is of interest only to the degree it relates to the situation of the primitive community in which the Gospels arose," and he approvingly cites Bultmann to the effect that a literary work is a primary source for the historical situation out of which it arose and only a secondary source for the historical details it narrates.[18] From this it is but a step to assert that the purpose of the study of the Gospels is to discover the theology of the evangelists rather than that of Jesus, which is scarcely recoverable. Norman Perrin preferred the title "composition criticism" to "redaction criticism," for it acknowledges the composition of wholly new sayings by the church's prophets and teachers.[19] He described Mark's gospel as "a mixture of historical reminiscence, interpreted tradition, and the free creativity of prophets and evangelists . . . in other words, a strange mixture of history, legend and myth,"[20] and concluded that "the nature of the Gospels and of the Gospel material is such that the locus of revelation must be held to be in the present of Christian experience."[21] Such conclusions I regard as unfortunate perversions of redaction criticism and in no way bound up with the method. A more sober estimate of its operation may be seen in Joachim Rohde's lengthy examination of the rise and

---

[18] W. Marxsen, *Mark the Evangelist* (ET; Nashville: Abingdon, 1969) 23–24.
[19] See N. Perrin, *What Is Redaction Criticism?* (Philadelphia: Fortress, 1969) 66.
[20] Ibid., 75.
[21] Ibid., 79.

practice of redaction criticism. In his view the study of the "third life-situation" means that

> each evangelist put the message differently in his own time, although he was bearing witness to one and the same Christ. The individual gospels are thus canonical examples of the way in which the problem of how the message of Christ is to be interpreted was answered in a new situation. To this extent redaction criticism is of supreme importance for practical theology today, and especially for homiletics, for the more successful it is in determining the setting of a gospel in the life and history of the earliest church, the more contemporary practical theology can learn how the message of Christ is to be presented in a new situation.[22]

That clearly implies the use of redaction criticism to learn from the evangelists how to do in our day what they did in theirs. I can think of no more worthy goal for a preacher of the gospel than to learn how to present the message of Christ to his or her own situation. It demands continuous dedication to the study of the Gospels, with a discriminating use of all the tools that Gospel research has made available, prayer for the love and compassion of the Lord who is their theme, and for the guidance of the Holy Spirit to grasp the message and make it effectively known to our contemporaries.

In this preliminary survey of the Gospels we have virtually ignored the Fourth Gospel, yet everything that we have said finds especial exemplification in it. In many respects the Gospel of John is an enigma to those who investigate it, not least because of the great variety of answers to the problems it presents. For example, critics are at odds in deciding whether the evangelist who wrote this Gospel knew and used the other Gospels. That's not so unimportant as it may appear, for from the second century on the churches have assumed that John's Gospel was written to supplement the other three, which is out of the question if he had not read them. A majority of critics today have, in fact, been persuaded that this Gospel is independent of the other three, even if the evangelist had been aware of their existence. To know of those Gospels is not the same as to use them.

According to John 21:24 the authority behind the Gospel is "the disciple whom Jesus loved." It reads: "This is the disciple who bears witness about these things and who wrote these things,

---

[22] J. Rohde, *Rediscovering the Teaching of the Evangelists* (ET; New Testament Library; London: SCM, 1968) 257–58.

and we know that his witness is true." The natural interpretation of that sentence is that the evangelist distinguishes himself from the Beloved Disciple, but that in his Gospel he has embodied the witness to Christ which the Beloved Disciple had left in his writings. There are many indications in the Gospel, from the first chapter to the last, that that "witness" is eyewitness. Unlike the Synoptic Gospels, the Fourth Gospel is largely set in Judea, with especial attention to the ministry of Jesus in Jerusalem, of which the earlier Gospels give no indication. This fact, together with the evangelist's knowledge of the attitude of the Jewish authorities to Jesus and of the decisions of the meetings of the Sanhedrin, the incidental remark that he was a friend of the High Priest (John 18:15),[23] and his knowledge of the trial before Pilate, is all explained if the Beloved Disciple had been a resident of Jerusalem during the ministry of Jesus.

One feature of the Gospel is abundantly plain to every preacher, namely that it is the preacher's Gospel *par excellence*. Every item in it calls out to be preached, and that for a simple reason: every item in it had been preached! The Fourth Gospel is the distillation of a lifetime's preaching. This hypothesis, set forth by various commentators, has been strengthened by the acute analysis of the Gospel by C. H. Dodd. He divided the Gospel, after its introductory chapter, into two main sections: chapters 2–12, the Book of Signs, and chapters 13–21, the Book of the Passion. The Book of the Passion is a declaration of the facts and interpretation of the redemption wrought in and through Jesus. The Book of Signs is more complex. It is in seven parts, each section consisting of a "sign" (sometimes two) with a discourse explaining its (or their) significance. The remarkable feature of the Book of Signs is that although there is a well marked progress to the climax of the ministry, each of the seven divisions is relatively complete and each enshrines within itself the whole Gospel, namely the manifestation, crucifixion, resurrection, and exaltation of the Son of Man. It would go beyond the scope of this chapter to describe how Dodd developed this remarkable observation, but merely to hear it stated, as I heard it in a lecture of Dodd's, was enough to cause scales to fall from my eyes. Any preacher with an eye for the gospel should be able

---

[23] See G. R. Beasley-Murray, *John* (Word Biblical Commentary 36; Waco: Word, 1987) 317 n. e.

to work it out, but in case of difficulty one may look it up in Dodd's book.[24]

A further consideration relative to the Book of the Passion may not be out of place. I described chapters 13–21 above as a narration of the facts and interpretation of the redemption in and through Christ. The "interpretation" is primarily made known in the Upper Room Discourses of chapters 13–17. It is within the bounds of possibility that these discourses have assumed their present form through their use by the Beloved Disciple in meditations at the communion service. This would explain how it is that some at least of the sayings of Jesus in the Upper Room Discourses occur earlier in the other Gospels, but still more striking that at least two addresses appear to have been combined into one, namely chapters 13–14 and 15–16. The last sentence of John 14:31, "Rise, let us be on our way," allows no doubt that Jesus here commands his disciples to depart from the Upper Room. Since this is followed by further discourse and prayer in chapters 15–17, it has often been assumed that Jesus continued to speak during the walk from the Upper Room to the garden of Gethsemane, but 18:1 is unambiguous: "After Jesus had spoken these words he went out with his disciples across the Kidron valley to a place where there was a garden." That means that everything in chapters 13–17 is set in the Upper Room. On reflection it is entirely fitting that the instruction of Jesus at his last meal with his disciples should be communicated at celebrations of the Lord's Supper, and that related teaching should have been associated with it also.

One final observation regarding the Fourth Gospel must be made. More than in any other Gospel the evangelist draws attention to the guidance of the Holy Spirit for understanding and communicating the revelation of God in Christ. John 14:26 is one of five passages in the last discourses concerning the Spirit's role in witness to Jesus: "The Paraclete (= Advocate or Counselor), the Holy Spirit, whom the Father will send in my name, will teach you everything, and will remind you of everything that I have said to you." Here is a promise that the Holy Spirit will not only enable the disciples to *recall* the words and deeds of Jesus but to *understand* their meaning—he will "teach" the disciples to grasp the

---

[24] C. H. Dodd, *The Interpretation of the Fourth Gospel* (Cambridge: Cambridge University Press, 1953) 383–89.

revelation of God in his Son. This is how it has been possible for this Gospel to present the ministry of Jesus in Palestine in closest relation to the ministry of the risen Lord in the world: the Holy Spirit enabled the Beloved Disciple uniquely to relate what Jesus said and did to the situation of the church in the world. The preacher under the guidance of the same Spirit may be enabled to relate the same word of God to his or her own generation. If this be so, we have yet further justification for the belief that the Gospel of John is especially the preacher's Gospel.

It would, of course, be unspeakably foolish to press this viewpoint and claim that the Gospels were written for the benefit of preachers! John 20:30–31 explicitly states that that Gospel was written to call unbelievers to faith in Jesus so that they may possess life in his name, and to confirm believers in their faith and deepen their life in Christ.[25] But it cannot be gainsaid that the man or woman called to expound the treasury of truth contained in these books reads them with increased understanding when he or she knows the process that brought them into existence; such a person should be able to grasp their import and make their message live for others.

To expound the Gospels worthily is no easy task. Just as the appeal of the gospel is simple to grasp, but its implications outrun the reach of the intellect, so the Gospels afford illumination to the humblest Christian, but their profundities elude us at every turn. It could hardly be otherwise, for they deal with the ultimate concerns of God and humankind, and in that region the plumb line of reason is a pitifully inadequate instrument. Yet the heart of the living God pulsates in the Life described in these pages. Anyone who ponders them long enough will enter into the mystery of the passion of God. Like the transfigured Lord, such a one will descend to the plain of humanity's need with a grace not of this world, and in company with the Spirit will bring his or her fellows out of the power of darkness into the kingdom of God's dear Son.

---

[25] See the exposition of John 20:31 in Beasley-Murray, *John*, 387–88.

2

THE GOSPEL IN THE

LIFE OF JESUS

A ctions speak louder than words." Most of us will agree with the proverb. In the life of the individual, in politics, and in international relations alike it is easier to promise than to perform, to utter sympathetic words than to give assistance. This is being fearfully illustrated as these lines are written by the "ethnic cleansing" that is going on in Bosnia, meaning the relentless destruction of the Moslem population, villages, and towns by Serbs and Croats. The rest of the European countries are aghast. They keep on persuading the warring countries to agree to cease fighting, agreements are made but instantly broken, calls are issued to organize force against aggressors, but are never followed up for fear of provoking attacks on troops supplying food, and meanwhile the "ethnic cleansing" continues unchecked. Perhaps this suggests why "actions speak louder than words" is commonly quoted as a judgment: some actions wholly negate words; where remedial actions are needed words can be hollow; and all too often smooth words are belied by deeds.

In a time when people revolt from propaganda promises and want to see things happening, it is significant that a new understanding of the Bible has emerged. It is looked on less as a book of wise sayings for the guidance of humanity (though such are to be found throughout its pages) and more as a book of God's action on behalf of the world. We have come to realize that God has been pleased to reveal himself not alone by communicating truths but by what he does. The book that follows the Gospels in the New Testament is traditionally known as "The Acts of the Apostles." Theology has preferred to think in terms of "The Acts of the Spirit of the Risen Lord." In any case it connotes God at work through his church to save the world. G. E. Wright and R. H. Fuller appropriated as a name for the whole Bible "The Book of the Acts of God."[1] And those acts are of a very special kind: not arbitrary acts of power, but acts by which people are saved and judged.

It is desirable, however, to ensure that we avoid misunderstanding on this. The God of creation is the God of redemption, achieving both by his acts of power. But in his wisdom he has sent men and women endowed with prophetic vision to explain his deeds. The Old Testament, for example, is like a two-leaf door. The one leaf hinges on the act of deliverance and salvation which we call the exodus. By it God rescued his people, who at that time were but a group of slave tribes, and he made them a free nation in covenant with himself and with a world mission. The other leaf hinges on the act of judgment which initiated Israel's exile, when the covenant nation was refined in the furnace of affliction. In both cases prophets were sent to act as spokesmen for God to make known what God was doing in those circumstances. Moses, viewed by the Jews as the greatest of all prophets, was God's instrument in leading his people from the land of slavery to the land of promise and the mediator of God's covenant with Israel; the prophets of the exile, notably Jeremiah and Ezekiel, warned the nation of the judgment that was coming unless they repented. But after the judgment prophets announced a third act, envisaged on the lines of the first: they declared that God was to bring about another exodus from their present distress and give them the "promised land" (the "inheritance") of the kingdom of God. The greatest announcer of that hope was the prophet known to modern scholars as Deutero-Isaiah, whose prophecies in Isaiah 40–55 form the Himalayas of the Old Testament. In the fullness of time

---

[1] G. E. Wright and R. H. Fuller, *The Book of the Acts of God* (London: Duckworth, 1960).

the doors swung open and the king of glory, the incarnate Lord, entered into his kingdom.

How did he manifest the kingdom? By the authoritative word he spoke? By the holiness and love of his life? By powerful deeds of deliverance? Answer: by all three! That is why, in face of the allegation that he was in league with the devil, Jesus could affirm, "If it is by the finger of God that I cast out the demons then the kingdom of God has come upon you" (Luke 11:20). The Pharisaic opponents of Jesus saw exorcisms happen through his authoritative word, but reacted by alleging that he was an instrument of the devil, and therefore as evil as the devil himself. Our Lord, through his parable of the Strong Man bound, showed that he was the victor over the devil, not his agent. Authoritative word, holy love, powerful acts all combined in his demonstration of the presence of God's kingdom.

It is, of course, unreal to divorce the words and character of Jesus from his deeds; his whole life constituted one divine "event" by which the gracious purpose of God was wrought out in flesh and blood. Nevertheless it is necessary to recall that the emphasis in the New Testament falls on the acts of Christ for the redemption of humanity, albeit acts of holy love as Jesus interpreted them. The speediest way of answering the question, "What is God like?" is to point to the cross of Christ and the empty tomb: there we see that God is holy love, acting in creative power for the salvation of the world. The gospel can be defined in such terms. We find it so described in the New Testament, especially in its hymns of celebration. Just such a hymn is cited (in part) by Paul in Philippians 2:6–11, prefaced by the appeal, "Let the same way of thinking be cherished by you which you have in union with Christ Jesus":

> who, though he bore the stamp of the divine image
> did not use equality with God as a gain to be exploited;
> but surrendered his rank,
> and took the role of a servant;
> accepting a human-like guise,
> and appearing on earth as the Man;
> he humbled himself;
> in an obedience which went so far as to die.
> For this, God raised him to the highest honour,
> and conferred upon him the highest rank of all;
> that, at Jesus' name, every knee should bow,
> and every tongue should own that "Jesus Christ is Lord."[2]

---

[2]The translation is that of R. P. Martin, *Carmen Christi* (SNTSMS 4; Cambridge: Cambridge University Press, 1967) 38.

There is a comparable hymn adapted by Paul in Colossians 1:15–20, while behind the prologue of the Gospel of John (John 1:1–18) there lies the stateliest hymn to Christ in the New Testament. The history of the incarnate Son is a story of redeeming action. To describe it is to tell out the Christian faith.

The Apostles' Creed was composed in the light of such a conviction. It is a trinitarian confession of faith, but the central clause is a description of saving acts of the Son of God. Doubtless the four evangelists, if they could have read it, would have entered a caveat on one score: it passes over the life of the Lord in silence.

> Born of the Virgin Mary,
> suffered under Pontius Pilate,
> was crucified, dead and buried.

Certainly they are key moments in the salvation history. But did nothing of importance for the saving sovereignty of God occur between the birth and death of Jesus? The evangelists, having records of the words and acts of Jesus in his ministry, saw that what lies between "born" and "suffered" is of vital significance for the kingdom of God. That is why they wrote their Gospels. They had no reservations about the apostolic gospel. That was the heart of their message also. But they saw the crucifixion-resurrection of Jesus as the climax of a unitary process, to be consummated in a chapter that no evangelist has yet been in a position to write, the parousia of the Lord in glory.

The evangelists were concerned about the "life in the flesh" of Jesus. Let us be clear, however, that they were not interested in presenting a "Jesus after the flesh," to use Paul's language (2 Corinthians 5:16). Mark, as well as Paul, could have penned the very sentence in which that phrase occurs: "Even though we once knew Christ according to the flesh, we know him no longer in that way," for it relates to knowing and judging Christ from a purely external point of view, as the majority of Jesus' contemporaries did. The task of the four evangelists was to present the life of Jesus as the story of salvation. In the preceding chapter we saw that the Gospel writers trod in paths laid out for them by the gospel preachers and wrote with a view toward making the good news of Christ plain to every reader. This applies equally to the narratives of the personal life of Jesus as to those of his interventions in other people's lives.

We must never forget that for the men who wrote of Jesus, the event that controlled a true understanding of him was that which made him their contemporary, namely his resurrection. We begin our consideration of the life of Jesus chronologically, with the story of his birth; they began it experientially, with the knowledge that he lives who died for them. Instead of beginning from the birth and looking along the avenue of time to the climax of his passion and resurrection, they began with the gospel of redeeming love and looked back on the life that brought the new age. Consequently they read every event in the light of the end and judged its significance accordingly. The famous picture by Sir John Millais of Jesus in the carpenter's shop shows our Lord as a boy, stretching his arms at the end of a day's work; the rays of the setting sun shine through the window on to his back, so that Mary, to her horror, sees on the wall a silhouette of a man on a cross. That situation is reduplicated for the evangelists a hundredfold, but to them, it betokens not horror but the outworking of God's eternal purpose in and through Jesus. The shadows and the glory of the cross and resurrection dovetail in the life of Jesus, coinciding with the shadows and the light of the life itself. The pattern of divine intervention, attested supremely by the suffering and glory of Easter, may be traced from Bethlehem onwards.

We shall examine the major events of our Lord's life, as narrated by the evangelists, and see how they relate to the theme of the Gospel as a whole.

THE GOSPEL OF THE INFANCY

European Continental theologians often characterize the narratives of our Lord's birth (in the first two chapters of Matthew and Luke) by this title. In view of the fact that these narratives stand at the beginning of Gospels written to set forth the good news of God, it is a legitimate title. They are dominated by the wonder of the birth, which is plainly stated to be the first stage in the process of redemption.

Attempts have been made, on textual and linguistic grounds, to show that the Virgin Birth is not an integral part of the sources on which Matthew and Luke drew. The majority of New Testament scholars not only agree that these attempts have failed, they affirm precisely the opposite, namely that it is the *sources* of the two evangelists which have determined their belief in the miraculous birth of Jesus, and that the evangelists have presented the material of their sources in accordance with their overall purpose in composing their Gospels.[3]

Let us acknowledge at once that we have no justification for asserting that without the Virgin Birth of Jesus the incarnation of the Son of God would have been impossible. We cannot set limits to what the creator God can and cannot do. We are called upon to recognize that this is the way God chose for the eternal Son to become one with "all flesh." Rather than think in terms of the necessity of the virginal conception of Jesus as a necessary condition for his divine nature to be united with humanity we should view it as a *sign,* pointing to the fact that the Son of God has become incarnate.[4] In that respect we may compare it with the empty tomb at the other end of the earthly life of Jesus; that was not an unmistakable proof that Jesus had risen from the dead; on the contrary virtually all the disciples, including the women, were puzzled and fearful at first sight of it, but it came to be recognized as a powerful sign of the authentic resurrection of Christ from death. Interestingly the virginal conception of Jesus and the resurrection of Jesus from the dead are both beyond the ability of human thought to explain, and both have been denied on that ground. With regard to the former Raymond Brown stated:

> It was an extraordinary action of God's creative power, as unique as the initial creation itself (and that is why all natural science objections to it are irrelevant, e.g., that not having a human father, Jesus' genetic structure would be abnormal). It was not a phenomenon of nature; and to reduce it to one, however unusual, would be as serious a challenge as to deny it altogether.[5]

Precisely the same comparison with creation has been made regarding the resurrection of Jesus. Walter Künneth, in his highly significant work on the theology of the resurrection, wrote:

> The fundamental miracle of the resurrection is God's creative act, which is essentially to be set in parallel with the fundamental miracle of the creation of the world.[6]

---

[3]See especially the magisterial work of R. E. Brown, *The Birth of the Messiah* (new updated ed.; New York: Doubleday, 1993), with its detailed discussion of the issue and his exegesis of Matthew 1–2 and Luke 1–2.

[4]So K. Barth, *Credo* (London: Hodder & Stoughton, 1936) 62–72, and Brown, *Birth of the Messiah,* 529.

[5]Brown, *Birth of the Messiah,* 531.

[6]*Theologie der Auferstehung* (4th ed.; Munich: Claudius Verlag, 1951) 63.

He, too, links the virgin birth with the resurrection as presupposing one another:

> The miracle of the incarnation is presupposed through the miracle of the resurrection, but similarly one can speak of the resurrection only because one knows about the birth of God's Son.[7]

The interpretation of the virgin birth as a sign of who Jesus is, namely the incarnate Son of God, needs amplification with respect to his relation to the Holy Spirit. Both Matthew and Luke draw attention to the conception of Jesus by the Holy Spirit (Matthew 1:18, Luke 1:35). Strictly speaking, the really important aspect of the birth of Jesus is not that he had a virgin mother but that his conception was by the Holy Spirit. That attests not only his relation to God but also his vocation regarding the kingdom of God. It is well known that in the Old Testament the manifestation of the Spirit is characteristically an intermittent phenomenon. Men were aided by the Spirit for specific tasks, but were not regarded as united with him. With Jesus something new came into being, a human life that began with the creative activity of the Holy Spirit and was sustained by him. In all probability Matthew, in seeing the fulfillment of Isaiah 7:14 in Jesus, wished his readers to recognize in the birth of Jesus the fulfillment of the Old Testament promises of the coming of the Spirit on the King-Messiah and Servant of the Lord. Isaiah 11:1ff. is a conspicuous example of such declarations, but above all the first of the four Servant songs (Isaiah 42:1–4), which tells of God bestowing on his Servant the Spirit to enable him to establish his kingdom on earth:

> Here is my servant, whom I uphold,
> my chosen, in whom my soul delights;
> I have put my spirit upon him;
> he will bring forth justice to the nations . . .
> He will not grow faint or be crushed
> until he has established justice in the earth;
> and the coastlands wait for his teaching. (NRSV)

The unusual feature of the Servant songs is their representation of the Servant as the one through whom the salvation

---

[7]Ibid., 120. Künneth cites K. Barth in affirming the same view. It is interesting to compare these robust statements with the cautious position of J. A. T. Robinson; without excluding belief in the possibility of the virgin birth and physical resurrection of Jesus, he opts for agnosticism rather than dogmatism relating to them, *The Human Face of God* (London: SCM, 1973) 138.

of the Lord comes. In the Old Testament generally the kingdom of God comes through the direct intervention of God, and the Messiah rules as his representative. The Servant songs, however, depict the Servant of the Lord as God's instrument for bringing to pass his saving purpose (see especially Isaiah 49:5–6, and 52:13–53:12). This the Servant does by virtue of his possession of the Spirit; he is thereby enabled to mediate the salvation of the kingdom to humankind. C. K. Barrett stated: "In the Old Testament the Spirit appears to act creatively only in relation to the primal creation of the world and man, and in the redemption of the people of God."[8] If, therefore, evangelists emphasize that the Spirit is creatively at work in the entry of the Messiah into the world, they thereby doubly underscore the fact that something momentous has happened for the deliverance of humanity. God has taken the decisive first step in the fulfillment of his promise to bring about the redemption of the world and the gift of his kingdom.

Both Matthew and Luke provide genealogies of Jesus, in accordance with Jewish custom. They differ considerably, but to no small degree because of the different purposes which the evangelists have. Matthew begins his Gospel with the sentence, "The book of the genesis of Jesus Christ, son of David, son of Abraham." In using the term "genesis" Matthew is echoing the Greek translation of Genesis 2:4 and 5:1—"the book of the genesis of the heavens and earth," and "the book of the genesis of Adam," which introduces a genealogy from Adam to Noah. But Matthew's primary intention is clearly to show that Jesus fulfills the promises to Abraham in Genesis 12:1–3 and to David in 2 Samuel 7:12 (David is promised an "offspring" who will rule a kingdom established by God; that was interpreted by the Jews to mean that David would have a "son" who would be Israel's Messiah). For that reason Matthew's genealogy reproduces a popular version of the royal line back to David. The division into three groups of fourteen generations is dependent on the "number" of David's name (the Hebrew language used letters for numbers: David = D-W-D = 14). Self-evidently Matthew writes to capture the attention of contemporary Jews. Luke has a different purpose: he sets his genealogy after describing the baptism of

---

[8] C. K. Barrett, *The Holy Spirit and the Gospel Tradition* (rev. ed.; London: SPCK, 1970) 20.

Jesus, which concludes with the words, "You are my beloved Son; with you I am well pleased"; there follows at once a genealogy going back to "Adam, the son of God" (Luke 3:22–37). Clearly Luke, writing for the Gentile world, wished to emphasize through his genealogy that Jesus was born as the Son of God to be the Savior of *the world*.[9]

One feature of Matthew's genealogy has fascinated Christians through the centuries, namely his inclusion of certain women in it. But what extraordinary women! The first is Tamar—an adulteress in defense of the law! (Specifically the levirate law, see Genesis 38:6–26.) Rahab was a harlot, saved by her act of faith (Joshua 2). Ruth, an unmarried woman, claimed her right under the same levirate law in a highly unusual manner, but was nevertheless praised by the man she lay with (Ruth 3:1–14). Bathsheba committed adultery with David, but her son Solomon was "beloved of the Lord" (2 Samuel 12:25) and was given preference over David's other sons to become king. Moreover, all four women were, in the sight of the Jews, foreigners! Tamar and Rahab were Canaanites; Ruth was a Moabitess, and therefore outside the scope of God's promises to Israel (Deuteronomy 23:3 says that a Moabite, a bastard and an Ammonite are not to enter the congregation "till the tenth generation," i.e., virtually forever); Bathsheba was the wife of Uriah the Hittite (2 Samuel 11:3). The surprising thing is that later teachers of the law did not judge these women adversely, but praised them for the initiative which each took (including Bathsheba, see 1 Kings 1:5–40), and attributed their actions to the Holy Spirit's guidance—doubtless since all of them were in the messianic line.[10] The later rabbis were not so kind to Mary the mother of Jesus. A tradition became established among the Jews that Mary committed adultery with a Roman soldier named Panthera (or Pantera), from whom Jesus was born, so that he became known as "son of Panthera." How early this allegation was made is uncertain—it is elaborated in various forms in Jewish literature of the Amoraic period (A.D. 200–500), and was known to at least some Christian teachers at the end of the second century (Tertullian, e.g., cites a Jewish claim that Jesus was the son of a prostitute). Did any such Jewish slander about the birth of Jesus circulate in the time that Matthew wrote? We

---

[9] On the genealogies of Matthew and Luke see Brown, *Birth of the Messiah*, 56–95.

[10] Ibid., 73–74.

cannot say, but if it did exist, the presence of the women in Matthew's genealogy would be the more comprehensible, not least in view of the Jewish preparedness to attribute their behavior to the prompting of the Spirit! The place of the women in the genealogy of Jesus could be held to clear him of unwholesome imputations, and at the same time reflect on the questionable nature of his ancestors: the Messiah was not born in sin, but he sprang from a sinful people! In distinction from some of his forebears, Jesus was born of a pure woman under the power of the Holy Spirit. But the foreign origin of those women taken into Israel's fold fittingly presaged the birth of the Jewish Messiah born to be the Savior of all nations.

The revelation of the Messiah's birth was made known in Matthew to "Magoi" and in Luke to shepherds. Tradition has set a halo about the heads of the former and has viewed them as kings. That was never intended by the evangelist. Magoi were astronomer-astrologer-priests, chiefly in ancient Parthia, which included territory now in northwest Iran and Armenia. Their religion was Zoroastrianism, which in its messianic hope was closer to that of Israel's prophets than any other ancient religion; its adherents looked for a savior-king who would rule in a kingdom of God, and who (in the belief of some at least) would arise in the West. The Magier-king Tiridates of Parthia caused an immense sensation when he journeyed to Rome in A.D. 66, leading sons of three Parthian kings, to do homage to Nero since the stars pointed to him as the awaited king of the world(!). The Magoi of whom Matthew wrote journeyed westwards because they saw the star of the Savior-king "at its rising"; that they should have sought him and prostrated themselves before him contrasts strikingly with the reactions of Herod and the Jewish rulers in Jerusalem. Luke makes a related point in the revelation of the birth of the Savior-Messiah to the shepherds in the fields (Luke 2:8–20); shepherds, by reason of their occupation, which kept them from strict observance of the law and from worship, were beyond the pale in the eyes of the "righteous," yet it was to such that the Messiah's birth was made known. What took place at the birth of Jesus was prophetic of the whole course of the gospel history and of the church itself: Jesus was rejected by the leaders of his people but accepted by common folk and representatives of the nations. Therein were fulfilled not only what stands written in the prophetic books of the Old Testament but also the age-old hopes of the nations which looked for salvation from the God of heaven.

THE BAPTISM OF JESUS

When considering the gospel in the *ministry* of Jesus we naturally begin with his baptism. This we view as an active step of Jesus in his service of God, not a passive one. In some respects it is a key to the ministry of Jesus.

The baptism of Jesus at the hands of John the Baptist has often been thought of as Jesus' acknowledgment of the authority of John's ministry (cf. Mark 11:27–33) and his dedication to the mission now beginning. There is truth in those assertions, but by themselves they are inadequate. It must never be forgotten that John's baptism was "a baptism of repentance for the forgiveness of sins" (Mark 1:4) undergone in preparation for the judgment and kingdom of the Messiah (Matthew 3:8–12). How should Jesus submit himself to that baptism? Some have concluded that since Jesus did so he was acknowledging that he was a sinner like all other human beings and sought to prepare himself for the Messiah's coming; then it was that he had a vision of heaven and the approbation of God for his action. In the judgment of the church through the ages, that flies in the face of all the evidence we have in the Gospels, above all the consciousness of Jesus from the outset of his ministry that he was the mediator of the kingdom of God, with authority to forgive sins (Mark 2:7–12) but himself being without sin (cf., e.g., Luke 11:13; John 8:46). When therefore Jesus was baptized "for sins," assuredly it was not in relation to his own sins but those of others. It was his first act of "numbering himself with the transgressors," as the last sentence of the last Servant Song puts it (Isaiah 53:12).

I can make sense of the baptism of Jesus, and indeed of the whole ministry of Jesus, only on the basis of the following assertion: *Jesus submitted to the baptism of John, among the repentant of Israel responsive to John's proclamation, to begin the messianic task as he interpreted it from the scriptures of the Old Testament.* This means that Jesus went to his baptism not to prepare himself for the coming of the Messiah but to consecrate himself for his service as Messiah. He advanced into the water not as a private person but as a representative person, i.e., on behalf of his own people, but also on behalf of all peoples, since the kingdom of God embraces all nations.

Accordingly when Jesus was baptized he saw the heavens "torn apart" (Mark 1:10)—a sign of the advent of the kingdom of God, confirmed by the descent of the Spirit of the kingdom on him, equipping him for his task of inaugurating the kingdom and making him the "bearer" of the Holy Spirit (cf. John 1:33). With that the voice of the Father came, "You are my beloved Son; with you I am well pleased" (Mark 1:11). The first clause echoes Psalm 2:7, interpreted of the Messiah by all Jews, plus Genesis 22:2 and 12, where the Hebrew term "only" (son, relating to Isaac in process of being sacrificed) is translated in the Greek text by "beloved" (an only son is naturally beloved!); the second clause cites the first Servant Song, Isaiah 42:1. The collocation of the three texts in the context of the baptism of Jesus is highly signifi-cant: the consecration of Jesus to his work as the Messiah who identifies himself with sinful humanity is acknowledged by the Father in terms that confirm his destiny as a messiah who shall fulfill the task of establishing the saving sovereignty through suffering that ends in victory.[11] Note that the Father *confirms* the destiny of Jesus as Messiah and Son rather than *reveals* it for the first time. To the Jews, Son of God was the status of the Messiah as king (so Psalm 2:7); for Jesus, consciousness of being the Son (of God) was primary, being rooted deeply in his soul, and messiahship was secondary, a matter of vocation. The latter will have been for him a growing realization in the years prior to his ministry, as he pondered in the light of the scriptures the way he must take. The scriptures will have led him to seek John's baptism. The Father confirmed that he was in the right way.

From this viewpoint the baptism of Jesus takes on a pro-found significance. Recognition of the voice of God as combining allusions to King-Messiah (Psalm 2), Isaac on the way to sacrifice (Genesis 22), and the righteous Servant whose service for the kingdom of God includes suffering for the guilty (Isaiah 42, 52:13–53:12) has led many scholars to see a straight path from the baptism of Jesus to his crucifixion, as though his baptism was a conscious dedication to death.[12] There is indeed a path from Jordan to Golgotha, but whether every step that Jesus was to take

---

[11] The conjunction of the three OT passages is the more striking if, as is likely, the Jewish belief was established, as early as the lifetime of Jesus, that all the sacrifices of Israel in the temple were acceptable to God in consequence of Abraham's sacrifice of Isaac.

[12] See, e.g., O. Cullmann, *Baptism in the New Testament* (ET; London: SCM, 1950) 15ff.; G. W. H. Lampe, *The Seal of the Spirit* (London: SPCK, 1951) 33–34; H. W. Bartsch "Die Taufe im Neuen Testament," *Evangelische Theologie* 8 (1948–49) 90ff.; G. Every, *The Baptismal Sacrifice* (London: SCM, 1958) 28.

on the journey was plain to him is dubious. The implications of Mark 13:32 hold good for the beginning of the ministry of Jesus as well as its end: as man he was not omniscient. That his God-ordained vocation included suffering will have been clear to him from the scriptures, and his unreserved obedience to his Father's will was integral to his baptism, including every step of the way ahead. But the opened heaven, the descent of the Spirit and the Father's voice, far from being a death sentence, indicate the initiation of divine intervention, the downfall of the powers of darkness, the dawn of the new creation, the promise of life from the dead. To achieve that, Jesus was ready for ultimate sacrifice; for that, his baptism was consecration without limit.

THE TEMPTATION OF JESUS

After the baptism of Jesus came his temptation. We are accustomed to reading the accounts of it in Matthew or in Luke, but it is much briefer in Mark, and dramatically described by him: "And the Spirit immediately drove him out into the wilderness. He was in the wilderness forty days, tempted by Satan; and he was with the wild beasts; and the angels waited on him." That the Spirit should "drive out" Jesus into the wilderness is striking. It was God's will that he should go there! The wilderness is a lonely place, and it has very diverse associations: the place of testing and temptation, as Israel found on the way from Egypt to the prom-ised land; but also the place of deliverance and salvation, as Isaiah 40:3–5 vividly declares. For Jesus it was to be both. He goes into the lonely place. Wild beasts are there. So is Satan. And so is the Spirit who has led him there.

Because of our knowledge of the accounts in Matthew and Luke, where Jesus is spoken of as standing on a pinnacle of the temple in Jerusalem, and then on a high mountain to view all the kingdoms of the world, we tend to think in literalist terms of Jesus actually going to Jerusalem and to a specific mountain; but he remains in the wilderness! And from which mountain can one see all the kingdoms of the world? By contrast William Sanday early in this century wrote a book on contemporary thought about Jesus and the Gospels, and set as a frontispiece in it a picture of Jesus in the wilderness being tempted by the devil: Jesus was depicted as sitting on a large stone, looking straight ahead— thinking! One must not object to that conception as taking the heart out of the temptation narratives, as though "wrestling with

. . . the rulers, the authorities, the cosmic powers of this present darkness, the spiritual forces of evil in the heavenly places" (Ephesians 6:12) requires wearing boxer shorts and fighting in a boxing ring. Did ever a more fearful struggle for any human being take place than when Jesus was on his knees in the Garden of Gethsemane? Oddly enough there is a possible reference to the temptation narrative in a little parable of Jesus, Mark 3:27: "No one can enter a strong man's house and plunder his property without first tying up the strong man; then indeed the house can be plundered." This was part of Jesus' reply to the charge of the Pharisees that his exorcisms were due to an agreement between himself and the devil; on the contrary, said Jesus, it was not because of an agreement with Satan but because he had defeated him, and henceforth Satan is powerless to stop Jesus from releasing his captives. When did Jesus show his superior strength and "tie up" Satan? The most likely answer is, When tempted in the wilderness.[13] The imagery of the parable is quite different from that in the temptation accounts of all the evangelists, but the reality is one with theirs: Jesus overcame the endeavor of Satan to turn him aside from his purpose to establish the kingdom of God; consequently his ministry was characterized by victory over Satan. The wild beasts made no attack on him, for he was "with" them—in peace! It is a reminder of the relations between man and beast at creation (Genesis 1:28, 2:19-20) and anticipated in the kingdom of the last days (Isaiah 11:6-9, 65:17-25). As Robert Guelich observed:

> Thus Jesus' peaceful coexistence "with the wild animals" boldly declares the presence of the age of salvation when God's deliverance would come in the wilderness and harmony would be established within creation according to the promise, especially of Isaiah.[14]

The temptation accounts in Matthew and Luke without doubt are concerned in the first instance with the attempt of the devil to sabotage the intention of his ministry. As has often been observed, fundamentally there is only one temptation—that of misusing divine Sonship to bring the kingdom of God in an easy way, and that would mean failure. Over against this temptation

---

[13] So J. Jeremias, *New Testament Theology* (ET; New York: Scribners, 1971) 72-73.

[14] R. E. Guelich, *Mark 1-8:26* (Word Biblical Commentary; Dallas: Word, 1989) 39.

stands the attitude, basic to the Gospels, that the Son of God came to do not his own will but that of his Father. He enunciated it as the "first" commandment, that of Deuteronomy 6:5, "You shall love the Lord your God with all your heart . . . soul . . . mind . . . strength" (Mark 12:30). It is central to the prayer that he taught his disciples. It is the secret of his life.

It is important to note that the temptations of Jesus did not end in the encounter with Satan in the wilderness. Luke records that at the last supper of Jesus with his disciples he stated, "You are those who have persisted with me in my temptations" (Luke 22:28; the Greek term *peirasmoi* here used has the dual meaning of tests and temptations, hence NRSV "trials"). It is not difficult to see how the temptations of the desert reappear in many disguises in the ministry of Jesus. The account in the Gospel of John of the feeding of the multitude ("in the wilderness"! Mark 6:31–44) relates that when the men saw the power of Jesus in that event they tried to seize him and make him king (what a leader he would have made against Rome!). To Jesus that was an attempt to force an anti-God messiahship upon him, and he "fled into the mountain alone" (John 6:15). It is noteworthy that the term "fled," preserved in a number of ancient manuscripts, appeared to later scribes as undignified and unworthy of Jesus, and they substituted an elegant word, rendered in our translations "withdrew." In so doing those scribes disguised the horror with which Jesus viewed the intention of the people. The event throws light on his normal habit of playing down the messianic issue before the crowds. When, later, certain Pharisees demanded of Jesus a sign "from heaven" he refused to give such; he knew the attitude of many Pharisees that he was an instrument of the devil and so could do earthly miracles; here he was being challenged to do something unmistakably from God; in that request Jesus saw a renewal of the old temptation and rejected it (Mark 8:11–12). Peter, in his supreme moment of insight, declared that Jesus was the Messiah, yet he tried to deter Jesus from the path of suffering and in so doing took the part of Satan instead of God (Mark 8:27–33). Gethsemane saw the battle at its height. Even after the victory there, when Jesus hung on the cross, Jewish leaders called on him to demonstrate his power and come down from it that they might believe (Mark 15:32). General Booth is reported to have said, "They would have believed in him had he come down; we believe in him because he stayed up."

To the bitter end Jesus resisted every conceivable temptation and remained faithful to his Father's will. In this he contrasted with two supreme examples of the opposite in the Bible: that of Adam and Eve in Eden, and that of the Israelites in the wilderness. Mark almost certainly had the former in view, and Matthew and Luke the latter. The contrast with Adam was important to Paul, who saw in Jesus the "last Adam" who reversed the disobedience of the first Adam and brought righteousness and life for all (Romans 5:12–21). The failure of Israel in the wilderness, and often in later history, caused the prophets to look for God to bring about a second exodus. Jesus in his wilderness temptation demonstrated that it had begun.

For the writer of the Letter to the Hebrews, the temptations in the life of Jesus brought great encouragement: "Because he himself suffered when he was tempted, he is able to help those who are being tempted" (2:18). That is encouragement for God's people in every generation.

THE CONFESSION OF JESUS AS THE MESSIAH

The next epochal event in the experience of Jesus was his self-revelation at Caesarea Philippi. It is generally seen as the watershed of his ministry. To it Jesus had led his disciples; from it he unfolds the nature of his mission and destiny. Unfortunately the passage in which it is narrated in the Gospels has led to great controversy in the history of the church, largely through Matthew's account of Jesus' statements made to Peter and the development of its exegesis in the Roman Catholic church. There are signs, however, of abatement of the controversy as exegetes, both Catholic and Protestant, are endeavoring to submit their own traditions to the judgment of the Word of God.

The context of the event is to be observed. It is a period when Jesus was seeking to be less involved in public ministry and to devote more time to his disciples for their instruction, since it was of vital importance that they should grasp more fully his identity, his calling, and their own calling. He therefore took them away to Caesarea Philippi, where he revealed the greatest lesson he had to teach them—who he was, and how he was to accomplish his mission.

"Who do people say that I am?" he asked the disciples. Their answers were surprising: John the Baptist risen from the dead, or Elijah returned to earth to prepare for the Messiah's coming, as Malachi said he would, or one of the prophets. "But who do you say that I am?" asked Jesus. "You are the Messiah," replies Peter. (Matthew's additional phrase, "the Son of the living God," is but an extension of "Messiah" that every Jew would take for granted, namely, the king is the Son of God, as in Psalm 2:7.)

At that point Matthew adds to Mark's account three sentences from his source that no other evangelist has recorded (other than 16:19b, cf. Matthew 18:18 and John 20:23). Many critical scholars have held that they are irreconcilable with the sharp reply of Jesus reported in Mark 8:30; that is a debatable judgment, but there is increasing agreement that the statements in Matthew 16:17–19 belong to later context(s), and that Matthew set them in this one because of their suitability to the theme.[15] It is often suggested that Jesus uttered these words in his resurrection appearance to Peter, with or without his fellow disciples (cf. the account of Peter's restoration to his apostolic service in John 21:15–17).[16] That is a plausible notion in view of the parallel statement to Matthew 16:19 in John 20:23, but it can hardly apply to the whole passage, since Jesus surely gave to Simon the name Cephas during his earthly ministry. Oscar Cullmann believed that the Last Supper was the most likely occasion for that, and he pointed to Luke 22:31–34 as the probable moment.[17] It is an ingenious suggestion and by no means impossible; nevertheless it remains a speculation. As with many of the sayings of Jesus it is less important to know when they were said than to understand their meaning, and to that we immediately turn.

Jesus declares that *Simon*—note the name—is blessed, because the Father has revealed to him that Jesus is the Messiah, confirming the early enthusiastic hopes. Jesus himself then gives to Simon a revelation: "And I tell you, you are *Kepha,* and on this *kepha* I will build my church." Observe: our Lord will not have said, "You are *Peter,*" for Peter is a Greek word, and Jesus was speaking in his own language. We should translate, "You are *Rock,*

---

[15] See e.g., W. Trilling, *Das wahre Israel: Studien zur Theologie des Matthäusevangeliums* (SANT 10; Leipzig: St. Benno Verlag, 1959) 156.

[16] This view was adopted and supported by the members of the group who issued the work, *Peter in the New Testament: A Collaborative Assessment by Protestant and Roman Catholic Scholars* (ed. R. E. Brown, K. P. Donfried, J. Reumann; Minneapolis: Augsburg, 1973) 86–101.

[17] O. Cullmann, *Peter: Disciple, Apostle, Martyr: A Historical and Theological Study* (2d ed.; London: SCM, 1962) 188–90.

and on this rock I will build. . . ." Simon's name became "Rock"! (This was literally so. In the Palestinian church Peter was known as *Kepha*, cf. Galatians 2:11, 14). Undoubtedly Jesus was using pictorial language—"I will build" almost certainly has in view a new temple that will replace the old (cf. Mark 14:58). It is my conviction that if Catholics had not conceived the extraordinary notion that our Lord would always provide his church with a "Peter" to rule it, we would readily see that Jesus was appointing Simon to play a special role in the beginning of the church. That role is indicated in the next sentence: "I will give you the keys to the kingdom of heaven." This was not an appointment to exercise authority over the church, as Isaiah 22:15–25 might suggest, but to open the door of the kingdom that people may enter it, as Matthew 23:13 unambiguously suggests. Those keys were used by Peter on the day of Pentecost in the proclamation of the gospel, and for the rest of his life.

The second half of Matthew 16:19 is extended to all members of the church in 18:18 with the same fundamental imagery: it is law-court language for declaring a defendant guilty (= "bound"), or innocent ("loosed"). It is therefore close to Paul's picture of forgiveness as "justification."[18] Apostles and all witnesses of Jesus are authorized by the Lord to make known that whoever believes the good news of the kingdom is truly forgiven, and all who reject it stand under judgment and should repent and turn to him in faith.

The last clause of 16:18 is a declaration of assurance regarding the future: "The gates of Hades will not have power against it (the church)" speaks of the powerlessness of death to hold in those who open their lives to God's saving sovereignty, for the Lord of the church is on his way to a redemptive death and resurrection. When Matthew wrote these words, Jesus was the Risen Lord who had brought life from the dead for all believers; his church is "The community of the resurrection"![19]

That is all very thrilling for disciples to hear. But Jesus administers a terrible shock to them. It is scarcely possible for us today to appreciate its enormity to the disciples who first heard that he must go to Jerusalem, suffer greatly through the leaders of

---

[18] So A. Schlatter, *Der Evangelist Matthäus* (6th ed.; Stuttgart: Calwer, 1963) 511.

[19] "The Community of the Resurrection" is the name given to an Anglican monastery founded by Bishop Gore, situated in Mirfield, near Leeds, England.

the Jews, be put to death, and after three days rise again (Matthew 16:21; cf. Mark 8:31; 9:31; 10:32). It not only contradicted everything they had ever believed about the Messiah, it was inconceivable that it could happen to *Jesus*. Nor was the shock mitigated by the addition "after three days rise again." Among the Jews "three days" was a common expression for a short time, and to hear that Jesus would rise from the dead "after a short time" would be understood by the disciples as denoting the resurrection of the dead for the kingdom of God, which was expected "shortly" (cf. Luke 19:11). Peter therefore expostulated, "God pity you Lord! This must never happen to you!" And then he receives a second shock: Jesus addresses him as a Satan—an adversary, a mouthpiece of the devil! A lot has to happen before Simon can be a rock on which Jesus can build his church! But Jesus goes on to indicate the consequences for the disciples of what he has said: the way of the Messiah is to be the way of the disciples; they must shoulder a cross and follow him—i.e., to Jerusalem, there to suffer and die as he is to do (Mark 8:34). That is the picture Jesus drew, and it is a terrible one. In the event none of the Twelve were ready to follow Jesus in that way, rather they fled from the place where the crosses were planted for execution. It was only after Jesus' death on the cross was illuminated by his resurrection that they found grace to follow in the steps of their Lord—including Peter (see John 13:36).

THE TRANSFIGURATION OF JESUS

Six days after the unveiling to the disciples of the Messiahship of Jesus, and the path he must tread to open the kingdom of God for all humanity, the glory of Jesus was revealed to three disciples, Peter, James, and John (Mark 9:2–8 and parallels). The event took place on "a high mountain." None of the evangelists gives its name. Through the years Tabor has been suggested as a possible location, but though Tabor may be termed a mountain by locals it certainly is not high. There was a Roman fort on its top in the day of Jesus, which made one commentator remark that the Lord could no more have been transfigured there than on a high road. Mount Hermon is a much more likely situation. It was outside Israel's territory, close to Caesarea Philippi, and loftier than any mountain in Palestine. Jesus would have seen its snowy peak frequently from Nazareth, but this may well have been the only time he ascended it. In view of the frequency with which revelation in the Bible takes place on mountains (cf. Genesis 22; Exodus 19; 24; 34; 1 Kings 18:20ff.; 19:8ff.) it was fitting that this manifestation of the glory of Jesus should have happened on Hermon at this time, for clearly it is bound up with the revelation of six days earlier.

Luke says that Jesus took the three disciples to the mountain in order to pray (Luke 9:28–29). We need not doubt that statement, but why go so far to pray? Why, but to ratify with the Father, in the company of a few trusted associates, the decision to undertake at this point the last journey to Jerusalem and to seek grace for the conflict? As in his baptism he identified himself with a sinful race and yielded himself to God for his saving task, so now he renewed his self-consecration to the Father for the accomplishment of the redemption of the world. His prayer was answered. In the experience of transfiguration the Father strengthened his Son for the task in view, and in the holy fellowship gave an anticipation of the glory to which it would lead.

Matthew cites Jesus as saying to the disciples, "Do not tell anyone about *the vision* . . . " (17:9). That was its nature, and the disciples were drawn into it. The grace and the glory were for the Son; the voice from heaven came less for his sake than for theirs: "This is my Son; hear him." *"My Son!"* Then they were right in their intuitions of his identity! *"Hear him!"* Then he was right in what he said about his call to suffer! Here was grace for the disciples, for they had need to listen to his message. We have earlier mentioned how difficult it is for us to enter into the astonishment and bewilderment of the disciples on hearing the revolutionary teaching of Jesus about the cross of the Messiah. Of this Dmitri Merezhkovsky wrote:

> In order to understand it we must shake ourselves from the two thousand year old habit, from dead dogma, even in our most reverential feelings and thoughts of the Cross. And this is not the same for us as to take off our clothes, but rather to tear the skin from the body.[20]

Where they had been certain that Jesus was terribly mistaken, the Father himself in his pity intervened, and the testimony of law and prophets was heard afresh.

Naturally there was no question that Jesus had given up his anticipation of ruling in the consummated kingdom. His path to

---

[20] Dmitri Merezhkovsky, *Jesus Manifest* (London: J. Cape, 1935) 237.

glory was strangely indirect, but to glory it most surely led. This is intimated in an extraordinary fashion in the vision on the mountain, inasmuch as its elements were all associated with the coming of the kingdom of God at the end: Jesus is glorified, as he will appear in his final coming; Moses and Elijah are with him, as representatives of the law and the prophets, but also as expected by Jews in the last days (cf. Malachi 4:5–6, and the use made of the expected appearance of Moses and Elijah in the end time in Revelation 11:3–12); the cloud that envelops the Lord, the prophets and the disciples is reminiscent of the theophanic cloud in which the Lord is to be revealed at his coming (Mark 13:26); the voice is often mentioned in visions of the end (e.g., Matthew 24:31); the two prophets from the past recall "the dead in Christ" and the three disciples "those who are alive and are left until the coming of the Lord" (1 Thess 4:15–17).[21]

Mark was undoubtedly aware of this feature of the vision, for he will have been responsible for setting the saying of Mark 9:1 as its introduction: "Amen I say to you, there are some standing here who will not taste death until they see that the kingdom of God has come with power." Whether Jesus himself had that in mind in uttering it is quite uncertain (it could be an alternative version of Mark 13:30), but there is a remarkable echo of this interpretation in 2 Peter 1:16–19:

> For we did not follow cleverly devised myths when we made known to you the power and coming [parousia, the final coming] of our Lord Jesus Christ, but we had been eyewitnesses of his majesty. For he received honor and glory from God the Father when that voice was conveyed to him by the Majestic Glory, saying, "This is my Son, my Beloved, with whom I am well pleased." We ourselves heard this voice come from heaven, while we were with him on the holy mountain. So we have the prophetic message more fully confirmed. (NRSV)

It is a striking concept that the Father's confirmation of the way that the Son must take is given in a vision not alone of the resurrection glory of Jesus (cf. John 13:31–32) but of his ultimate coming in glory. The light of Hermon thus penetrates the darkness of Golgotha. Though Jesus is to die in a gloom impenetrable to human eyes, his path is from glory to glory (cf. 2 Corinthians 3:18). The cross and the throne are alike glorious.

---

[21] This whole theme was developed by G. H. Boobyer in *St. Mark and the Transfiguration Story* (Edinburgh: T. & T. Clark, 1942).

This the disciples had painfully to learn. It is still an essential part of the gospel.

THE GOSPEL OF THE PASSION OF JESUS

To speak of the "passion" of our Lord (i.e., his sufferings and death as recorded in the Gospels) is to come to the heart of the gospel. It is a complex of events from which it is hard to exclude anything as irrelevant. Of all the features emphasized by the evangelists, one of the most striking is their conviction that the events of the passion are in complete accord with the will of God revealed in the scriptures. It will be found, on examination, that most of the key passages in the Gospels concerning the end of our Lord's life are enforced by explicit references to the Old Testament, or implicitly have such in view. For example the triumphal entry in Matthew (21:1–9) and Luke (19:28–38) is described with a citation of Zechariah 9:9 and Psalm 118:25–26. In Mark the temple cleansing (11:11, 15–19) is supported by Isaiah 56:7; the betrayal of Judas (14:17–21) by Psalm 41:10; the prophecy of Peter's denial (14:26–31) by Zechariah 13:7; the distress in Gethsemane (14:32–42) by Psalm 43:6; the arrest of Jesus (14:43–52) by a general allusion to the necessity for prophecy to be fulfilled (v. 49); the trial before the Sanhedrin (14:53–72) by the joint quotation of Psalm 110:1 and Daniel 7:13 (in v. 62). The association of the conspiracy of the Jewish leaders and the trial with Psalm 2 deeply impressed itself on the mind of the early church, as Acts 4:25–30 illustrates. The narration of the crucifixion recalls Psalms 22 and 69; the passages are so familiar, Mark does not feel it necessary to call attention to them.

The special features of the passion narratives by Matthew, Luke, and John as compared with Mark can be traced to the use of other scriptures which had impressed them. Compare, for example, the details concerning the end of Judas recorded by Matthew (27:3–10) with Zechariah 11:12–13 and Jeremiah 39:6–15; 18:2–3. John's description of the soldiers refraining from breaking the legs of Jesus, as he was dead already, yet thrusting the spear into his side, just to make sure (19:31–37), is particularly instructive: the evangelist emphatically calls attention to the fulfillment of scriptures by these actions, which appear to include the death of Jesus as God's Passover lamb (Exodus 12:46; Numbers 9:12; cf. John 1:29), the suffering righteous man (Psalm 34:19) and the pierced representative of God (Zechariah

12:10). It is conceivable that the different passion narratives in the Gospels are ultimately due to their being formed on different "skeletons" of Old Testament prophecies. In any case none can doubt how fundamental it was to the evangelists to show that the sufferings and death of our Lord were in accordance with the eternal counsels of God (cf. Acts 2:23; 1 Peter 1:19–20; and Revelation 13:8?). In this conviction they were surely right.

It is not possible for us to consider here all the elements of the passion story in their relation to the proclamation of the gospel. In view of our limited space we shall restrict our attention to the Last Supper, the agony of Gethsemane, and our Lord's utterances of desolation and victory on the cross.

We include consideration of the Last Supper of Jesus with his disciples, not only because it was the climax of his ministry to them, and its critical importance to the church, but because it provides the most important evidence as to how Jesus interpreted his death. A. E. J. Rawlinson gave expression to this belief in some striking words:

> Interpreting in advance the significance of his coming Passion, he was in effect making it to be, for all time, what it otherwise would not have been, viz. a sacrifice for the sins of the world. It is the Last Supper which makes Calvary sacrificial. It was not the death upon Calvary per se, but the death upon Calvary as the Last Supper interprets it and gives the clue to its meaning which constitutes our Lord's sacrifice.[22]

To be a little more precise I think we should modify that last sentence to make it read "not the death per se, but *the death upon Calvary as our Lord in the Last Supper interprets it. . . .*" For it was Jesus himself who uttered the words "This is my Body . . . ," as he handed the broken loaf to the disciples and "This is my new covenant blood . . . " as he gave the cup to be shared among them. In so speaking and acting he was declaring and enacting a double parable of his death as a sacrifice, not for the disciples alone, but for all humanity.

The same thought is found in the prayer of Jesus in John 17, notably v. 19: "On their behalf I consecrate myself. . . . " The whole ministry of Jesus had been one of dedication to the service of God, but here his consecration reaches its climax. In sacrificial

---

[22] A. E. J. Rawlinson, "Corpus Christi," in *Mysterium Christi* (ed. G. K. A. Bell and A. Deissmann; London: Longmans, Green, 1930) 241.

contexts in the Old Testament the term "consecrate" can be synonymous with "sacrifice" (see Deuteronomy 15:19, 21). In the context of this prayer Jesus solemnly consecrates himself to death in order to mediate the saving sovereignty of God to all humankind. His prayer accordingly makes his death a voluntary offering of himself for the salvation of the human race. Thereby (plus the singularity of his identity!) his death on the cross is distinguished from that of the two men crucified on either side of him. At the table Jesus relates his death to his disciples ("on your behalf," Luke 22:19–20; 1 Corinthians 11:24) as he gave them the loaf and the cup. Hence the continuation of his prayer in John 17:19 has special reference to them: "I consecrate myself, that they themselves also may be consecrated in truth." In the Old Testament to "consecrate" can denote the setting aside of persons to priestly or prophetic ministry (cf. Exodus 28:41; Jeremiah 1:5). The consecration of Jesus to death is made in order that they too may be consecrated to the task of bringing the saving sovereignty to the world in like spirit as he brought it. He alone can open the gates of God's kingdom to the world, but his followers are called to be its instruments as they make it known to the world by proclamation in word and by suffering love.

We must not, however, forget that at the Last Supper Jesus explicitly related his death to the whole people of God and the whole world. The saying regarding the cup in Mark 14:24 reads, "This is my blood of the covenant poured out on behalf of many." No less than three significant passages of the Old Testament are echoed in this statement. Exodus 24:8 records that Moses took blood of the sacrifices offered for Israel at Sinai and sprinkled it on the people with the words, "See the blood of the covenant that the Lord has made with you." Paul and Luke have the expression "the *new* covenant," which recalls Jeremiah's prophecy of the new covenant which God is to make with Israel and Judah in the last days, when the law will be written in their hearts, and all the people will know him and experience his forgiveness (31:31–34). Finally Isaiah 52:13–53:12 tells of the Servant of the Lord bearing the sin of "many," which in its context refers to the world of nations, astonished alike at the sufferings of the Servant for the guilty and his exaltation as Lord of all.

An endlessly discussed problem relating to the Lord's Supper is whether or not it was a celebration of the Passover. The evidence of the Gospels appears to be conflicting. The Synoptic Gospels clearly represent the meal as a Passover. In Mark 14:22

the disciples ask, "Where do you want us to go and prepare the Passover for you?" which proves to be the Last Supper. But in John 18:28 it is stated that after the arrest of Jesus the chief priests refused to go inside the governor's palace "so that they should not be defiled but eat the Passover," and in John 19:14 the hour of Pilate's sentencing Jesus to death by crucifixion is recorded—twelve noon on the day of preparation for the Passover, which was the time when the Passover lambs were being prepared for slaughter. Many solutions to the conundrum have been offered. The most plausible one is the existence at that time of two different calendars, namely solar and lunar, which determined the date of religious festivals; the former was a year of 364 days, so that on its basis the festivals always occurred on the same day of the week, the Passover always falling on a Tuesday; the Qumran group adhered to that calendar, the Sadducees to the lunar system; if Jesus followed the former and the fourth evangelist recorded the official view, all would be explained.[23] It's a brilliant solution of the problem and has attracted many scholars, but not commanded the assent of all. Whatever the truth of this matter, one fact is acknowledged by all who have investigated it: *the Passover associations of the Last Supper are presupposed in all the Gospel accounts,* curiously enough, most emphatically in the Gospel of John. A major motif in that gospel is the fulfillment of Israel's festivals by Jesus, above all that of the Passover, as John 19:31–37 illustrates. One result of that emphasis is to show the ministry, death and resurrection of Jesus as the realization of the prophetic anticipation of God's gift to Israel of a second Exodus leading to the kingdom of God. In the time of Jesus that was a major element in the Jewish mind at Passover: celebration of the redemption of Israel at the first Exodus under the first redeemer, Moses, and eager anticipation of the second Exodus under the second redeemer, the Messiah. Hence the Last Supper of Jesus is not only heavy with the thought of his impending sacrifice but illuminated by that of the feast of the kingdom of God, participation in which is made possible through the sacrifice which leads to resurrection and the glory of his final appearing.

The account of Jesus in the garden of Gethsemane gives us a glimpse into the darkness of the Passion. Jesus "began to be

---

[23] See the discussion by I. Howard Marshall in *Last Supper and Lord's Supper* (Carlisle: Paternoster, 1980) 57–75.

terrified and in distress," writes Mark (14:33), using language that Matthew and Luke hesitate to repeat. John, however, comes close to Mark, in that he reports Jesus as saying, "Now my heart is in turmoil" (12:27), a term that signifies an agitation, horror, convulsion, and shock of spirit. He takes with him his close associates, Peter, James, and John, to pray, and in words that echo Psalm 42:6 tells them, "I am deeply grieved, even to death; remain here, and keep awake" (Mark 14:34). His command, "Keep awake," was in order that they also should pray—for themselves and for him, for he evidently felt that he needed the help of his Father more than he had ever done in his life, but they also needed to pray for themselves, for the hour of crisis was to come upon them as well as on him. In the event they had no heart to respond to his bidding. He turned to his Father in an intensity of prayer that resembled a battle (note Luke's description of the sweat of Jesus falling to the ground "like great drops of blood," 22:43–44), but they were overcome with weariness and slept. The crisis found him prepared and them unprepared. He overcame the temptation to retreat; they surrendered to it and fled.

The heart of our Lord's prayer on this occasion is in Mark 14:36, "Father, all things are possible to you; remove this cup from me; yet not what I want, but what you want." Jesus knows that even now it is possible to defeat the Jewish opposition to him (cf. Matthew 26:53), and to resist Pilate and the might of Rome (John 19:11). His natural wish is for deliverance, but his deepest desire is to pray with all his heart, "Not what I want, but what you want." The battle consisted in affirming the first clause of his prayer ("All things are possible for you"), eliminating the second ("Remove this cup from me"), and meaning the third ("Not what I want, but what you want"); i.e., in recognizing that God could take the cup from him but being willing to receive it at his hands. The fearfulness of the cup lay precisely in the fact that it was from God and not from man. The figure of a cup given by God to people is a standing symbol in the Old Testament to represent his judgments on them, for strong drink makes people reel in drunkenness and fall to the ground. Isaiah 51:17 is particularly illuminating, for it refers to Israel as having drunk a cup given to them by God:

Rouse yourself, rouse yourself!
Stand up, O Jerusalem,
you who have drunk at the hand of the Lord
the cup of his wrath,

who have drunk to the dregs
the cup of staggering. (NRSV)

The "cup" has entailed "devastation and destruction, fam-
ine and sword," and Jerusalem's "children" are "full of the wrath
of the Lord" (vv. 19–20). They are consoled, however, by the
promise that the cup they have drunk will be handed to their
tormentors. Such associations of the symbol of a cup which God
wills that Jesus should drink ("what *you* want"!) is a hint of the
reason why Jesus shrank so fearfully from taking it from the hand
of God, in contrast to the frequent readiness of later Christian
martyrs to go to death for the name of Jesus: it was not the
prospect of crucifixion alone that made Jesus "terrified and in
distress," but what was entailed in giving his life "a ransom for the
many" (Mark 10:45). Nevertheless the Spirit who was with him
led him, as always, to obedience and wholehearted acceptance of
the Father's will. The greatest battle of prayer was won, and no
power on earth or in hell could henceforth deflect him from
his goal.

The darkness of Gethsemane found its counterpart in the
darkness on the cross and the cry of dereliction, "My God, my
God, why have you forsaken me?" (Mark 15:34). What did that
cry signify to Jesus? The question has been raised since the
words cite the opening of Psalm 22, and it is generally acknowledged that to quote a sentence of the Old Testament scriptures
may cover its context also. That has led to a curious controversy
with respect to this citation. Commenting on the passage A.
Menzies wrote:

> He who quotes the first words of a poem may be thinking not of these
> words only but of some later part of the poem or of its general course
> of thought, and the twenty-second Psalm, while it opens with a cry
> like that of despair, is not by any means a Psalm of despair, but of
> help and salvation coming to one brought very low.[24]

The suggestion is in line with a tendency to view the cry
of Jesus as expressing not an agony of mind, but a consciousness
that the will of God is being performed. Sir Edwyn Hoskyns
went further in this direction. He thought that the cry "It is
finished" (John 19:29) sums up the latter half of Psalm 22 and
accordingly wrote:

---

[24] A. Menzies, *The Earliest Gospel: A Historical Study of the Gospel according
to Mark* (London: Macmillan, 1901) 281.

The Matthaean-Markan word, "My God, my God, why have you forsaken me?" and the Johannine, "It is finished," have the same significance; the former cites the first words of the psalm, and in so doing involves the whole; the latter sums up its meaning and is less open to misunderstanding.[25]

I reproduce this view to be just to men of undoubted insight into the scriptures, notably Sir Edwyn Hoskyns, whose commentary on the Gospel of John is outstanding, but it seems to me a most implausible interpretation. Psalm 22 certainly finishes up with triumphant praise, but that does not diminish the reality of the agony described in the first twenty-one verses; the praise of the next eleven verses is added when the situation has changed and God has answered the prayer of the psalmist for deliverance. Exactly the same phenomenon is apparent in Psalm 69, which is quoted more frequently in the New Testament than any other psalm relative to the sufferings of Jesus, but which ends in half a dozen sentences of thanksgiving. The ordinary reader of the Gospels cannot resist the impression that the so-called cry of dereliction is precisely that: Jesus voicing through scripture language a fearful sense of God-forsakenness. Jurgen Moltmann does not hesitate to affirm the truthfulness of that impression. On the terrible cry of Jesus from the cross he writes as follows:

> God-forsakenness is the final experience of God endured by the crucified Jesus on Golgotha, because to the very end he knew that he was God's Son. God's silence, the hiding of his face, the eclipse of God, the dark night of the soul, the death of God, hell: these are the metaphors for this inconceivable fact that have come down to us in the traditions of Christian experiences of God. They are attempts to describe an abyss, a sinking into nothingness; yet they are only approximations to Jesus' final experience of God on the cross, his Job-like experience. The uniqueness of what may have taken place between Jesus and his God on Golgotha is therefore something we do well to accept and respect as his secret, while we ourselves hold fast to the paradox that Jesus died the death of God's Son in God-forsakenness.[26]

I have long been convinced that there is no section of the Old Testament scriptures which Jesus pondered more than

---

[25] E. Hoskyns, *The Fourth Gospel* (2d ed.; ed. F. N. Davey; London: Faber, 1947) 531.
[26] J. Moltmann, *The Way of Jesus Christ: Christology in Messianic Dimensions* (San Francisco: Harper, 1990) 167.

Isaiah 40–55, with its songs of the Servant of the Lord, and above all the final one, Isaiah 52:13–53:12. There the tribulation of the innocent Righteous Servant on behalf a guilty world is set forth with all clarity. The cry of dereliction is a clue to the cost to Jesus of being the bearer of humanity's guilt. But the pain of it was not borne by him alone. That is implied in Paul's famous words, "God in Christ was reconciling the world to himself" (2 Corinthians 5:18f.). Perhaps the greatest contribution of Moltmann to our understanding of atonement is his insistence on the suffering of the Father in the suffering of the Son. "The theology of surrender is misunderstood and perverted into its very opposite," he affirmed, "unless it is grasped as being the theology of the pain of God, which means the theology of the divine co-suffering or compassion."[27] Commenting on the Gospel phrase "for us" he added:

> The inner secret of Christ's vicarious act "for us" is the vicarious act and self-giving of God: "If God is for us, who can be against us?" The whole Trinity is caught up in the movement towards self-surrender, which in the passion of Christ reaches lost men and women and is revealed to them.[28]

It should be stated that the cry of dereliction was not the last word of Jesus on the cross recorded by Mark. He added, "Jesus uttering a great cry breathed his last" (15:37). What that cry was Mark did not know. May we assume that it was that recorded by the fourth evangelist—"It is finished"? (John 19:30, which also states that Jesus then "gave up his spirit"). Therein the sacrificial obedience of the Son was concluded. The veil of the temple was rent from top to bottom, God's testimony to the fulfillment of atonement by his Son. The Roman centurion superintending the crucifixion exclaimed, "Truly this man was God's Son" (Mark 15:39). What exactly he intended by that witness we cannot tell, but Mark recorded it as a foreshadowing of the confession that multitudes of the Roman world were to make, thenceforward more than even Mark could possibly know. From his cross Jesus draws "all" to himself (John 12:31–32).

---

[27] Ibid., 178. This conviction is the theme of Moltmann's earlier work, *The Crucified God* (London: SCM, 1974).
[28] Moltmann, *The Way of Jesus Christ,* 167.

THE GOSPEL OF THE RESURRECTION OF JESUS

In one of Luke's summary statements of the life of the earliest church in Jerusalem, Acts 4:32–35, he states, "With great power the apostles gave witness to the resurrection of the Lord Jesus" (v. 33). That was intended as a summary of the apostles' preaching of the gospel. Certainly the accounts of Peter's preaching in the first five chapters of Acts have one theme: the Jewish rejection of Jesus and their handing him over to the Roman authority for crucifixion, and God's reversal of their judgment by raising him from death. The preaching of Paul recorded in Acts has a similar emphasis, but is frequently related to the risen Lord's appearance to him. In itself that message was extraordinary, but it was far more than the simple news of the resuscitation of a dead prophet. Peter tells his Jewish hearers in the temple, "You killed the originator of life, whom God raised from the dead" (Acts 3:15). The term "originator" (Greek *archēgos*) was used of a hero who founded a city state, or a military leader, or a pioneer. It is evident that the expression "originator of life" had the meaning of one who by his resurrection brought life for all, and gives them to share in his power and glory. Interestingly, the writer to the Hebrews speaks of Jesus as "the originator of salvation" (Hebrews 2:10), which in Aramaic would be exactly the same wording as Peter used, for "salvation" and "life" are identical in that language. That in itself is an indication of the significance of the resurrection of Jesus to its earliest preachers.[29]

In our modern times the question inevitably is asked, "But did it really happen? Is it conceivable that Jesus was raised from the dead to become the Savior of the world?" We know the typical answer of the rationalist: "Dead men don't rise." That's not modern. Some members at least of the church at Corinth wrote and told Paul that (1 Corinthians 15:12), which is why Paul wrote the lengthy chapter on the resurrection in his reply to them. Strangely, there has been no little hesitation on the part of Christian scholars to commit themselves to a clear affirmation of belief in the bodily resurrection of Jesus. In part it is due to the notion that the resurrection is not a historical event but belongs to the spiritual order, and so is for faith alone. Emil Brunner was strongly committed to belief in the resurrection, but affirmed:

[29] See G. Delling, "ἀρχηγός," *TDNT* 1.487–88.

Easter, the resurrection of the Lord, is not an "historical event" which can be reported. . . . It is itself revelation, the divine self-testimony, which, as such allows of no objectivity, because it is addressed to faith.[30]

As long ago as 1913 James Denney responded to this "dogmatic concept of history," as he called it, by saying, "It is vain to controvert such a dogma by argument, it may be demolished by collision with facts."[31] Brunner had supported his view by stating that the only people named as witnesses of the resurrection of Jesus were believers. That's not correct. Paul was most certainly not a believer when Jesus appeared to him. It is likely that the same was true of James, the brother of Jesus (for the appearance to him see 1 Corinthians 15:7). John 7:5 declares that the brothers of Jesus did not believe in him. It is altogether likely that James would have been confirmed in his opinion when Jesus was arrested and crucified, and we have no knowledge of a change of attitude if and when reports of the resurrection of his brother reached him.

Brunner also held that the empty tomb, observable to any secular person, plays no part in the New Testament as a foundation for faith in the resurrection of Jesus.[32] That, too, is highly disputable. Paul's statement of the primitive kerygma in 1 Corinthians 15:3–4 includes three items: Christ died for our sins, he was buried, he has been raised on the third day; the separate clause "he was buried" is in all probability an allusion to the empty tomb. We recall that the purpose of the chapter was apologetic with regard to the reality of resurrection. All four Gospels give clear accounts of the discovery of the empty tomb. Mark's gospel, as we have it, ends with a report of women arriving at the tomb and finding it empty; a "young man" (angel?) told the women that Jesus was not there: "He was raised . . . *Look, there is the place where they laid him.*" (The list of appearances of the risen Lord that follows is a later addition to the Gospel.)

We earlier drew attention to the view that the empty tomb was not so much a proof of the resurrection of Jesus as a sign of

---

[30] E. Brunner, *The Mediator* (Philadelphia: Westminster, 1947) 575, and K. Lake and H. J. Cadbury, *English Translation and Commentary,* vol. 4 of *The Beginnings of Christianity,* part 1: *The Acts of the Apostles* (ed. F. J. Foakes-Jackson and K. Lake; London: Macmillan, 1933) 36.

[31] J. Denney, *Jesus and the Gospel* (London: Hodder and Stoughton, 1913) 108.

[32] Brunner, *The Mediator,* 576.

it. But let none underestimate the effect of the sign. Paul Althaus affirmed that the proclamation of the resurrection "could not have been maintained in Jerusalem for a single day, for a single hour, if the emptiness of the tomb had not been established as a fact for all concerned."[33] The Jewish leaders did not dispute that the tomb in which Jesus was laid was empty; they did not, because they could not; in self-defense they could only claim that his disciples had stolen his body (Matthew 28:11–15). (Justin, in his *Dialogue with Trypho*, 108.2, reports that his Jewish counterpart in the dialogue repeated the allegation.) Neville Clark, accordingly, was justified in asserting:

> The Empty Tomb stands as the massive sign that the eschatological deed of God is not outside this world of time and space or in despair of it, but has laid hold on it, penetrated deep into it, shattered it, and begun its transformation.[34]

Let us freely acknowledge that the "sign" of the resurrection was confirmed by the appearances of Jesus to his disciples, and that it was largely these experiences that turned the disciples to an unwavering faith in Jesus the risen Lord. Not that anyone witnessed the resurrection of Jesus itself, naturally, for that was an act of God of creative proportions, hidden from human view. The disciples were witnesses to the fact that Jesus had been raised to life by the power of God, and were themselves transformed by their experiences. The list of such appearances in 1 Corinthians 15:5–8 must have been compiled and taught very early. Paul would have been informed about them in Damascus at the time of his own conversion, and later had many opportunities to speak with those named in it. The date of his conversion is generally reckoned as not earlier than two years after the crucifixion-resurrection of Jesus, but not later than seven years after it, and is commonly agreed to be about four years after it. That is far too early for supposed "legends of the resurrection" to arise.

James Denney (and many other theologians) became convinced that the supreme evidence for the resurrection of Jesus is its effect in the creation of the Christian church.

---

[33] P. Althaus, *Die Wahrheit des kirchlichen Osterglaubens* (Gütersloh: Bertelsmann, 1940) 25, cited by W. Pannenberg, *Jesus, God and Man* (London: SCM, 1968) 100.

[34] N. Clark, *Interpreting the Resurrection* (London: SCM, 1967) 98.

The real historical evidence for the resurrection is the fact that it was believed, preached, propagated, and produced its fruit and effect in the new phenomenon of the Christian church, long before any of our Gospels were written. . . . Faith in the resurrection was not only prevalent but immensely powerful before any of our New Testament books were written. Not one of them would ever have been written but for that faith. It is not this or that in the New Testament—it is not the story of the empty tomb, or of the appearing of Jesus in Jerusalem or Galilee—which is the primary evidence for the resurrection; it is the New Testament itself. The life that throbs in it from beginning to end, the life that always fills us again with wonder as it beats upon us from its pages, is the life which the Risen Savior has quickened in Christian souls. The evidence for the resurrection of Jesus is the existence of the church in that extraordinary spiritual vitality which confronts us in the New Testament.[35]

Granting this eloquently stated conviction, there is one question we have not yet raised, namely the nature of the resurrection of Jesus itself. Are we to think of it as a bodily resurrection, or an essentially spiritual event witnessed only in vision? That has been hotly debated by scholars, but why do we have to choose between the alternatives? Paul, in his discussion of the nature of the future resurrection gave us a needed clue: "If there is a physical body, there is also a spiritual body. Thus it is written, 'The first man, Adam, became a living being'; the last Adam became a life-giving spirit" (1 Corinthians 15:44–45). The entire New Testament is written in agreement with the primitive kerygma cited by Paul: "Christ died . . . was buried . . . has been raised. . . . " This language assumes that the Lord in his body was crucified, buried and raised from death. But according to Paul, in resurrection the body of Jesus was so completely transformed that in him, the risen Lord, the new creation was present, and through him humanity may know its transforming power even now (2 Corinthians 5:17: "If anyone is in Christ, there is a new creation: everything old has passed away; see, everything has become new!"). The resurrection event accordingly is both bodily and spiritual. The transformation of the body of Jesus presupposed is sheer miracle and mystery beyond understanding. We do well to acknowledge that fact candidly. The miracle and the mystery will be revealed in the event which it anticipates, namely the parousia—the coming of the Lord in power and glory. That is a mystery of the same order,

---

[35] Denney, *Jesus and the Gospel*, 111–12.

for through both God achieves his purpose in creation, and both are "eschatological" acts.

Here we grasp the ultimate significance of the resurrection of Jesus: as the incarnate Son of God he is the representative Man in whom the destiny of humanity, i.e., resurrection from death, was realized. It follows that the Easter resurrection was more than God's reversal of the Jewish leaders' rejection of Jesus, more than God's revelation and vindication of Jesus as the Messiah through whom God's kingdom was coming, more even than God's revelation that the death of Jesus had brought about the redemption and reconciliation of the world. It was all these things and more, inasmuch as in Jesus the saving sovereignty of God was inaugurated through his living, his dying, and his rising, and in him, the risen Lord, the new creation is present and is available for all humankind. That theology is assumed by the evangelists in the first three Gospels, but it becomes explicit in the Fourth Gospel. John 12:31-32 reads: "Now is the judgment of this world, now the prince of this world shall be thrown out, and I, if I am lifted up from the earth, will draw all to myself." Here the death and resurrection of Jesus are viewed as one event, through the use of the verb "lift up" to denote being lifted up on a cross and being lifted up to the throne of God. (The Aramaic term *zeqaph,* "lift up," was actually employed for the verb "crucify." It occurs in the Syriac version at Mark 15:24.) That makes the death of Jesus integral to the eschatological act whereby the judgment of the world takes place—at once a revelation of the sin of humanity, the bearing of that sin by the Son of God, and the "casting out" of Satan through the completeness of the sacrifice achieved and through the enthronement of Jesus by resurrection to the right hand of God; that having taken place Jesus will draw "all" to himself—not to the cross, but to himself as the risen Savior.[36]

This interpretation of the unity of the death and resurrection of Jesus appears to be assumed by Paul in his exposition of the importance of Christ's resurrection for our salvation in 1 Corinthians 15:12-19. "If Christ has not been raised then our proclamation is empty and your faith is empty. . . . If Christ has not been raised your faith is futile, you are still in your sins." Paul does not say, "If Christ has not been raised you don't know whether his sacrifice was accepted by God"; he declares, "Our

---

[36] See Beasley-Murray, *John,* 213-15.

preaching and your faith are empty of meaning and you are still in your sins." What appears to be in Paul's mind is the doctrine of Christ as the representative Man, alike in his death and in his resurrection, by means of which humanity is rescued (redeemed!) from sin and death for life in the kingdom of God. That is applied in the immediately succeeding paragraph, "As in Adam all die, so also in Christ all will be made alive." It is the Pauline equivalent of the utterance of Jesus in John 11:25: "I am the Resurrection and the Life." Jesus has been appointed by the Father to be the means of resurrection, the life-giver, in accordance with John 5:21, "As the Father raises the dead and gives them life, so also the Son gives life to those whom he wishes." That holds good from Easter on and until the coming of the Lord, as John 11:25 indicates:

> Whoever believes in me, even though he dies, will come to life, and everyone who lives and believes in me will never die.

The first clause is an assurance of resurrection after death, when through Christ the saving sovereignty of God reaches its consummation. The second clause is a declaration that every believer in Jesus has the life of the kingdom of God and therefore will never "die," for such a person has "crossed over from death to life" (John 5:24).

Jesus then is the life of his people—through the Holy Spirit, sent by the risen Lord as an Easter gift on the day of Pentecost (Acts 2:33). That means that justification, as an element of Christian experience, can never be reduced solely to a matter of legal status before God, even though the term comes from the law courts. When God declares a person righteous in his sight, his creative word accomplishes its verdict, as truly as when God said, "Let light be," light came to be. Moreover, the Christian is justified not in his own right but "in Christ." This is plainly stated by Paul in Romans 8:1-2: "There is now no condemnation *for those who are in Christ Jesus*. For the law of the Spirit of life in Christ Jesus has set you free from the law of sin and death." The righteousness displayed in the life of Jesus, supremely in his obedience unto death, becomes ours as we share his risen life. United by the Spirit with the risen Christ, believers possess a moral dynamic, so that far from escaping "the just requirement of the law" they are enabled to fulfill it (Romans 8:4). That is the outcome of the Christian being a "new creation" in Christ (2 Corinthians 5:17). And that, according to Paul, is the meaning of one's baptism. Romans 6:4 states the purpose of baptism thus: "buried with him through baptism to death, in order that as Christ was raised from the dead through the glory of the Father, so we also should walk in newness of life." Resurrection life in Christ should find expression in living that is characteristic of the new age.

Since Christ is the life of his own by the Spirit, his life binds them into a closely knit group, the church. This is part of the gospel of the resurrection. We are delivered from one solidarity into another, from the old race into the new humanity, that together we might experience fellowship with Christ and all others in unity with him, and serve him in the world as he served it. The distinguishing mark of the church is that it is the church of the risen Lord who has sent his Spirit to believers to make of them his "body." Two ideas are entailed in that concept: the first is the unity of members of the church in Christ, the second is the church as the instrument through which the risen Lord continues his mission in the world, every member of which has a part to play in that work ("members" = "limbs" of the body!). Both aspects are important. Sinful people are lifted from their sense of isolation in the universe to being part of the company of the redeemed in Christ. They are delivered from associations that drag them from God and are set in the fellowship that binds them to God. In that fellowship they find common thought, common life, and a love that takes its inspiration from the love of the redeemer (John 13:34–35). The center of all is the Christ who binds each to himself and each to all and to the Father (John 17:21–23). And the purpose of it all? "That the world may believe that you sent me" (John 17:21). The most frequently mentioned aspect of the work of Christ in the Fourth Gospel is that he was sent by the Father. The commission laid upon his followers by the risen Lord was: "As the Father has sent me I also am sending you" (John 20:21). The mission of the Son continues (the perfect tense "has sent" in Greek implies continuance in God's mission); he fulfills it through all whom he sends.

The relation of the risen Lord to humankind extends beyond his church. He is Lord of all flesh. A primitive Christian confession ran, "To this end Christ died and lived again that he might be Lord of the dead and living" (Romans 14:9). To such a statement there is no exception; every individual stands in relation to the risen Lord. The world has never been without the providential government of God. Having prepared the world for the advent of his Son, God has been pleased to invest the Son with authority over it (Matthew 28:18). Despite the counterclaims of men and the opposition of every antichrist, there is one Lord only who has right to exercise universal sovereignty. He has entered on that right and will continue to use it until the last enemy is destroyed (1 Corinthians 15:22–26). As a corollary of this all life must be claimed for his sovereignty. His it is by right, and his it must be in fact. We who have yielded to his sovereignty and are experiencing the redeeming powers of his kingdom are called to mediate them to our fellows, alike through the call to repentance and through the quality of our lives as we claim every sphere of life for God.

The risen Christ is therefore Lord of the future. We have seen that the Easter resurrection was the beginning of the new creation and of the resurrection of all humanity, and as such it anticipated the coming of the Lord at the end. The consciousness of the crucial significance of the resurrection of Christ regarding the end finds striking expression in 2 Timothy 1:10: Christ Jesus "annulled death and brought life and incorruption to light through the gospel." The unusual feature of this statement is that the annulment of the power of death and bringing to light of life and incorruption is attributed to the "appearing" of the Lord, i.e., his appearance in the flesh, and everything entailed in it. That must denote his whole mediatorial work in ministry, death, and resurrection. The entire process in word and action revealed the truth of life in the kingdom of God, now and in the future, and in particular the assurance of resurrection through Christ on the last day. The prospect before the believer is nothing less than sharing the glory of Christ. The Lord of Easter has promised that it shall be so ("Because I live you too shall live," John 14:19). He will come to ensure that it happens.

Our gospel is thus the description of the saving acts of Christ on behalf of the world. Through his life, death, and resurrection salvation was achieved for all humanity, and his appearing at the end will bring it to perfect fulfillment. The process is one—God in action in our Lord Jesus Christ, who was born for us, lived for us, died for us, was raised for us, communicates his grace to us, and at the last shall come for us.

Let his messengers pray that their lips may worthily and effectively proclaim the gospel in the life of Jesus!

3

THE GOSPEL IN THE

MIRACLES OF JESUS

But miracles don't happen!" So we are told by typical secular-minded persons who have no time for the church and no interest in religion. It is not uncommon to hear the miracle stories of the Bible grouped along with the fairy stories of childhood; to relate the miracles of Jesus to children in Sunday schools does no harm, but adults shouldn't be expected to believe them! This attitude, very prevalent among nonliterary viewers of television in the Western world, is to no small extent a remnant of the deism that flourished in the seventeenth and eighteenth centuries and a mechanistic view of science which developed, ironically, from the deeply religious Sir Isaac Newton.

The idea that miracles do not and cannot happen is particularly associated with the eighteenth-century philosopher David Hume. He declared:

> A miracle is a violation of the laws of nature; and as a firm and unalterable experience has established these laws, the proof against a miracle, from the very nature of the fact, is as entire as any argument from experience can possibly be imagined.[1]

---

[1] D. Hume, *An Enquiry Concerning Human Understanding,* Section 10, Part 1. This citation is from Colin Brown's *That You May Believe: Miracles and Faith Then*

Observe, Hume here spoke in purely general terms. He did not consider any specific miracles, such as the resurrection of Jesus. His dictum ruled out the possibility of miracles as such, and so he considered it not worth spending time on individual cases.

This concept of a miracle as a "violation" of the laws of science became widely accepted, and was believed to be confirmed by the apparently immutable laws of science with which it was linked. This confidence in a mechanistic view of the universe, however, has been shaken by the development of quantum theory, for whereas the universe had been assumed to be determined by unchangeable laws, the quantum theory of particles implies that the universe is fundamentally indeterministic, and therefore appears to leave room for impartial investigation into reported miracles. Admittedly, those versed in the philosophy of science are cautious about making overconfident claims for the validity of miracles on the basis of quantum theory. Nevertheless Mary Hesse, a lecturer in the philosophy of science in Cambridge University, stated:

> There is no doubt that abandonment of the deterministic world-view in physics has made it more difficult to regard the existing state of science as finally legislative of what is and what is not possible in nature.[2]

But Ms. Hesse had to admit that for the scientific mentality the presumption is still strong that the kinds of things that demonstrably do not happen most of the time never have happened.[3] Unfortunately it is also true that there have been a significant number of theologians who maintain a similar position. Rudolf Bultmann set the German church on its ear some years ago by an essay in which he pleaded for courage to rid the gospel of its "mythology." He had in mind primarily the entire structure of the gospel, and the miracles came in for merely incidental treatment, but what he said about them was plain enough:

> The miracles of the New Testament, as miracles, are finished. . . . One cannot use electric light and radio apparatus, accept the claims of modern medicinal and clinical methods in cases of illness, and

and Now (Grand Rapids: Eerdmans, 1985) 19; I am indebted to the author for his insights into this subject and the history of thought concerning it.

[2]M. Hesse, "Miracles and the Laws of Nature," in *Miracles: Cambridge Studies in Their Philosophy and History* (ed. C. F. D. Moule; London: Mowbray, 1965) 38.

[3]Ibid., 40.

at the same time believe in the spirit and miracle world of the New Testament.[4]

It is not to be wondered at that Bultmann raised a storm through this position of his. Many who sympathized with his attempt to present the gospel in modern terms felt compelled to part company with him in this total rejection of miracles. The notion that a miracle is a violation of the laws of the universe is false, despite the fact that Christians have themselves frequently believed that they had to accept that view. On the contrary, it is fundamental to biblical faith that God is creator of the universe and is in continuous relation with it. God does not have to break laws of the universe he has made whenever he intervenes in the affairs of humankind, but is free at all times to work in and through the universe for the accomplishment of his beneficent will. To consider that man's modern technological accomplishments, including the remarkable advances in the treatment of diseases, eliminate all belief in the miracles of Jesus is beyond comprehension.

Colin Brown entitles a chapter of his book on miracles "The Curious Case of the King of Siam." He cites a story told by John Locke, the famous English philosopher in the seventeenth century, of the king of Siam being entertained by the Dutch ambassador. The king was fascinated by the stories which the ambassador told of his own country. The ambassador explained that sometimes in the winter the water became so hard that people could walk on it—even an elephant could do so! At that point the king broke in and said, "Hitherto I have believed the strange things you have told me, because I look on you as a sober fair man; but now *I am sure you lie!*"[5] Interestingly, Hume echoed that story, only in his version it was an Indian prince who refused to believe that there was such a thing as ice. Hume, however, commented that the prince reasoned justly, for he had had no experience of water ever becoming solid. The notion of ice did not conform to his experience, and so he was justified in refusing to believe it. That is a most extraordinary comment. How is it that Hume didn't acknowledge the obvious fact that it was because the

---

[4]R. Bultmann, *Kerygma und Mythos,* vol. 1 (ed. H. W. Bartsch; Hamburg-Volksdorf: Reich, 1951) 18; cf. idem, *Kerygma and Myth* (ET; trans. R. H. Fuller; London: SPCK, 1953) 5.

[5]C. Brown, *That You May Believe,* 33. The story is in John Locke's *Essay Concerning Human Understanding,* book 4, ch. 15.

prince (or king) was ignorant of what was possible in other areas of the world that he could not bring himself to accept the authentic witness of one who came from a different climate; that there was a vast range of experiences beyond the man's knowledge by reason of his insularity, on account of which he was greatly mistaken about the nature of this world; and that if only the man took steps to expand his experience, he would increase his knowledge of what was really possible in this universe? The answer is that it never occurred to Hume so to think, because he was in exactly the same situation as that "prince"! A whole realm of experience lay beyond his ken, namely a personal experience of God such as multitudes of people have had through the ages, the validity of which science is not in a position either to affirm or deny because the experience of God is not bound by the natural order.

In fairness one must acknowledge that Hume had a considerable knowledge of religious people, and indeed spent three years in a Catholic institution in France, where he studied and wrote his first book, *A Treatise of Human Nature*. Moreover he frequently discussed miracles, notably of a crass kind revered by uneducated and religiously superstitious people, who in his view were the typical believers in miracles. Nevertheless he was an *observer* of religion, and that from an atheistic viewpoint, not in a position to attest from his own experience the impact of God on the life of a human being. Hence when Hume maintained that the Indian prince was justified in rejecting the idea that ice existed, he had in view the unreasonableness of religion, and of miracles in particular, and stuck to his position that the report of a miracle must either be false or have a natural explanation, instead of perceiving the lesson that one can be mistaken about the interaction between God and the world on account of the limitations of one's own experience. Christians naturally take a different stance from that of Hume, but not because they are all ignorant of logic or philosophy or science (there are plenty of Christians who are expert in those areas), but because of the witness that the Bible gives to the activity of God in and through this world, and the experience of the transforming power of Christ in their lives. And that, moreover, is not restricted to individuals alone, but includes the corporate experience of the people of God through millennia.

It is important to note that there has been a change of attitude of late to the function of miracles relating to the Christian faith. Whereas formerly it was customary to hold that miracles proved the truth of the gospel, it is nowadays more usual to reverse the statement and assert that if we believe the gospel we shall be inclined to believe also the miracles of the Gospels. Alan Richardson, in his book *The Miracle Stories of the Gospels,* voiced this conviction:

> The history which the Evangelists write is their good news, their gospel. . . . If we accept their gospel, we accept the history which they record, and we do not find it difficult to believe with them that the form of the revelation which God made in Christ included the working of the "signs" which proclaimed to the opened eyes the fulfillment of the age long hope of the prophets of Israel, the promise that God would visit and redeem his people.[6]

This is a commonsense attitude to maintain, and on the basis of it Canon Richardson dealt with the miracles of Jesus in an unusually helpful manner. I confess to not knowing how often non-Christians are converted to the Christian faith by reading or hearing about the miracles of Jesus, but I am quite sure that many Christians are *confirmed* in their faith by studying his miracles. Nevertheless it appears to me evident that the authors of the Gospels, and their forebears the gospel preachers, related the miracles to vindicate and clarify the claims of Jesus. In his sermon on the day of Pentecost, Peter described Jesus as "a man marked out by God among you by miracles and wonders and signs which God did by him in your midst, even as you yourselves know" (Acts 2:22). According to this, the acts of Jesus were such as God alone could do, and accordingly were God's testimony to his Son.

This conviction forms a leading motif of the Fourth Gospel. "I have greater witness than that of John" (the Baptist), says Jesus to the Jews; "the work which the Father has given me to accomplish, the very works that I do, bear witness of me that the Father has sent me" (John 5:36). To the disciples in the Upper Room, he says, "Believe me that I am in the Father, and the Father in me; or else believe me for the very works' sake" (14:11). The evangelist towards the close of his Gospel makes a significant statement as to its purpose:

> There were many other signs that Jesus did in the presence of his disciples that are not recorded in this book; but these have been written so that you may believe that Jesus is the Christ, the Son of God, and that through believing you may have life in his name. (20:30–31)

---

[6]A. Richardson, *The Miracle Stories of the Gospels* (London: SCM, 1941) 126.

The evangelistic intention of this Gospel seems transparent: the evangelist wrote about the "signs" of Jesus and their meaning in order that people might believe in him and have eternal life. I do not doubt that that was, in fact, integral to his purpose. It so happens, however, that there is a slight variation in some of our earliest manuscripts of the New Testament as to the spelling of the term "believe," which makes it mean *"continue to believe"* (that Jesus is the Christ), and so to know increasingly "life in his name." The two statements of purpose are not contradictory, but fit the Gospel as a whole; it is likely that both were in the evangelist's mind as he wrote. The dual intention is characteristic of the very nature of the miracles of Jesus.

To the problem of the historicity of the miracles of Jesus recorded in the Gospels the following considerations have relevance.

(i) The Gospels, as we have already pointed out, were composed by men who, as they wrote, stood by the cross and the empty tomb. That is, their thinking was dominated by the twin facts of the crucifixion and resurrection of Jesus. And so were their Gospels. They were penned in the light of these events and move towards them. The resurrection was the crowning revelation of Jesus as the Son of God (cf. Romans 1:4). Whoever believes that has no difficulty in believing that the God who wrought this miracle on him in his death also wrought lesser miracles through him in his life. But there is more to this than the size, as it were, of the miracle of the resurrection in comparison with the miracles of his ministry. We have already affirmed the conviction of the writers of the New Testament that when Jesus was raised from the dead the new world was manifest in him. Now for the Jews the "new world" they were awaiting signified the "new age" when the kingdom of God was to appear (the Hebrew term ʿolam meant both "world" and "age"). The presence of the kingdom of God in Jesus, however, did not begin with his resurrection; its presence in him is the key to his entire ministry in Israel. He made it known that he was sent to fulfill God's promise to Israel of establishing the "saving sovereignty," or kingdom of God, in their midst; the fulfillment of that promise he declared alike by his words and deeds. Observe, by his *deeds* as well as *words!* On various occasions Jesus spoke of his "acts of power" as manifestations of the kingdom of God (e.g., Matthew 11:5–6, 12:28, 13:17). The miracles of Jesus thus were kingdom-of-God acts, and so were anticipations of his resurrection, and like the latter were works of God in him. The miracles of Jesus were of the same order as his resurrection, the incursion of the new world into this one. This may not "prove" their factuality to the satisfaction of non-Christians, but it should give food for thought to believers who doubt that Jesus did perform miracles.

(ii) We possess extraordinary testimony from our Lord's enemies to their conviction that he worked miracles. They alleged that he was in league with the devil, "the prince of the demons" (Mark 3:22). Of the veracity of the evangelists' report that such a charge was made there can be no doubt. It was no credit to Jesus that the spiritual leaders of his nation accused him of being an associate of the devil. What made them do it? They were compelled to it by the extraordinary deeds which he performed, above all his exorcisms, which simply awed the populace at large (see Mark 1:27–28). The lawyers ("scribes") of the Pharisaic party had to admit that Jesus was endowed with supernatural powers, yet they could not bring themselves to ascribe those powers to God, for in their estimate his teaching was false. They believed that the traditional exposition of the law of God, which they taught the people, went back to Moses, and so was as authoritative as the scriptures themselves. Jesus rejected this oral law, and accused the Pharisees and their lawyers of setting aside the law of God for the sake of their tradition (see Mark 7:5–9). Here is the major difference between Jesus and the Sadducees, who also rejected the oral tradition: Jesus not only *taught* that the Pharisees misinterpreted the law through their adherence to the complicated oral tradition, he *lived* his rejection of it; he freely associated with the allegedly "unclean" ordinary people, and denounced the Pharisees and their lawyers as hypocrites. They were enraged at that accusation, and perforce concluded that Jesus was an accomplice of the devil and performed his works through Satan's power. No clearer testimony concerning the beliefs of those who watched Jesus at work could be asked for than this: in the view of even those desirous of discrediting him, Jesus worked miracles!

Now this had deadly results. Deuteronomy 13 contains detailed instruction as to what to do with Jews who seek to lead astray their people religiously: they should be put to death. In the estimate of Jews contemporary with Jesus, the Bible was the law contained in the five books of Moses; the rest of the books were exposition of it. For those who viewed the oral law as of similar authority as the written law, the rejection of the former was heretical. To gain the ear of the populace by miracles and persuade them to reject it was doubly serious. This is why the

Pharisees were so strong in their opposition to Jesus: in their view he was leading the people astray and therefore, according to Deuteronomy 13, he should die (cf. Mark 3:6). It so happens that there is a passage in the Talmud which seeks to justify the Jewish decision to have Jesus put to death. It reads:

> On the eve of the Passover they hanged Yeshu and the herald went before him for forty days saying: "Yeshu of Nazareth is going forth to be stoned, in that he has practised sorcery and beguiled and led astray Israel. Let everyone knowing anything in his defence come and plead for him." But they found nothing in his defence, and hanged him on the eve of the Passover. (*b. Sanhedrin* 43a)

The expression "practised sorcery" is clearly an echo of the allegation that Jesus cast out demons by the prince of demons. Thus the reminiscence continued through the years.

It should be mentioned at this point that the record in John 11 of the miracle of the raising of Lazarus ends with an account of a meeting of the Sanhedrin in Jerusalem, called to consider what should be done with Jesus in view of the report of his raising the man. The event, apparently, is viewed as the last straw in the exacerbation of the Jewish leaders by Jesus, and on the recommendation of the high priest Caiaphas a formal decision to have him executed was taken (11:49–53). The account is significantly in accord with the outlook of the chief priests, and throws light on the reports of the trial of Jesus in the four Gospels.[7]

(iii) Some of the teaching of Jesus, which bears the stamp of his own originality, is so intertwined with his miraculous acts as to be inseparable from them. We read, for example, of John the Baptist in prison, hearing of the works of Jesus, sending disciples of his to Jesus with the message, "Are you the coming one, or are we to await somebody different?" (Matthew 11:2–3).

It is clear why John made that inquiry. He had preached that the Messiah was to come with scourge in hand: "His winnowing fork is in his hand, and he will clear his threshing floor and will gather his wheat into the granary; but the chaff he will burn with unquenchable fire" (Matthew 3:12). What, then, did all these stories mean of Jesus going about healing sick people and consorting with tax gatherers and other unsavory persons? When

---

[7] See the article by E. Bammel, "Ex illa itaque die consilium fecerunt . . . ," in *The Trial of Jesus: Cambridge Studies in Honour of C. F. D. Moule* (ed. E. Bammel; SBT 2d series; London: SCM, 1970) especially 20–40.

was the real action going to begin—the baptism of fire and the judgment of the wicked, in particular the destruction of Herod, who had clamped him in prison for his rebuking Herod's incestuous relation with his brother's wife? Jesus replied in the following terms:

> Go and tell John the things that you hear and see: The blind are receiving their sight, the lame are walking, the lepers are being cleansed, the deaf are hearing, the dead are being raised, and the poor are having the good news brought to them. And happy is the person who is not made to stumble by reason of me. (Matthew 11:4-6)

These words are meaningless unless they corresponded to the deeds of Jesus. If the opening clause is to be taken seriously ("Go and tell John what you hear and see") John's messengers witnessed that very day examples of this kind of healing. The incident is too artless to be a later construction, and no evangelist would turn John the Baptist into a doubter without warrant. The incident and teaching alike bear witness to the reality of the phenomena attested.

We earlier cited Mark's account of a paralyzed man carried to Jesus by four friends (2:1-12). They were unable to reach Jesus because of the crowd inside and outside the house where he was teaching, so they carried their friend via the outer stairway to the roof, opened it up, and let him down in front of Jesus. The response of Jesus to the faith of the group was to say to the sick man, "Your sins are forgiven you." The lawyers objected that God alone had the right to forgive sins, whereupon Jesus demonstrated his God-given authority to do precisely that by healing the man of his paralysis. This issue is presented in the narrative in such a way that I cannot believe it was devised by an artful preacher to present new light on the authority and power of Jesus. His claim to forgive sins is in Mark's narrative as integral to the healing of the paralytic as are the flesh and bones of a human body, and it is implausible to attempt to separate them, as some critics do.[8]

Yet a third circumstance comes to light in the laments of Jesus over unbelieving cities which had witnessed his ministry but refused his message.

---

[8]As Bultmann, followed by not a few, argued: *History of the Synoptic Tradition* (1963, reprint; Peabody, Mass.: Hendrickson, 1993) 14-16.

He began to reproach the cities in which most of his deeds of power had been done, because they did not repent. "Woe to you Chorazin! Woe to you, Bethsaida! For if the deeds of power done in you had been done in Tyre and Sidon they would have repented long ago in sackcloth and ashes. But I tell you, on the day of judgment it will be more tolerable for Tyre and Sidon than for you.

"And you, Capernaum,
will you be exalted to heaven?
No, you will be brought down to Hades!

"For if the deeds done in you had been done in Sodom, it would have remained until this day. But I tell you that on the day of judgment it will be more tolerable for the land of Sodom than for you." (Matthew 11:20–24, NRSV)

Strong words like these from Jesus demand an adequate cause, and one is given in the nature of the unbelief shown to him. Tyre and Sidon, like Sodom, had become bywords for heathen wickedness and were frequently denounced by the prophets (see, e.g., Isaiah 23; Jeremiah 24:22; 47:4; Ezekiel 26–28). Sodom above all was viewed as beyond redemption, as rabbinical maxims attest: "The people of Sodom will not rise again" (*'Abot de R. Nathan* 36); "The people of Sodom have no part in the future world" (*m. Sanhedrin* 10:3). The deeds of power witnessed by the people of Chorazin and Bethsaida and the message of Jesus heard by them were so compelling that they would have been sufficient to turn even those sinful pagans to God in repentance, had they been able to see and hear them. This language is inconceivable without the presuppositions (a) that Jesus did, in fact, perform miraculous deeds which *he* considered authentications from God, and (b) that in the sight of Jesus only the evil within men and women could refuse such credentials, an evil so radical as to call forth the severest judgment of God. As evidence from the lips of Jesus, this demands most serious consideration.

THE PURPOSE OF THE MIRACLES OF JESUS

After that preamble we should now be prepared to consider why Jesus performed miracles. Some suggest that we need look no further than the surface to find this: the miracles of Jesus were performed simply out of pity for people in need; to think up theological motives for them is to introduce an atmosphere of artificiality alien to the human Jesus. One sympathizes with this viewpoint, but perhaps it is another instance of "both/and" rather than "either/or." The surface view is hardly sufficient by itself. Certainly Jesus was perpetually "moved with compassion" in the presence of needy folk, but we must ask, "Why did he move among them at all?" Out of pity for them? Yes, but still more out of obedience to the call of God. He had a foreordained ministry to fulfill. He had come to reveal the kingdom of God in word and deed. His ministry of healing was an integral part of his deliverance of human beings, and it belongs to his mediation of the kingdom of God as much as his preaching does. His miracles and his proclamation were integral to the redemptive process whereby the saving sovereignty of God was inaugurated in the world.

In this connection we should not overlook the parabolic nature of a number of the actions of Jesus. His cleansing of the temple embodied more than one lesson; not least it expressed his indignation at the defilement of the one court into which Gentiles were allowed to enter, hence the citation of Isaiah 56:7 in Mark 11:17; but still more, it was a sign of the judgment of God on the temple through the priestly authorities making it "a den of robbers"; the latter phrase comes from Jeremiah 7:11, the context of which tells of the impending destruction of the temple and the scattering of Israel from its land (so Jeremiah 7:8–15). The triumphal entry of Jesus into Jerusalem is to be placed in the same category. It is hardly likely that Jesus rode into Jerusalem on a donkey merely because he was tired;[9] the great majority of scholars view it as a deliberate symbolic act. The time had come for Jesus to show his colors; he accordingly presents himself to the people as Messiah, yet not as the warrior king to lead them to battle, but as the Prince of Peace of whom Zechariah spoke. Even more plainly than either of these incidents, the actions of Jesus at the Last Supper, the breaking of a loaf and distributing of a cup of wine, were of a symbolic nature. So, also, many of the miraculous acts of Jesus may be viewed in this manner.

For example, the withering of the fig tree (Mark 11:12–14), takes on a more significant aspect if, as many think, this act was intended to be prophetic of judgment about to fall on the guilty nation.[10] Jesus' frequent actions on people brought for healing, like touching a person (an especially significant act when a leper

---

[9] So K. Lake in K. and S. Lake, *An Introduction to the New Testament* (London: Christopher, 1938) 30.

[10] See W. R. Telford, *The Barren Temple and the Withered Fig Tree* (Sheffield: JSOT Press, 1980) passim.

was concerned), laying hands on eyes, and putting saliva on tongue and ears, would all be comprehensible to a people used to symbolism in act as well as in speech. In fact, all the miracles of Jesus may be viewed as *signs* of the inauguration of the saving sovereignty of God according to the promise of the scriptures (the fourth evangelist uses that term exclusively of the miracles of Jesus—never the term *dynamis*, miracle).

At this juncture an objection is sometimes raised to the view here maintained. How can this interpretation of the miracles of Jesus be reconciled with his refusal to give a sign to certain Pharisees when asked for one? His statement was unusually strong: "Why does this generation seek a sign? Amen I say to you, a sign will certainly not be given to this generation" (Mark 8:12). Before pronouncing a hasty judgment about this, we should also recall that Jesus uttered woes on cities that had witnessed his signs but had not repented (see Matthew 11:20–24), a circumstance we have already had occasion to note. In the light of this, the statement of Jesus to the Pharisees must have had reference to the *kind* of signs they wanted. They had asked for a sign "from heaven," i.e., from God. They had probably known of the accusation of fellow Pharisees that Jesus was hand in glove with the devil, and that his miracles were due to the power of the devil in him; it could well have been a challenge to Jesus to perform a miracle that was manifestly of God—"from heaven," proof positive that it was not "from hell!" Mark in any case considered that the motive that inspired the request was insincere (8:11—the Pharisees came "tempting him," suggesting that they had no intention of repenting, even if Jesus had granted what they asked). To that kind of attitude Jesus had nothing to say, whether it showed itself in Pharisees, or Herod (Luke 23:8–9), or Pilate (Mark 15:4–5; John 19:9).

We take it, then, that the miracles of Jesus were significant beyond expressing his sympathy for people, and that they were of a piece with his message and even declarative of it. Actions always show a person's character. In the case of so unique a person as Jesus they were more than usually significant. It involves no reading of forced interpretations into the miracles of Jesus to affirm that on the least estimate they reveal *his* character. In reality, when we examine them we are led to postulate that they testify to (a) the fact of his messianic lordship, and (b) the nature of that lordship. Both these aspects of their message are indissolubly bound up with his teaching on the kingdom of God.

There can be no doubt that the *evangelists* believed that the miracles testified to Jesus as Messiah and Lord of the saving sovereignty of God, finally revealed in the climax of his miracles, his Easter resurrection. The latter in their estimate confirmed the former (so Acts 2:22–24). That is powerfully illustrated in the story of Thomas, which was intended to be the conclusion of the Gospel of John. Thomas had been absent from the disciple group on Easter day and refused to believe that Jesus had risen from the dead. The following Sunday Jesus appeared to the disciples again, and Thomas was present. Jesus addressed him, and stretching out his hands he invited Thomas to touch the nail prints and thrust his hand into his side. There surely can be no doubt, despite the artists' impression, that Thomas did *not* do so. Overwhelmed, he broke down and confessed with an adoring heart, "My Lord and my God" (John 20:28). When the evangelist penned those words he fulfilled his purpose in writing his Gospel. Thomas's confession was his confession too, and he wrote that others might make it theirs. "Jesus did many other signs . . . but these are written that you may believe that Jesus is the Messiah, the Son of God" (John 20:30–31). On this issue the Fourth Gospel, viewed as the last of the four, was formerly contrasted with Mark's, commonly thought to be the first of the four, in which the dogmatic purpose is less visible. That notion is now generally regarded as untenable. We have no Markan conclusion comparable to that of John, so we are unfavorably placed in this respect. Nevertheless Mark has provided the equivalent in the opening words of his Gospel: "The Gospel of Jesus Messiah, Son of God." What follows is written with the intention of demonstrating that Jesus is the one of whom such claims are made. The deeds and words of Jesus reveal him as Messiah and God's Son.

It is instructive to compare the way the four evangelists present the ministry of Jesus in their respective Gospels. Mark's introduction begins with his description of the work of John the Baptist, the baptism and temptation of Jesus, and then a summary of the message of Jesus:

> The time is fulfilled,
> the kingdom of God has come upon you.
> Repent,
> and believe the good news.

When C. H. Dodd first suggested that this statement should be interpreted as the proclamation of the presence of the kingdom of God[11] he was disbelieved by a majority of New Testament scholars. Two generations later the majority now agree that he was right, not least on the ground that if the time of waiting for the promised kingdom is over, the time of the kingdom has arrived.[12] Mark then records the calling of the earliest disciples (1:16–20), and a series of miracles performed by Jesus which illustrate the presence of the saving sovereignty of God operating through him (1:21–45).

Matthew follows Mark closely but replaces Mark's description of miracles with a summary statement of Jesus' ministry of preaching the gospel of the kingdom and healing people "of every disease and sickness" (Matthew 4:23–25), followed by the new law of the kingdom, i.e., the Sermon on the Mount (chs. 5–7), and then a lengthy account of miracles of Jesus of all kinds (chs. 8–9). Luke does not reproduce Mark's summary of Jesus' proclamation of the kingdom of God, but he supplies a more dramatic equivalent. After two short sentences recording the commencement of Jesus' ministry (4:14–15), he describes the visit of Jesus to Nazareth, which Mark places halfway through his account of the ministry. Jesus reads in the synagogue the prophets' passage for the day, Isaiah 61, which was seen by the Jews as an announcement of the kingdom of God in terms of the great Jubilee emancipation of the end time (cf. Leviticus 25). Luke summarizes in a single sentence the exposition given by Jesus of the passage: "Today this scripture has been fulfilled in your hearing" (4:16–21). The message thus presented is essentially the equivalent of Mark 1:15, and Luke follows it up by immediately reproducing Mark's account of the miracles performed by Jesus (4:31ff.).

John does something similar, but characteristically in another idiom. His account of the call of the disciples concludes with a statement of Jesus to them, "Amen, amen I tell you, you will see heaven opened and the angels of God ascending and descending to the Son of Man" (John 1:51). That is a reflection of Jacob's dream of a ladder reaching from heaven to the wilderness where he was, with angels ascending and descending on it, showing that, though far from home, he was not alone, for God was with him. Jesus uses that figure to indicate a new lesson of that

---

[11] C. H. Dodd, *The Parables of the Kingdom* (London: Nisbet, 1935) 44.

[12] See the review of the discussions on Mark 1:14–15 in the author's *Jesus and the Kingdom of God* (Grand Rapids: Eerdmans, 1986) 71–75.

dream: He is the point of communication between heaven and earth to which heaven's blessings are to flow. It is another way of representing Jesus as the mediator of the saving sovereignty of God, and it applies to his whole ministry. That is at once illustrated by the account of Jesus' first miracle, the changing of water into wine at a wedding feast (John 2:1–11). The meaning of that "sign" is seen in the Jews' favorite biblical picture of the kingdom of God, Isaiah 25:6–9:

> On this mountain the Lord of hosts will make for all peoples
>   a feast of rich food, a feast of well-aged wines,
>   of rich food filled with marrow, of well-aged wines strained clear.
> And he will destroy on this mountain
>   the shroud that is cast over all peoples,
>   the sheet that is spread over all nations;
>   he will swallow up death for ever.
> Then the Lord God will wipe away the tears from all faces. . . .
> It will be said on that day,
>   Lo, this is our God; we have waited for him that he might save us.
>   This is the Lord for whom we have waited;
>   let us rejoice and be glad in his salvation. (NRSV)

If the evangelist had wished to add an explanation for the sign that Jesus performed that day he could have quoted this passage and used exactly the same words that Luke cited from Jesus in the synagogue at Nazareth: "Today this scripture has been fulfilled in your hearing." Jesus had inaugurated the kingdom of God promised through the Old Testament prophets, and that not alone by words but by deeds that revealed the presence of the saving sovereignty. The lordship of Jesus is exercised through love and compassion combined with power.

It will not be overlooked that the preceding statement is equally true of the exorcisms of Jesus, which his opponents interpreted as evidence of his alliance with the devil. In rebutting that allegation Jesus spoke a single-sentence parable:

> No one can enter the strong man's house and plunder his property without first tying up the strong man; then indeed he will plunder his house. (Mark 3:27)

The thought embodied in that parable reflects a well-known passage from Isaiah 49:24–25:

> Can the prey be taken from the mighty,
>   or the captives of a tyrant be rescued?
> But thus says the Lord:
> Even the captives of the mighty shall be taken,

> and the prey of the tyrant be rescued,
> for I will contend with those who contend with you,
> and I will save your children. (NRSV)

What God promised that he would do in the day of deliverance Jesus was now doing as his representative. His exorcisms were due not to an agreement with the devil but to his overcoming him, making "the strong man" helpless to prevent the one stronger than he from rescuing his victims. A distinguishing mark of the kingdom of God is precisely its conquest of the evil powers and the triumph of the good. "If it is by the spirit of God that I cast out demons, then the kingdom of God has come upon you" (Matthew 12:28). There is no need for Jesus to say, "Then am I the Messiah." That is implied in his acts of deliverance. In Jesus kingdom and person are one.

Throughout the Gospels, where the polemic atmosphere is not present, the miracles are narrated in this consciousness of their revealing the kingdom of God in action in Jesus. The evangelists were not slow to use them for their didactic value, and this they have done in a variety of ways. In Mark 8:22–26 a blind man is brought to Jesus with a plea that he might touch him—evidently in the belief that that would be sufficient for his sight to be restored. Jesus took the blind man out of the village, put saliva on his eyes, laid his hands on him and asked whether he could see anything. "I can see people," he replied, "but they look like trees walking." Jesus laid hands on him again, and he was able to see clearly. Matthew and Luke omit this incident, perhaps because they did not wish to include what appeared to be an imperfect miracle. Mark had no such scruples. He saw in it an excellent illustration of a theme he was carefully working out. Several times he had pointed out the lack of insight of the disciples. At the stilling of the storm they had been "utterly astounded, for they did not understand about the loaves, but their hearts were hardened" (6:52). In this very chapter Jesus had rebuked them for their lack of comprehension of his warning against the "leaven of the Pharisees and of Herod" (8:14–21). The disciples admittedly had a better understanding of Jesus than most others, but it was still a very imperfect one. They were like the partially healed blind man: to *him* men looked like trees, to *them* the image of Jesus was still blurred. Mark, however, records the journey to Caesarea Philippi immediately after this narrative. Here Jesus "lays hands" again on the eyes of the disciples, and they see him properly, and confess him to be the Messiah. Mark has used the story well. He would not have dreamed of claiming that Jesus performed this miracle on the blind man for such a purpose, but he had no hesitation in employing it to convey this lesson.

Mark's procedure here is the more impressive when we note that the last healing miracle he had recorded was not unlike this one; Jesus healed a man who was deaf and "spoke with difficulty," i.e., he had a speech impediment (Mark 7:31–37). The unusual term "speaking with difficulty" (a single Greek word, *mogilalos*) occurs in a passage which we know was important to Jesus, Isaiah 35:5–6:

> Then the eyes of the blind shall be opened,
>   and the ears of the deaf unstopped;
> then the lame shall leap like a deer,
>   and the tongue of the *speechless* sing for joy.

It is altogether likely that Mark's use of the term is intended to recall that scripture, which tells of the wonders that will take place in the day of the kingdom's coming, implying that this is an instance of its fulfillment through Jesus. If so, it indicates what care Mark used in the composition of his Gospel. It further illustrates how he and his preacher friends must have been accustomed to drawing more than one kind of lesson from the miracle stories they narrated.

This prepares us for considering the second of our points regarding the miracles of Jesus, namely that they bear witness to the nature of the lordship of Jesus.

JESUS THE SAVIOR OF THE WORLD

In the Old Testament, God is Savior of Israel, and the only Savior of the nations. This message is sounded out above all in Isaiah 40–55, e.g., Isaiah 43:3: "I am the Lord your God, the Holy One of Israel, your Savior," and 45:15: "Truly, you are a God who hides himself, O God of Israel, the Savior." The prophet who writes in such a vein declares time and again that there is no other God, therefore Israel's Savior is the Savior of the world. Consider for example 45:21–22:

> There is no other god besides me,
> a righteous God and a Savior,
>   there is no one besides me.
> Turn to me and be saved,

all the ends of the earth!
For I am God, and there is no other.
By myself I have sworn . . .
"To me every knee shall bow,
    every tongue shall swear." (NRSV)

It is therefore comprehensible that the representative and mediator of the saving sovereignty of God should become the Savior of
Israel and of the nations. This axiom is made visible in the
miracles of Jesus.

A typical example is the account of the woman suffering
from a hemorrhage, who presses in the crowd to get near to Jesus.
We are informed that she had suffered for years. She had spent all
her money on physicians, but they had been unable to help her;
rather their efforts had only made her worse. Having heard of the
power of Jesus to heal, she sought to contact him. She had not the
courage to speak to him but believed that simply to touch his
clothes would be enough. When she arrived where he was, crowds
were thronging him. Out of sheer physical necessity many were
touching him, though without any perceptible effect. But she
became close enough to clutch at a tassel on the fringe of his
cloak. That was, indeed, enough: she was healed. When Jesus
discovered who she was he said to her, "Daughter, your faith has
saved you; go in peace and be healed of your disease" (Mark 5:34).
The term "saved" in such a context means "cured" of disease, but
such a use will have been too good an opportunity for a preacher
to miss! Every detail of her sufferings and of the unavailing efforts
of others to help her is significant in the light of the gospel; in her
desperate need she sought the Lord, came to him, "touched" him
believingly, confessed her faith in him, and was "saved"—in body,
mind, and spirit. By the terms employed a healing miracle has
become an illustration of the power of the crucified and risen Lord
to liberate men and women from bondage for life under the
saving sovereignty of God.

If the evangelists needed any warrant from Jesus for their
procedure they could have pointed to his own description of his
vocation as that of a physician: "Those who are well have no need
for a physician, but those who are sick; I have come to call not the
righteous but sinners" (Mark 2:17). The utterance is universally
recognized as rightly reflecting the nature of Jesus' ministry, but
some have queried whether he actually spoke of any as "righteous," and so not needing his message of repentance in light of
the dawn of God's saving sovereignty. The terms "righteous" and

"sinners," however, are surely not to be pressed, but are due to the comparison between the sick and the well. Robert Guelich perceptively commented on the saying:

> Jesus came to offer God's redemptive fellowship by announcing the coming of God's sovereign rule in history and "calling" all to respond. This invitation went to all to declare a time of wholeness and the establishment by God of a new relationship with those who respond to his action in history. Thus, the kingdom in one sense includes all who are "well" and offers healing to the sick; includes all the "righteous" but invites the "sinners" to come into this new relationship. To that extent Jesus' ministry was all-inclusive. The shepherd did not dispense with the ninety-nine sheep when he sought and found the one lost sheep (Luke 15:3–7); nor did the woman discard the nine coins in favor of the one she found (Luke 15:8–10). Rather Jesus focused his ministry on reaching out to those aware of their need of God's redemptive activity in their lives. In the process, however, some of the "healthy" and "righteous" showed themselves to be less than whole and in need of a right relationship with God (Luke 15:25–32). Consequently, to the extent that Jesus' ministry was rejected by the "healthy" and "righteous" it was exclusive. But the accent of 2:17 is on the positive ministry to those in need.[13]

When this message was taken to the Gentile world it would have sounded like very good news, for it was generally thought that the gods were interested only in the healthy and the strong. One of the most popular cults of the day was that of Asclepius, the god of healing, for he was believed to be concerned about the weak; historians tell us that, in the conquest of Greek religion by Christianity, his fortress held out longest. People need one who can deal with them as they are, not as they ought to be. Jesus came as the healer of the sickness of humankind, and none was in too desperate a plight for him.

The church has not been at fault in following in the evangelists' footsteps in its treatment of the healing miracles of Jesus. To heal a man of leprosy,[14] for example, offers one of the best

---

[13] Guelich, *Mark 1–8:26*, 105.

[14] It is evident that the term "leprosy" (Greek *lepra*, Hebrew ṣaraʿathy) is ambiguous, since it was applied in ancient societies to a number of skin diseases. Arndt and Gingrich maintain that in Greek prior to the LXX translation of the Hebrew Bible the term meant psoriasis. It is, however, generally agreed that in the Bible the term can denote leprosy, as well as other diseases. See the discussion, and the various attempts to render the word in languages that do not have a term for leprosy, in R. G. Bratcher, *A Translator's Handbook on the Gospel of Mark* (published for the United Bible Societies; Leiden: Brill, 1961) 64–65; also H. van der Loos, *The Miracles of Jesus* (Leiden: Brill, 1965) 465–68.

parallels to spiritual cleansing that one can find, for among Jews the most notorious feature of leprosy was precisely its nature as defilement, and the consequent necessity for isolation of a leper from society. Its religious significance in Israel was increased by the fact that only a priest could declare a leper clean, its tragedy that none could cure it. The habit of Jesus of touching a leper must have had a deep emotional effect upon the individual concerned, for no ordinary person would do such a thing. For preachers of the gospel, the healing of leprosy would be equally significant; they would see in it a picture of the Lord taking upon himself the burden of man's defilement, by reason of which all who believe are pronounced "clean" in the sight of God. Every incident of a leper being healed therefore would serve as an illustration of the gospel. We can hardly doubt that the story of the ten lepers healed by Jesus, of whom only one returned to thank him for his mercy, was often repeated, with an appeal for corresponding thankfulness on the part of hearers who had experienced the power of Christ's redemption in their own lives.

It is a curious fact that the only instances reported in the Gospels in which Jesus healed people at a distance concerned Gentiles. Matthew tells of a centurion who came to Jesus, pleading with him that he should heal his "boy,"[15] who was ill and was suffering grievously (Matthew 8:5ff.). Modern English translations render the Lord's reply as a statement, "I will come and heal him," but a question was probably intended: "Am *I* to come and heal him?" Jesus was a Jew, and the centurion should have known that Jews do not enter the houses of Gentiles. But he did know! And this almost certainly will have been in his mind as he contemplated the possibility of Jesus' healing his boy. It makes his well-known reply the more startling when we realize that it was premeditated: "Sir, I am not a fit person for you to enter under my roof (i.e., I am a Gentile and you are a Jew), but only speak a word and my boy will be healed." The logic on which this reasoning is based is plain: "I am a man under a superior authority, from which I have received authority that has to be obeyed by those over whom I have been set; the like applies to you, for you have been commissioned by God, and he has authorized you to exer-

---

[15] The Greek term *pais* can mean "boy" in the sense both of "child" and "servant." Luke uses the term *doulos,* "slave," whereas John, in an account which relates to the same healing, employs the terms *huios,* "son," *pais,* "boy," *paidion,* "little child."

cise his power in this world." The amazement and delight of Jesus at hearing a Gentile soldier so speak knew no bounds. He said to those around him, "I have not found such faith with anybody in Israel," and he told the father that he could go home, with the further word: "Let it happen in accordance with your faith." That was the only authoritative word uttered by Jesus on that occasion—"Let it happen!" But it was enough: "The boy was healed in that hour" (8:13).

Matthew then brings to this context a saying of Jesus placed by Luke elsewhere (Luke 13:28-29). Jesus tells of people coming from all parts of the world to enjoy the feast of the kingdom of God at its future manifestation, but he adds that in that time "the sons of the kingdom will be banished into the outer darkness." "Sons of the kingdom" are they for whom the kingdom is intended—"citizens of the kingdom." That saying must have utterly shocked those who heard it. Taken at face value it sounds as if Jesus was asserting that no Jew, but only their forbears Abraham, Isaac, and Jacob, will be found in the worldwide celebration when the kingdom of God comes in its glory and power. For that reason some scholars flatly refuse to believe that Jesus could possibly have said it.[16] But the saying is not to be taken at face value. It is a warning directed to Jews who opposed his message of the kingdom of God, for they were in danger of being shut out of it. The emphasis falls on the joyous prospect of the nations streaming into the kingdom of God, which contemporary hostility to the proclamation of the kingdom cannot prevent. The threat of judgment is added for those who maintain that hostility, for the promise of the kingdom is for those who respond to God's call to repentance. The saying is not intended to exclude the whole nation from the final kingdom; after all, Abraham, Isaac, and Jacob are *representative* Israelites![17]

---

[16] So D. Zeller, "Das Logion Mt 8:11f/Lk 13:28f und das Motiv der Völkerwallfahrt," *BZ* 16 (1972) 88-91. He follows E. Käsemann in his belief that the saying was "an eschatological judgment of holy law," uttered by a Christian prophet in face of the Jewish rejection of the Christian mission, see Käsemann, *New Testament Questions of Today* (London: SCM, 1969) 100.

[17] That the saying was intended as a warning was perceived by Luke, who placed it immediately after Jesus' answer to the question, "Master, will only a few be saved?" Jesus had replied, "Strive to enter through the narrow door; for many, I tell you, will try to enter and not be able." Luke follows that with a further parable of the door that is locked against those who had heard Jesus in their streets, Luke 13:22-27.

The other occasion of Jesus' healing at a distance concerned a Syrophoenician woman whose daughter was demon possessed (Mark 7:24–30). She came to Jesus and asked him to exorcise her daughter. According to Matthew, Jesus gave her no reply, and his disciples asked that she be sent away, "for she keeps shouting after us" (Matthew 15:23). Jesus was unwilling to do that but said, "I was sent only to the lost sheep of the house of Israel," a saying reminiscent of Matthew 10:5–6. When she nevertheless persisted in her plea, he replied, "It is not fair to take the children's bread and throw it to the dogs." (Mark precedes that with, "Let the children *first* be fed," implying that the dogs will get their share afterwards!) "Dogs" was a common term among Jews for Gentiles. The woman certainly had more than her share of rebuff, but she refused to be put off. She answered Jesus in his own imagery: "Yes Master, yet even the dogs eat the crumbs that fall from their owners' table." As with the centurion, Jesus was deeply impressed with the woman's faith, and he spoke in a similar fashion to her as he had done to the centurion: "Woman, great is your faith! Let it happen for you as you want." The evangelist adds that her daughter was healed at that hour (cf. Matthew 8:13; Luke 7:10; John 4:50–53).

We may experience some surprise that Jesus hesitated to help Gentiles, and could even use his own people's language in referring to them ("dogs"!), but despite the reluctance of some scholars to accept the authenticity of Matthew 15:24, its particularity argues for its genuineness. We must take seriously the consciousness of Jesus that he was sent as the Messiah of Israel, to fulfill first of all the promises of God to his people. It appears that these two "foreigners" who came to Jesus with outstanding faith are the only two Gentiles for whom he performed healings, and in each case he appears somewhat reluctant. As Jeremias remarked with regard to the Syrophoenician woman, "Jesus does not grant her request until she has recognized the divinely ordained division between God's people and the Gentiles. This division 'remains sacred.' "[18] It "remains sacred" for the period of our Lord's ministry only—until the curtain dividing the holy place

---

[18] J. Jeremias, *Jesus' Promise to the Nations* (SBT 24; London: SCM, 1958) 30. The last sentence is a citation from A. Schlatter, *Der Evangelist Matthäus*, 489, who added: "There is a power that overcomes this limitation, for the rule holds good for the Gentile woman that God's goodness brings near needed help, and that faith is never put to shame and shattered."

from the most holy place in the temple was "torn from top to bottom" (Mark 15:38), after which the division has no more place. The servant nation must then fulfill its task to serve the nations by making known the gospel of the kingdom to all (cf. Isaiah 49:3-7).

THE MASTER OF THE EVIL POWERS

A second aspect in which Jesus is presented in the miracle stories shows him as the great exorcist, the Lord of the powers of evil. However strange to our modern Western culture exorcism may appear, it made a deep impression on the contemporaries of Jesus and was presented by the evangelists as an integral part of the good news. It is evident that Jesus attached great importance to this aspect of his ministry. Not only did he himself frequently engage in the activity, but he commissioned his disciples to do likewise. All three Synoptic Gospels tell of Jesus sending out his disciples on mission, and it is evident that all the sources on which the evangelists depended had a record both of the mission and the mission charge that Jesus gave his disciples.[19] That led T. W. Manson to write, "The mission of the disciples is one of the best attested facts in the life of Jesus."[20] It is interesting to compare the account in Mark with that in the Q source. The latter is briefly reproduced by Luke: "He sent them to proclaim the kingdom of God and to heal" (9:2). Matthew expands it to read:

> As you go, proclaim and say, "The kingdom of heaven is upon you." Heal the sick, raise the dead, cleanse lepers, cast out demons; freely you received, freely give. (10:7-8)

That represents a command to the disciples to reproduce the ministry of Jesus in all respects. The fact that it belongs to a context in which Matthew brings together all the sayings of Jesus

---

[19] For Mark see 6:6-13. For Q see, e.g., Matthew 9:37-38/Luke 10:2-3; Matt 10:7-8/Luke 9:2-3; Matt 10:12, 13, 15/Luke 10:6, 7, 12. (It is evident that in the Markan passages taken over by Matthew the latter conflated Mark and Q). For M see, e.g., 10:5-6. Luke's source records a further mission of seventy (or seventy-two) disciples sent to Israel (Luke 10:17-20); he will have reproduced that account as an intimation of the later mission of the church to the nations. (Genesis 10 in the Hebrew text numbers the nations of the world as seventy, LXX gives the number as seventy-two; the Greek mss. at Luke 10:1 vary between seventy and seventy-two disciples.)

[20] T. W. Manson, *The Sayings of Jesus* (London: SCM, 1949) 73.

relating to mission indicates his conviction that the churches also should continue to reproduce the mission of Jesus, just as the apostles were commanded to do.

Mark's account, however, places the accent significantly differently. Omitting the Lord's instructions as to how the disciples are to carry out their mission it reads as follows:

> He called the Twelve and began to send them out two by two, and gave them authority over the unclean spirits. . . . He said to them, "If any place will not welcome you and they refuse to hear you, as you leave, shake off the dust that is on your feet as a testimony against them." So they went out and proclaimed that all should repent. They cast out many demons, and anointed with oil many who were sick and cured them (6:7–13).

The only reference in these words of Jesus to a command that the gospel should be preached is in the statement, "If any place will not welcome you and *they refuse to hear you.* . . . " Mark's emphasis is revealed in the descriptive statement before and after his citations of Jesus' sayings: "The Lord gave the disciples authority over the unclean spirits. . . . They went out and preached that all should repent, and they cast out many demons and cured people who were ill. . . . " Matthew and Luke do, in fact, reproduce Mark's description of the commission of Jesus to the Twelve, Luke more clearly than Matthew (9:1–6), for in Matthew's greatly expanded account of Jesus' instruction on mission (chapter 10) the stress on exorcism is lost. But the place given by Jesus to exorcism in his own and the disciples' mission is striking in view of its strangeness to modern Western culture.

In the context of the first century of our era, however, it is comprehensible why such emphasis was laid on demon possession. To be under the sway of a demon was not a mark of wickedness; it was part of the tragedy of a world in which human beings are victims of powers stronger than themselves. People were terribly aware of them at that time, not least in Palestine. Hugh Schonfield, in a description of first-century Galilee, tells of the pathetic condition of many of its inhabitants:

> A physician visiting the towns and villages could not hope to cope with the enormous number of nerve-cases, the blind, the deaf, the dumb, lepers, epileptics and paralytics, many of them owing their sufferings to the political and economic conditions. Women were hysterical, men frightened at shadows. The land was ridden by a great fear of the Evil One and his demons. Superstition and religiosity flourished. Many resorted to magical practices. Many made pilgrim-

ages to the shrines of saints and to holy springs. There were those who gave themselves up to agonized prayer and severe fasting, and poor souls who ran wild and naked in the waste places and sheltered in tombs in the rocks.[21]

Against such a background, the news that by his ministry, death, and resurrection Jesus revealed himself as Lord of the invisible world would be welcomed by many with greatest relief. And thus it was preached. Peter found it possible to summarize the ministry of Jesus with the terse description: "He went about doing good and healing all who were oppressed by the devil" (Acts 10:38). All the healing miracles of Jesus would be comprehended by the phrase "doing good"; the deliverance from evil powers was set in a class by itself. On this Lake and Cadbury passed a remark in similar spirit to that of Schonfield:

> It is scarcely possible to over-emphasize the extent to which Jesus appeared to his immediate followers as the great Conqueror of the devil and demons. Not chiefly as a preacher of good conduct and high ethics—of which neither the Jewish nor the heathen world was ignorant—but as the triumphant Conqueror over the source of evil does he appear in the Synoptic Gospels.[22]

From this viewpoint it is easy to see why such a circumstantial narrative as that of the epileptic boy was preserved by Mark (9:14–29). The pitiable condition of the child, the helplessness of the disciples and Jewish teachers alike, the agony that wrung the confession of faith from the father, and the power of Christ to heal by a word all present a unique parallel to the deliverance which he performs for every believer. There is no reason why we moderns should hesitate to use such a story today, for the sufferings of the lad are characteristic of the agonies of multitudes of our age.

But, it may be asked, are we really justified in using narratives about exorcism in preaching the gospel today? Many would protest against doing so, on the basis that demons and demon possession have no place in our sophisticated society; belief in a personal devil and his legions belongs to an outmoded view of the world like the notion that the earth is flat. Caution, however, needs to be exercised towards that kind of talk. Precisely that mode of argument is brought forward by rationalists to reject

---

[21] H. Schonfield, *The Authentic New Testament* (London: D. Dobson, 1955) xxxv.

[22] Lake and Cadbury, *The Acts of the Apostles,* 127.

belief in God. That there still exist primitive and superstitious ideas of God has no bearing on the reality of a personal yet transcendent God who is creator and redeemer. Whereas mathematical or scientific proofs of the existence of God cannot be produced—a God who transcends creation cannot be *proved* by elements within creation—it is enough for most Christians to recognize in Jesus the ultimate revelation of the God who has shown himself throughout history.

But here is a fact that is to be weighed carefully: the supreme revelation of God was given in terms of redemptive action in the ministry, death, and resurrection of Jesus, which Jesus interpreted as the coming of the saving sovereignty or kingdom of God; if one feature of the ministry of Jesus is certain, it is that he performed acts which he and all eyewitnesses regarded as casting out demons, and that activity he spoke of as clear evidence of the inbreaking of the kingdom of God—"If it is by the finger of God that I drive out demons, then the kingdom of God has already come upon you" (Luke 11:20/Matthew 12:28). Significantly, that is one of the few eschatological sayings of Jesus that critical scholars unanimously declare to be authentic. Rudolf Bultmann said of it that it "can, in my view, claim the highest degree of authenticity which we can make for any saying of Jesus; it is full of that feeling of eschatological power which must have characterized the activity of Jesus."[23] The Swedish New Testament scholar Ernst Percy saw that the exorcisms of Jesus were more than signs that the kingdom of God was simply near; he affirmed, "They are a piece of the kingdom itself. Where Satan is driven back, the rule of God begins."[24] These two citations should be pondered; they eloquently express the profound significance that the exorcisms of Jesus must have had for him. The kingdom of God was not a peripheral theme to Jesus; it was at the very heart of his thought and the driving motive of his life, and this was an important element of it.

The Gospels leave us with the clearest impression that in this feature of his ministry Jesus is not sharing primitive beliefs of his age, but is manifesting his consciousness of being in conflict with evil powers, i.e., with Satan and his demonic agencies, a consciousness also expressed in the temptation narratives. But it

---

[23] Bultmann, *History of the Synoptic Tradition,* 162.
[24] E. Percy, *Die Botschaft Jesu* (Lund: Gleerup, 1953) 179.

is a conflict in which he is the victor on behalf of humanity, and therein lies the promise of the redemption of humankind (cf. Mark 3:27; John 12:31–32). This conflict and this victory are of such fundamental importance to Jesus and his work for the saving sovereignty of God, alike in his ministry and in his death and resurrection, it would seem that the preacher of the gospel of the kingdom should acknowledge that the recognition of Jesus as Lord and victor over all evil powers is integral to the Christian message.

THE PRINCE OF CREATION

The title "Prince of Creation" may appear a little unusual, but the more familiar "King of Creation" or "Lord of Creation" belongs to the status of the risen Lord rather than to the role that he had in his ministry. Hence the use of "Prince of Creation" to point to an aspect of the miraculous works of Jesus that has been vigorously debated.

There is a group of miracles recorded in the Gospels which are referred to as nature miracles, i.e., not healings of people who are ill, but actions which affect inanimate forces of nature. These include the changing of water into wine (John 2:1–11), the calming of the storm (Mark 4:35–41), the walking on the water (Mark 6:30–44), the withering of the fig tree (Mark 11:12–14). For many readers of the Gospels these incidents raise grave doubts, for in their case the alleged "violation of the laws of nature" is held to be more obvious, not to say crass, than with the healing miracles. For this reason endeavors are frequently made to give rationalistic explanations of the events, e.g., the changing of the water into wine is held to be an application to Jesus of the claim of adherents of the Dionysus cult that Dionysus provides wine and the fullness of life experienced in intoxication; the calming of the storm and the walking on the water are variants of one story, the truth of which is that Jesus did not walk on the water but beside the water, and owing to the waves the disciples did not realize that he was standing on land; the feeding of the multitude was a real event, but it took place through a spontaneous sharing of food by those who had some with those who had none; and the withering of the fig tree was a development of a parable told by Jesus about an unfruitful fig tree which its owner wished to cut down, but which was given a temporary reprieve through the plea of his gardener (Luke 13:6–9).

R. H. Fuller tended in this direction and cautiously expressed himself thus:

> The rarity of nature miracles, their absence from Q, from other sayings of Jesus and from Mark's summaries, and the fact that only the disciples witness them, throw serious doubt on their having happened exactly as they are recorded. We think that there is probably some historical basis for some of them, for traditions are rarely created out of nothing. All we can safely say is that they probably came into the tradition somewhat later than the healings and exorcisms.[25]

Reflection on this issue has led me to the conviction that there is less difference between the so-called nature miracles and the miraculous healings of Jesus than is commonly thought. We have already seen that the objection that miracles are a "violation of nature" has been applied to healings as well as the "nature" miracles, and we have rejected that notion in favor of the belief that the creator God is free to work in and through his creation according to his will. Moreover the healing miracles of Jesus are expressly attributed to the power of the Spirit in him and the authority of his word (cf., e.g., Acts 10:38; Mark 1:22, 27; Luke 11:20). Colin Brown speaks of these events as "speech-actions" of Jesus, and points out that they are parallel to the "speech-actions" of God in the Old Testament, notably in relation to creation.[26] This is an illuminating parallel, for it covers all the miracles of Jesus, the healing and the nature miracles, as the work of God in and through Jesus. The God who brought about creation by the power of his word and the presence of his Spirit (Genesis 1:2, 3, 6, etc.) was bringing about a new creation in and through him. The miracles of Jesus were the recreative acts of the Triune God! In such circumstances, distinctions between healing miracles and nature miracles are subsidiary to the fact that God Almighty was at work in Jesus, a reality which he is reported to have readily affirmed (e.g., John 5:19–20; 14:10–11).

It is noteworthy that in the nature miracles of the Gospels we constantly hear echoes of Old Testament works of God. The power of God in the Old Testament was conspicuously seen in his mastery over storm and sea. The calming of the sea by Jesus reminds us of Psalm 93:3–4:

---

[25] R. H. Fuller, *Interpreting the Miracles* (London: SCM, 1963) 39.
[26] C. Brown, *That You May Believe*, 122–23.

The floods have lifted up, O Lord,
   the floods have lifted up their voice;
   the floods lift up their roaring.
More majestic than the thunders of mighty waters,
   more majestic than the waves of the sea,
   majestic on high is the Lord! (NRSV)

Many similar passages, some of them echoing the ancient story of the conflict between the sea and the gods of heaven, hold that the God of Israel alone has power to subdue heaven and earth and sea, and every rebellious political power as well. Psalm 106, which celebrates the deliverance of Israel from Egypt at the exodus, says at v. 9:

He rebuked the Red Sea, and it became dry;
   he led them through the deep as through a desert. (NRSV)

The parallel in Mark 4:39 is closer than is sometimes realized, for there we read that Jesus stood up in the boat and called out, "Silence! *Be muzzled!*" There is no need to interpret this as meaning that Jesus addressed Satan seeking to destroy him through the sea.[27] The personification is similar to that in Psalm 106, and appears again in the withering of the fig tree. It shows Jesus expressing kingdom authority in the same creative manner as does God in the Old Testament.

From this point of view we can understand the episode of Jesus walking on the water (Mark 6:22–33). It is not really a variant of the calming of the storm, although the situation is explicitly said to be one of a driving wind that makes progress across the lake difficult (v. 48). The narrative is closely bound up with the feeding miracle, for the disciples were crossing the lake because of the order of Jesus (v. 45 "he compelled them to embark in the boat"). Jesus had gone to the hills to pray. In the small hours of the morning he saw that the group were in difficulties, so he went to their aid, walking on the water. The account would be unbelievable in relation to anyone else, but in Jesus we are dealing with the one who in his humanity was in a unique relation to God, the incarnate Son of God, in the process of inaugurating the kingdom of God through his living and dying

---

[27] John Wimber interpreted the cry of Jesus as indicating that Jesus "saw in nature's attack the work of Satan. This was a classic power encounter in which Jesus was at war with the perpetrator of destruction," *Power Evangelism: Signs and Wonders Today* (London: Hodder & Stoughton, 1985) 106.

and rising. If no one else in history has walked on water, neither has any other human being had that origin, that calling, and that destiny. It is worth noting that the fourth evangelist relates that when Jesus drew near to the terrified disciples, he said to them, "I am (he), stop being afraid" (6:20). All translations of the Gospel render that, "It is I. . . . " The idiom could have that meaning, but the evangelist knows passages like Isaiah 43:10, 13, 25, where "I am he" is uttered by God, and he interprets this as the first "I am" saying of his Gospel. We recall Old Testament parallels to this incident. Job 9:8 speaks of God the Lord as he who "alone stretched out the heavens and trampled the waves of the sea." But closer in thought is Psalm 77:16–19, another exodus recollection:

> When the waters saw you, O God,
> when the waters saw you, they were afraid;
> the very deep trembled. . . .
> Your way was through the sea,
> your path, through the mighty waters;
> yet your footprints were unseen. (NRSV)

Bultmann spoke of Jesus' statement to the disciples, "I am, do not be afraid," as "the traditional formula of greeting used by the deity in his epiphany."[28] That is an illuminating comment, but Bultmann was referring to Gentile usage; the evangelist was describing Jesus as the revelation of God, coming to his disciples in distress—in the second exodus!

The feeding of the multitude, which according to the Gospels took place immediately before the walking on the water, is the only miracle of Jesus that is reported in all four Gospels. All too frequently modern preachers tend to draw attention to the boy who gave his lunch that others might eat, rather than to the significance of the meal thereby made possible. The Synoptic Gospels place the eating of the meal in the wilderness; it is pretty certain that all the evangelists saw in the miracle a repetition of the feeding of Israel in the wilderness (Exodus 16:15–18, 31–36), but through a greater than Moses. The general Jewish expectation that the second redeemer, the Messiah (the first redeemer being Moses), would restore the manna was now being fulfilled. But further, the meal was, in fact, an anticipation of the feast of the kingdom of God, but on a greater scale than the wedding at Cana.

---

[28] R. Bultmann, *The Gospel of John: A Commentary* (trans. G. R. Beasley-Murray; Oxford: Blackwell, 1971) 216.

In John 6 we see the yet deeper meaning expounded of Jesus as the bread of life, who also gives bread "that one may eat of it and not die" (v. 50).

Attempts to give a "natural" explanation of what is admittedly an incomprehensible nature miracle have earlier been alluded to. In my judgment, one factor in John's account of the event rules out all such explanations. He, and he alone, tells of the outcome of the meal:

> When the people saw the signs that he had done, they said, "This is in truth the prophet who was to come into the world." Jesus therefore, knowing that they were about to come and take him by force to make him king, withdrew again to the hill country by himself, alone. (John 6:14–15)

Here is the record of an attempted messianic revolt, an attempt to force Jesus to become the people's "king" and lead them to overthrow their enemies. Assuredly that required a far more powerful cause than the mere encouragement of people to share fish rolls.

The hope of a king who would lead the people in a movement of liberation from their oppressors was strong among the Jews, especially among the peasants, and it facilitated the rise of messianic pretenders. Josephus tells of leaders of revolts at this time who "claimed the kingship" or "were proclaimed king" by their followers. The fact that Jesus was able to feed a crowd of thousands with no resources at all had the effect of making some in the crowd say, "This must be the prophet like Moses who is to come at the end time"—the very man, able to work the miracles that Moses did! Yet others saw in Jesus a man of unprecedented power who could lead the nation to victory over its enemies.

John records that it was Jesus who saw that "they were about to come and take him by force to make him king." How did he react? Almost all the manuscripts of the Gospel say, "he withdrew into the hill country." That term "withdrew" is an elegant Greek word which occurs nowhere else in the Fourth Gospel. One Greek manuscript, the original hand of the famous *Codex Sinaiticus,* supported by a few versions, reads the startlingly inelegant word, "he *fled.*" No sane copyist could accidentally read that for the other term, nor would any replace the respectable word by "he fled." But it evidently astonished an early copyist to read that Jesus actually ran away after the great miracle; he concluded that someone must have made a mistake, and replaced it by the more dignified "he withdrew." Even *Codex Sinaiticus* was altered by a later "corrector"!

But there was reason for Jesus to "run away." His whole ministry was endangered. Everything for which he had labored and was then laboring was at stake, for such a revolt would have been instantly condemned by the Jewish leaders, crushed by the Romans, and his teaching about the kingdom of God discredited.

This unexpected turn of events has been described as the most dangerous moment in the ministry of Jesus. No wonder he got away from the crowd as quickly as possible! But before he left, it was urgently necessary to send off his disciples. They, after all, were also Jews, and as prone to messianic enthusiasm as any—especially when Jesus was at the center of the excitement. This explains Mark's apparently unmotivated note: "Immediately (i.e., after the feeding miracle) he compelled his disciples to embark in the boat and go ahead of him to the other side, to Bethsaida." When they were safely out of the way Jesus himself speedily went into the hill country—to pray, as Mark noted (6:45-46), doubtless to seek the guidance of the Father in this crisis and to pray for the avoidance of further trouble.

We have considered this miracle of the feeding of the multitude at length because of its importance in our discussion on the "nature" miracles of Jesus. It is easy to dismiss them airily, even superficially, as many have done, and thereby miss their profound significance as "signs" of the kingdom of God. It so happens that no "sign" of Jesus is more complex and rich in meaning for faith than the feeding miracle, but our congregations have no idea of that. The witness of all four Gospels is needed to grasp its profundity. It is good for our souls and for our congregations to plumb its depths and make them known.[29]

THE REVEALER OF GOD

Among the healings of Jesus reported in the Gospels, his giving of sight to blind people holds a prominent place. We recall that in his reply to the enquiry of John the Baptist as to whether he really was "the coming one" (an expression from Psalm 118:26

---

[29] For an illuminating discussion of the significance of John 6:14-15 see the article by Hugh Montefiore, "Revolt in the Desert," *NTS* 8 (1961-62) 135-41.

applied to the Messiah), Jesus cited Isaiah 35:5–6 as a description
of the works he was performing:

> Then the eyes of the blind shall be opened,
>   and the ears of the deaf shall be unstopped;
> then the lame shall leap like a deer,
>   and the tongue of the speechless sing for joy. (NRSV)

Luke 7:21 states that Jesus had just then accomplished such acts
of healing, and thereby made the opening words of his answer
peculiarly relevant, "Go and tell John what you have seen and
heard. . . . " There was reason for this prominence given to Jesus'
healing of blind people: blindness was seen as a figure for the
moral darkness of the world and its ignorance of God, in contrast
to the saving grace that comes from knowing God. So the apostle
speaks of people in the pagan world as "darkened in their understanding, alienated from the life of God through their ignorance
and hardness of heart" (Ephesians 4:18). The obverse to that is
seen in the gospel call, epitomized in a snatch of a hymn in the
same letter (5:14):

> Awake, you sleeper!
> Rise from the dead,
> and Christ will shine upon you.

I cannot resist at this point passing on a story told me by a
colleague of mine in Louisville, Kentucky, Dale Moody, professor
of systematic theology. He was invited to speak at a vacation Bible
school for children. In his talk he chose to teach the children that
song in its original Greek wording, putting it to a simple and lively
tune. One of the children went home singing it, and on arrival
found her father slumped in a chair, dead drunk. She went on
singing, and the father woke up. After a moment or two listening
without comprehension he asked, "What's that queer song you're
singing?" She replied, stretching out her hand and pointing to
him: "Wake up, you sleeper, rise from the dead, and Christ will
give you light!" He was dumbfounded, not to say shocked, and
couldn't get over what his daughter had said to him. He inquired
where she had learned it, and where it was found, and by the end
of the week went to the church where his daughter had been and
opened his life to the light of the world. That is precisely the
rationale of the inclusion in the Gospels of stories about Jesus
making the blind to see.

The well-known story of the giving of sight to blind Bartimaeus is recounted by Mark in such a manner as to convey that

lesson (10:46–52). Jesus was with the group of Galileans on their way to Jerusalem to celebrate the Passover, and was making his way through Jericho. Bartimaeus was sitting by the roadside begging and heard the crowd passing by. On learning that Jesus was among them he kept on shouting, "Son of David, Jesus, have mercy on me!" Jesus stopped, and had him brought to him. When he heard what he wanted, namely his sight, he healed him with the words, "Go, your faith has saved you." Again, we recall that "Your faith has saved you" can mean "has healed you," but the language has deliberately been retained—by and for the preacher! Mark's closing sentence reads, "Immediately he regained his sight and followed him in the way." That means, of course, that the healed blind man joined the crowd walking on the road to Jerusalem, but we do not forget the name given very early to the Christian faith: "The Way." Blind Bartimaeus became a believer, a member of the church, in all probability a well-known Christian, like Simon of Cyrene, who was forced by Roman soldiers to carry the cross beam that had been tied to the shoulders of Jesus, and which he could no longer carry (Mark 15:21). Mark's addition to Simon's name, "the father of Alexander and Rufus," indicates that Simon's experience led him to become a Christian, and the whole family with him, which will have been widely known among the Christian communities of Mark's time.

The story in which all this is supremely exemplified is that of Jesus giving sight to the man born blind in John 9. It is one of the most vivid narratives in the New Testament and a classic example of conversion.

The man was *born* blind. That motif runs through the whole episode. The disciples, on learning that the man was so born ask a typical Jewish question: "Who sinned, this man or his parents, resulting in his blindness?" It reflects the belief that all suffering is due to sin, and therefore all suffering is punishment for somebody's sin. The possibility of prenatal sin was discussed by Jewish scholars. Genesis 25:22 tells of the twins Jacob and Esau "struggling together" in Rebekah's womb. One scholar suggested that they went around trying to kill each other. Another thought that when Rebekah passed a synagogue Jacob struggled to get out (cf. Jeremiah 1:5), but when she passed a heathen temple Esau struggled to get out (cf. Psalm 58:4)! Jesus dismissed the conundrum, "Who sinned, this man or his parents?" His condition, said Jesus, was that the works of God be revealed in him, and he added, "So long as I am in the world I am the light of the world." The act of giving sight to this man, accordingly, was a sign of Jesus as the light for all humanity of all nations of the earth.

Jesus had made that claim in the Festival of Tabernacles. Great candelabra were lighted each night in the temple, bringing to mind the pillar of fire that accompanied the people in the wilderness wanderings, a symbol of God's presence with his people as he guided them to the promised land. They were also an anticipation of the light of God's presence at the second exodus, at the coming of the kingdom of God in the end time (see Isaiah 60:19–22; Zechariah 14:5–7). In this salvation history context Jesus spoke of being light *for the world*. Joseph Blank saw in this "the universal saving character of the revelation and the universal saving significance of the person of Jesus."[30] Such is the evangelist's assumption in telling this story.

Jesus, then, proceeded to make a paste with his saliva mixed with some earth, smeared it on the blind beggar's eyes, and told him to wash in the pool of Siloam. These were all symbolic acts, to encourage the faith of the blind man. The evangelist pointed out that Siloam means "sent." The significance of that observation was perceived by Chrysostom, the great preacher of the eastern church, who commented, "Jesus is the spiritual Siloam"; the blind eyes of the beggar were opened not only through paste and washing in the pool, but through Jesus, sent by the Father to open the blind eyes of all people. The rest of the account centers on the blind man and the confused reactions to his gaining sight.

Especially interesting is the interaction between the Pharisees and the once blind man who can now see. The former were in a dilemma: the man had been made to see on the Sabbath; the miracle pointed to Jesus as used by God, but the breaking of the Sabbath pointed to him as a sinner! They therefore asked the man's parents if he really was born blind; they confirmed that he was, but were too scared to say how it was that he could now see. They then questioned the man himself, on the assumption that he was lying; they told him to "give glory to God," i.e., confess his sin and tell the truth (cf. Joshua 7:19). He confessed the truth—once he was blind, but now he could see, but he could not understand why they knew so little about Jesus and denied the

---

[30] J. Blank, *Krisis: Untersuchungen zur johanneischen Christologie und Eschatologie* (Freiburg: Lambertus, 1964) 184.

good he was doing. The Pharisees were furious and replied, "You were born in sin, and are you trying to instruct us?" In so speaking they were admitting that he was telling the truth—he *was* born in sin, and so born blind!—but since he now could see, he had in truth been healed—by Jesus! In their anger they threw him out.

Jesus found the man and completed the healing process: he opened his spiritual eyes that he should know who he was. There is a certain poignancy in the situation: it is the first time the formerly blind man has been able to see the face of Jesus, and he now learns that he is looking on the Son of Man. No wonder that he prostrated himself before him!

The end of the story is discomforting. "For judgment I came into this world," said Jesus, "that those who do not see might see, and that those who see might become blind" (John 9:39). That reads strangely in the light of John 3:17, "God did not send his Son to judge the world, but that the world might be saved through him." The latter states the primary purpose of the sending of the Son; he came to open eyes to see God and his new world and the way to gain it. But salvation is given to faith, and where the Son is spurned judgment ensues. To reject the light is to condemn oneself to self-chosen darkness. Such is the result of the coming of the revealer of God.

THE BESTOWER OF LIFE

There is a sense in which all the miracles of Jesus testify to him as the giver of life. On the one hand his healings released men and women from the constraints of suffering for life of a higher quality, a transformed life, especially for those who suffered from severe illnesses such as paralysis, leprosy, blindness, and demon possession. On the other hand they are all understood as kingdom of God acts; they are signs of the presence in this world of the saving sovereignty of God, which is pressing forward to its final revelation. It is plain that of all the blessings of that kingdom the greatest is "life," whether described simply by that term alone or as "eternal life"; both denote life in God's eternal kingdom.

It is possible to find passages in the Gospels in which "life" or "eternal life" and "kingdom of God" are virtually synonymous. The clearest example is that of the encounter of the rich young man with Jesus (Mark 10:17–31). He comes running to Jesus and asks what he has to do to "inherit eternal life." Jesus tells him to keep the commandments, and on his protesting that he has done that since his childhood, Jesus bids him to sell his goods and give the money to the poor, and he will have "treasure in heaven," i.e., with God; he then invites him to become one of his disciples. This he cannot bring himself to do, and Jesus looking at the retreating figure says, "How hard it will be for those who have wealth to enter the kingdom of God." The astonished disciples ask, "Who then can be saved?" Jesus replies, in effect, "Nobody! Only God can do that!" When their astonishment turns to indignation, and they ask, "What then shall we have?" he says that everyone who has left home and brothers and sisters, etc., will receive a hundredfold in this time, and in the coming age "eternal life." The synonyms are instructive: "inherit eternal life," "treasure in heaven," "enter the kingdom of God," "be saved." Strictly speaking "kingdom of God" is God himself putting forth his sovereign power to save, and "life" or "eternal life" is existence under the beneficent, saving sovereignty. The miracles of Jesus are signs of that saving sovereignty in action in the present and to be openly revealed in the future.

This was grasped with complete clarity by the fourth evangelist. Of the miracles performed by Jesus of which he knew he selected seven as preeminently setting forth the purpose for which Jesus came, namely to initiate God's kingdom of salvation, long promised to his people and in process of realization in his life, death, and resurrection. As mentioned earlier, the evangelist does not use the term "miracle" but consistently employs the term "sign," thereby emphasizing the function of the miracles of Jesus as signposts that point to the kingdom actually operative in Jesus, the nature of the salvation that he brought, and the light they throw on who Jesus is. The one simple word which sums it all up is "life." In the Fourth Gospel the saving sovereignty is seen as the bestowal of life, and Jesus as the life-giver.

A mere glance at the seven signs narrated in the Gospel suffices to confirm what has been said. The changing of water into wine at the wedding feast in Cana is illuminated by the description of the feast of the kingdom in Isaiah 25:6–10, wherein several highly significant features are emphasized: (1) the feast is for all nations; (2) it is a feast of "rich food, well-aged wines . . . of well-aged wines strained clear"; (3) death is destroyed for the feast, "the shroud that is cast over all peoples"; (4) the Lord God for whom his people have waited has done this, hence the call is sounded, "Let us be glad and rejoice in his salvation." The link between kingdom, life, festival, and joy is unmistakable. The establishment of that link began at Cana's wedding, it characterized the whole ministry of Jesus right up to the Last Supper, and it was intended to characterize his church's life and worship till the final celebration of the coming of the kingdom in glory (1 Corinthians 11:26).

The account of the healing of the king's officer's son, who was at the point of death, is dominated by the saying of Jesus to the officer: "Go on your way, your son lives" (John 4:50). The man believed what Jesus said and departed. His servants met him while on his way with the news, "Your boy lives." On learning when the change in the boy's condition occurred he realized that it happened when Jesus told him, "Your boy lives." Three times in the short narrative that statement is made, showing plainly the nature of the healing as a sign that Jesus gives the life of the kingdom of God.

The same lesson is set forth in the immediately following narrative of the healing of the paralytic at the Pool of Bethesda, only this time the subject was a man who had been ill for most of his life. Unlike the father of the boy whom Jesus healed, this man displayed no faith; in fact he had lost heart and hope. Jesus took pity on him and told him to get up, pick up his pallet, and walk. And so he did. But it happened to be the Sabbath day, and some Pharisees were more concerned that the man was breaking the Sabbath than that he was walking for the first time in nearly forty years. The defence of Jesus is stated in 5:17: "My Father is working right up until now, and so am I." That alludes to an extraordinary rabbinic doctrine that after creation God rested, and his Sabbath still continues; but in the present time he shows to the righteous something of the reward he has laid up for them and to the wicked something of the "recompense" that awaits them in the future. Jesus emphatically rejects the teaching and declares:

> As the Father gives life to the dead and makes alive those whom he wills, so the Son also gives life to those whom he wills. In fact, the Father judges nobody, but he has handed over all judgment to the Son (5:21–22).

The healing of the paralytic at Bethesda is a sign of the truth of that claim.

The feeding of the multitude and the walking on the water we have considered at length. The former is viewed as an anticipatory celebration of the feast of the kingdom, and stresses the feature of Jesus as the bread of life—given "for the life of the world" (6:51). The walking on the water, closely bound up with the former, is a sign that Jesus is one with him whom the covenant people know as the "I am"; it is given to him to use that expression, and with it the Father's sovereign power to deliver his followers in distress.

The giving of sight to the man born blind is a further sign of the fulfillment of prophetic promises about healings that usher in the advent of the kingdom of God, and in particular of the light of life that Christ is and brings to the world. The raising of Lazarus is the outstanding example of the Lord's exercise of his authority to give life to the dead, which is the very heart of the saving sovereignty of God. It is epitomized in the saying of Jesus to Martha (11:25–26):

> I am the resurrection and the life;
> whoever believes in me, even though he dies, will live,
> and whoever lives and believes in me will never, never die.

The first clause affirms Jesus as the one through whom resurrection life is given. The Father has vested in him that power (see 5:21–22, 25–26). The second clause is an unambiguous declaration that the believer in Jesus will be raised from death for life in the consummated kingdom. The third clause is not a repetition of the second for emphasis; it states that the believer in Jesus, already possessing the life of the kingdom of God, has a life which death cannot touch; he lives, as Jesus promised that he would after his own resurrection! (See 14:19; the same teaching occurs in 2 Corinthians 5:14–15.)

The cumulative effect of the signs of Jesus in John is overwhelming: they exhibit more powerfully than any spoken words could do the truth of Jesus as the life-giver for the whole world—life of the kingdom of God now, and life of the kingdom in the future, eternal life. God himself has set his seal on the truth of that: he raised the Son from death, never to die again! The ultimate sign of the kingdom of God in the life of Jesus is Easter, and that anticipates the final sign at his coming for the revelation of the kingdom.

Such is the message of the miracles of Jesus. The messenger who has perceived some of their many aspects in the Gospels will not hesitate to declare Christ by means of them. That is why they were recorded. Then let us go to it!

4

THE GOSPEL IN THE

TEACHING OF JESUS

It has become a commonplace of New Testament studies, thanks to C. H. Dodd, to distinguish between "preaching" and "teaching" in the church of the New Testament. "Preaching" *(kērygma)* has relation to the gospel, and is primarily directed to those who are not Christians; it is declaring what God has done in Christ to redeem the world through his life, death and resurrection, with the promise of his coming at the End. "Teaching" *(didachē)* is instruction for those who have responded to the gospel in repentance and faith; it explains the implications of the good news, notably the nature of redemption, and therefore Christian doctrine, and moral counsels for behavior, and so Christian ethics. To preach the gospel is the prime task of the evangelist, to expound the teaching is an important element of the work of a pastor-teacher of a local congregation.

This distinction has proved valuable, and has clarified our approach to the Gospels and the New Testament letters. It is plain, however, that it must not be pressed beyond warrant. The "teaching" may be a handmaid of the gospel, and the "preaching" may be presented through teaching. That holds good of Jesus himself, notably of his parables, and of the church through the ages. The experience of not a few pastors has convinced them that the most effective means of convicting people of their need of God is to set forth positively the character of Christ; the contrast with their own condition often has power to lead people to repentance and faith in the Holy One of God. Similarly it is not unknown for an individual to be confronted with the teaching of Jesus, and for it to dawn on the person that this is what he or she has been seeking. Such an effect has been especially known through reading the Sermon on the Mount.

An acquaintance of mine as a student in Cambridge came to the conclusion that he ought not to be as ignorant as he was about the teaching of Jesus; he therefore took a New Testament, and on a sunny afternoon sat down beside the river Cam, and for the first time in his life read through Matthew chapters 5–7, the Sermon on the Mount. Its effect on him was electric: he leaped to his feet in excitement, exclaiming that this teaching would transform the world if only people listened to it. It led him to seek the Lord, and, remaining in Cambridge for all his working life, he exercised a highly influential ministry among students in the university.

T. W. Manson suggested, with great probability, that the teaching of Jesus was preserved in the first place for the instruction of new believers, secondly to satisfy the sheer interest of people in Jesus himself, thirdly for open-minded pagans who were concerned to find the truth and live by it, and fourthly for Jewish communities, all too many of whom had heard misrepresentations of Jesus—not only to put them right, but also to enlighten Jewish scholars who might show some sympathy towards the Christian way.[1] The first and the last concerns could equally apply to the collection of sayings of Jesus common to Matthew and Luke but not reproduced by Mark (the Q tradition).

Interestingly, there is one letter in the New Testament which conceivably was written with a similar motive, namely the Letter of James. It is addressed to "the twelve tribes in the Dispersion" (1:1), and although written in uncommonly good Greek, is in many respects the most Jewish book in the New Testament. Several features of this letter are unusual: (i) its lack

---

[1] Manson, *Sayings of Jesus*, 9–10.

of characteristic elements of the gospel (there is no mention of the death and resurrection of Jesus, forgiveness of sins through his mediatorial work, the advent of the kingdom through his redemption and therefore new life in the Spirit, baptism and the Lord's Supper); (ii) its equally surprising lack of mention of characteristic marks of Judaism, despite its Jewishness (there is no mention of Moses, circumcision, ceremonial laws, Sabbath, temple, etc.), but 2:2–4 describes a rather disgraceful scene in a synagogue ("assembly" is literally the term "synagogue"), 4:1–4 rebukes conflicts and murders that happen among the readers, and 5:1–6 threatens judgment to come on wealthy landowners who hold back laborers' wages and murder the righteous; (iii) the letter includes many themes of the Old Testament and moral aspects of Judaism, but also cites many sayings of Jesus, especially from the Sermon on the Mount. It is likely that the letter is addressed to Jewish synagogues, particularly in Palestine, in the period when Jewish Christians attended worship along with their non-Christian Jewish neighbors, and the teaching of Jesus could be tactfully given without offense. James, the brother of Jesus, was honored both among Jews and Christians for his exceptional piety.

It is not surprising that some Christian scholars and preachers have adopted the position that the real, authentic gospel is the teaching of Jesus. The preaching about the crucified and risen Savior is held to be a later dogmatic structure, due above all to the apostle Paul, which caused the message of Jesus to recede into the background. The Sermon on the Mount is then seen as the supreme example of the good news preached by Jesus, standing in irreconcilable contrast with the dogmatic point of view prevailing in the Gospels generally. This interpretation is less common now than it once was, though it is being revived in some sophisticated groups in Europe and in the United States. To most students of the New Testament it is rendered difficult of acceptance by the simple critical consideration that the Sermon is not *one*, but a *compilation* of many sayings of Jesus originally spoken on various occasions. The so-called Sermon on the Plain in Luke 6:20–49 is almost entirely found in Matthew's Sermon on the Mount, and in the same order, hence this common material is acknowledged to be from the Q source; to this Matthew has added material drawn from his own special source. There is, however, a great deal more teaching material in both Q and Matthew's special source, much of which can only be described as "gospel," declaring who Jesus is and calling people to faith in him, just as in the kerygma, the gospel of the crucified and risen Lord. It is manifestly arbitrary and unjustified to fasten on the portions of these two collections contained in the Sermon and assert, "These are authentic," and of the other sections of the same collections outside the Sermon, "These are spurious." That would be a misuse of evidence. Moreover, if we compare the teaching of the Sermon with the rest of the recorded instruction of Jesus we see that there is no discrepancy between the two; the Sermon harmonizes with the other teaching and presupposes its fundamental content relating to the kingdom of God.

We may further affirm that in the light of contemporary studies on the Gospels it is no longer justified to divorce sayings reflecting our Lord's consciousness as to his person and ministry from the other accounts of his teaching and his acts. The saying in Matthew 5:17, "Do not think that I came to abolish the law or the prophets; I did not come to abolish but to fulfill," is a key utterance to understanding the ministry of Jesus. It doubtless reflects the belief of many Jewish opponents of his that Jesus did, in fact, seek to destroy the law and prophets by his teaching and mode of life. This charge Jesus repudiated. But Christians have often read the statement as though he said, "Do not think that I came to abolish the law or the prophets; I did not come to abolish the law, but to fulfill the prophets." He came to fulfill both. That conviction conditioned the form and substance of his teaching and manner of life. Matthew grasped that fact perfectly; it led him to collect in the fifth chapter of his Gospel Jesus' interpretations of major elements of the law of Moses. The intention of that section of the Sermon on the Mount is not to contrast our Lord's teaching with the Mosaic legislation, as though he rejected it, but rather to unfold the underlying principles of God's demands enshrined in the Old Testament law. Nor is that to be confined to the interpretation of ideas and language of the law, as though "fulfillment" meant primarily "carry through to completion the concepts of law and prophets"; Jesus believed that his mission was to fulfill the law as truly as he was sent to fulfill prophecy, namely in his life and action. That determined his way from his baptism to his cross.

There are admittedly scholars who protest that Jesus did not order his life according to prophecy, and that to maintain that he did is to contradict his manifest sense of inner freedom and his known attitude to the scriptures. That opinion, I am persuaded, is due, at least in measure, to the misreading of Matthew 5:17, to which I alluded above. Jesus was a Jew, and every Jew who looked on the Hebrew Bible as the revelation of God sought to order his life according to it. Christians in measure seek to do the same, but that was a duty doubly serious for Jews, in view of their belief that the Bible was primarily the law of God made known in the Pentateuch, and that the rest of the books were added for its fuller understanding. Their life was dominated by the endeavor to live according to the law, which accounts for the multifarious applications of the commandments in the rabbinic tradition. The difference between Jesus and his Jewish contemporaries was that he went back directly to the prime authority of the Old Testament and rejected the complex casuistry of the tradition (cf. Mark 7:5–13; Matthew 23:4). In the years prior to the commencement of his ministry Jesus had opportunity to meditate long on the text of the Old Testament. For him the revelation of God was given in the Hebrew Bible, and he found therein a path marked out for him.

We do not mean to imply by this that Jesus seized on a few isolated, generally forgotten sayings or proof texts for a novel way of interpreting the Bible. Israel's lawyers (the "scribes") were the exegetes of the Bible for the people, but none of them thought to interpret it as Jesus did. They were acquainted with the Servant songs of Isaiah 40–55, but were puzzled as to how to relate them to other prophetic scriptures; by contrast those songs corresponded to the intuition of the messianic task of one Man only, just as the vision of "one like a son of man" in Daniel 7 found an echo in his heart such as was perceived by no one else. One Man alone was able to fuse the prophetic teaching about the Son of David, the Son of God, the Servant of the Lord, the Righteous Sufferer of the Psalms, and the Son of Man, and that was because he alone attained the insight that his destiny was to fulfill these intimations of the divine revelation.

C. H. Dodd wrote a highly original book on the use of the Old Testament in the New. He maintained that, contrary to long-standing opinion, no primitive collection of isolated Old Testament texts was available in the primitive church, but at a very early date a certain method of biblical study was established and became part of the equipment of Christian evangelists and teachers. This method covered large sections of the scriptures, especially from Isaiah, Jeremiah, and certain Minor Prophets and Psalms. They are cited in all the main sections of the New Testament, and are interpreted as setting forth "the determinate counsel of God." These scriptures relate to the day of the Lord and the kingdom of God; the figure of the Messiah, but notably as the Servant of the Lord, the Righteous Sufferer, and the Son of Man; Israel, judged and renewed; and such passages as Genesis 12:1–3; Deuteronomy 18:15; Psalms 2; 8; 110. A unified "plot" is discernible in these scriptures: they describe God's intervention in judgment and redemption to achieve his purpose for his creation; it is realized through one who suffers shame and torment, but by the grace of God is delivered and raised up and glorified. Dodd comments on this scheme as follows:

> The New Testament avers that it was Jesus Christ himself who first directed the minds of his followers to certain parts of the scriptures as those in which they might find illumination upon the meaning of his mission and destiny. . . . To account for the beginning of this most original and fruitful process of rethinking the Old Testament we found need to postulate a creative mind. The Gospels offer us one. Are we compelled to reject the offer?[2]

We certainly are not! The "creative mind" was that of Jesus, and a digest of its working is revealed in the Sermon on the Mount. The Sermon can be rightly understood only in the context of the redemptive sovereignty of God, to which he bears testimony in the Gospels, and which he brought about by his living and dying and rising.

We do well steadily to bear in mind that Jesus himself publicly taught and preached. Matthew summarizes the early ministry of Jesus thus: "Jesus went about teaching in their synagogues, preaching the gospel of the kingdom, and healing every disease and every sickness among the people" (4:23). Our records reproduce both the teaching and the preaching. The Sermon on the Mount itself contains both elements. Significantly the Sermon begins with the gospel (the Beatitudes) and ends with a parable of judgment (the Two Houses). That which lies between comprises instruction on the greater righteousness (cf. 5:20), which Jesus elucidates from the law and by admonitions and warnings.[3]

---

[2] C. H. Dodd, *According to the Scriptures: The Substructure of New Testament Theology* (London: Nisbet, 1952).

[3] See R. A. Guelich, *The Sermon on the Mount* (Dallas: Word, 1982) 33–36, 107–10.

We shall consider the leading themes in our Lord's teaching and preaching that are of prime importance for preaching the gospel today.

THE KINGDOM OF GOD

The introduction to the Gospel of Mark reaches its climax in a description of the proclamation of Jesus (1:14–15):

> Jesus came to Galilee, preaching the good news of God,
> and saying,
> "The time is fulfilled,
> and the kingdom of God has come upon you;
> repent, and believe the good news."

Almost certainly Mark wished his readers to understand these words as a summary of the message of Jesus, and not as a statement which he made on a single occasion. Jesus could, of course, have uttered the sentence exactly as it stands, for it is wholly in accord with the rest of his teaching; but one cannot imagine Jesus journeying around Palestine constantly repeating these words. The suggestion has been made, with great likelihood, that the declaration was taken by Mark from the so-called "catechesis," i.e., the instruction that was drawn up in the early days of the church for new believers; it may have been selected as a representative statement of Jesus or formulated on the basis of the sayings and parables preserved in the catechesis.[4]

There is admittedly a certain ambiguity in this statement. The verb translated "has come upon you" (Greek *ēngiken*) literally means "has drawn near." Most earlier scholars understood the affirmation to mean that the kingdom of God is near at hand, but not yet here; the message of Jesus to his nation was, "The kingdom of God has come close to us; therefore repent, so as to be ready for its coming." But it was overlooked that the clause in question is parallel to the one before it: "The time is fulfilled," i.e., "The time of waiting for the kingdom has ended"; or, if the precise meaning of the term translated "time" *(kairos)* is pressed, it could mean, "God's appointed time for his kingdom has come to pass." Either way the emphasis is on the arrival of the time for the kingdom to be revealed. Yet the next clause normally signifies that

---

[4] So E. Lohmeyer, *Das Evangelium des Markus* (14th ed.; Göttingen: Vandenhoeck & Ruprecht, 1957) 29–30.

the time for the kingdom to come is "near"! The apparent contradiction in terms is resolved when one takes into account that Jesus, as the earliest disciples who passed on his teaching, will have taught and preached in Aramaic and not in Greek, and there is more than one term in that language which can signify both presence and nearness in the future. It was C. H. Dodd's contention that the same Aramaic word behind Mark 1:15 was also behind that in Matthew 12:28: "If it is by the spirit of God that I drive out the demons then the kingdom of God *has come to you*."[5] It so happens that the statement as it stands is admirable, for it signifies that the time is over for crying "How long?" for the kingdom of God; it has made its entrance into history, though in a hidden fashion, and it will come in increasing measure as God's saving acts are accomplished until its final revelation in glory. In other words, the kingdom of God has been *inaugurated* and is pressing on to its consummation. That interpretation naturally takes into account other sayings of Jesus that fill out this summary statement, but as a summary of his teaching it requires that expansion.[6]

One further question needs clarification before we leave Mark 1:15: what did Jesus mean by the expression "kingdom of God"? There are still enough "kingdoms" in this world for the impression to be gained generally that "kingdom" means a country ruled by a king. I do not doubt that most people in the Western world assume that "United Kingdom" denotes the country of Britain, but that is not so; by the Act of Union passed in the year 1800 the expression "United Kingdom" signifies the *peoples* of England, Scotland, Wales and (Northern) Ireland, who come under the rule of the one sovereign of the four countries. In reality the English term "kingdom" signifies primarily kingship, i.e., the authority or power of a king, sovereignty, supreme rule; secondly it denotes an organized community having a king at its head, and so a monarchical state; then thirdly a territory or country ruled by a king, and so a realm. The *Oxford English Dictionary* illustrates the first meaning of "kingdom" by a sentence from Hobbes written in

---

[5]The Greek term in Matthew 12:28 is *ephthasen*, "has arrived." See Dodd, *Parables of the Kingdom*, 43–45.

[6]The passage has been discussed by many writers through the twentieth century. See the review given in the present author's *Jesus and the Kingdom of God* (Grand Rapids: Eerdmans, 1986) 71–75, with the literature cited 355–56, and the excellent summary by Guelich, *Mark 1–8:26*, 41–46.

1679; he defined monarchy as a form of government "which, if he limit it by law, is called Kingdom; if by his own will, Tyranny." The contrast between "kingdom" as the just exercise of royal power and "tyranny" as the unjust exercise of such power is striking. It is precisely this first meaning of kingdom which the Hebrew term *malkuth,* the Aramaic *malkutha,* and the Greek *basileia* all have in mind. This meaning of *basileia* is most clearly seen in the book of Revelation (12:10): the song that is sung to celebrate the expulsion from heaven of the defeated Satan begins:

> Now have come about the salvation and the power
> and the kingdom of our God
> and the authority of his Christ. . . .

Those four terms salvation, power, kingdom, authority are here clearly related; they are all dynamic in their emphasis, and in this context "kingdom" is better translated "sovereignty."

Strangely the expression "kingdom of God" does not occur in the Old Testament, but the reality signified by it is there, namely the promise that a time is to come when God will exercise his almighty, sovereign power in judgment upon the evil powers of this world and in the deliverance of his people (and in some prophets at least, the deliverance of all nations). Such is the meaning of "kingdom of God" in the teaching and proclamation of Jesus, but with emphasis on the deliverance. For him "kingdom of God" is virtually a synonym for "salvation." In contrast, however, to the usage of modern preachers, the term "salvation" is hardly ever on his lips, whereas "kingdom of God" (or its equivalent "kingdom of heaven") is continually used with reference to God's redemptive purpose for humankind.[7] "God in action to fulfill his purpose of grace for the world" is what Jesus ever had before him when he spoke of the kingdom of his Father. And that action was taking place through him.

The proclamation of the kingdom by Jesus is inseparably bound up with a call for response from his hearers. This is indicated in the conclusion of Mark's summary of Jesus' message:

---

[7]In the expression "kingdom of heaven," heaven is a substitute for the name God, used by the Jews out of reverence for his name (an early example is seen in Daniel 4:25–26). In rabbinic literature outside the Targums "kingdom of heaven" is always used. Matthew, writing with an eye on the Jewish people, alone among the evangelists uses "kingdom of heaven," but also "kingdom of God" five times and other periphrases for the name God. On the usage of Jesus himself see G. Dalman, *The Words of Jesus* (Edinburgh: T. & T. Clark, 1902) 91–93, 194–234.

"Repent, and believe the good news." "Repentance" should never be reduced to mere sorrow for having done wrong. Still less should we be misled into thinking that the Greek term for repentance *(metanoia)* adequately expressed what Jesus demanded. *Metanoia* signifies change of mind or opinion; it is primarily an intellectual change, and even when ethical it can be from good to bad as well as from bad to good. J. Behm stated, "For the Greeks *metanoia* never suggests an alteration in the total moral attitude, a profound change in life's direction, a conversion which affects the whole of conduct." Reviewing the various meanings the term had for the Greeks, Behm concluded, "These ideas do not constitute a bridge to what the New Testament understands by *metanoia*."[8] Jesus rather had in mind what the Old Testament prophets meant when they called on Israel to repent. The Hebrew term for "repent" is "turn" *(shub)*. It is particularly important to Ezekiel, but his appeal to Israel is typical of the prophets:

> Therefore I will judge you, O house of Israel, all of you according to your ways, says the Lord GOD. *Turn,* and *turn* from all your transgressions, so that iniquity may not be your ruin. Cast away from you all the transgressions that you have committed against me, and get yourselves a new heart and a new spirit. Why will you die, O house of Israel? For I have no pleasure in the death of anyone, says the Lord GOD. *Turn, then, and live!* (18:30–32; NRSV, adapted)

The call of Jesus to his people, accordingly, was, "Turn to God, and believe the good news!" What good news? The "good news of God," as Mark describes the preaching of Jesus in 1:14. It recalls some significant passages in the book of Isaiah, e.g.:

> Climb up to a mountain top,
> you who bring good news to Zion,
> Raise your voice and shout aloud,
> you who carry good news to Jerusalem.
> Raise it fearlessly,
> say to the cities of Judah,
> "Here is your God!" (40:9, REB, adapted)

Similar references to God's good news are found in Isaiah 52:7 and 61:1–3; the theme of both chapters is that of God putting forth his sovereign power to save and redeem his people, and extending his beneficent rule to all nations (so 52:10 and 61:11). "The good news of God" proclaimed by Jesus, therefore,

---

[8] J. Behm, "μετάνοια," *TDNT* 4.979–80.

was wonderful news for his contemporaries. In their oppressed condition none better was conceivable! God had initiated the process of the salvation of his promised kingdom. All they had to do by way of response was "turn and believe." That meant conversion to God, and commitment to the way of the kingdom as revealed by Jesus. The excitement roused by the good news must have been tremendous. The genuineness of the response was another matter.

This teaching concerning the inauguration of the kingdom of God in the ministry of Jesus is attested in a number of his utterances. We have already cited Luke's account of his preaching in the synagogue of Nazareth, how Jesus stood up and read the passage in Isaiah 61:1–2, which describes the kingdom of God in terms of the great year of Jubilee. In the so-called Melchizedek fragment of the Qumran community it is interpreted as the last year of Jubilee, which is to begin with a day of slaughter carried out by Melchizedek, his liberation of Israel, and making atonement for Israel's sins. That identification of the judge of the nations and redeemer of Israel with Melchizedek is a characteristic twist of the Qumran group. As a community of priests who had renounced the temple of Jerusalem and its worship, they looked either for two messiahs to arise—a king of David's line and a priest of Aaron's line—or a single messiah who combined both functions.[9] We recall that Melchizedek was a king who was also "priest of the Most High God!" (Genesis 14:18).

The conjunction of "day of slaughter" with "day of liberation" is equally typical of the Qumran community in its interpretation of scripture. In Isaiah 61 the anointed messenger speaks of being sent:

> to proclaim the year of the Lord's favor,
> and the day of recompense of our God;
> to comfort all who mourn. . . .

The entire chapter is positive, with not a hint of judgment in it; the continuation of the consolation of the prophecy appears to make it certain that the "recompense" is for the people of God

---

[9]The former view is seen in the *Manual of Discipline* (1QS 9:10–11), which refers to "the coming of a prophet and the Messiahs from Aaron and Israel" (cf. also 1QS 2:11f.). The concept is the presupposition of the *Testaments of the Twelve Patriarchs*.

who look for his salvation, not for the judgment of his enemies (see especially vv. 7–8).[10]

Through Luke's restriction of the citation of the Lord's reading of Isaiah 61 to vv. 1–2a (thus omitting the clause about the "recompense"), it is evident that he viewed Jesus himself as interpreting it of the grace of the kingdom, for Luke summarized Jesus' exposition of the passage in a single sentence: "Today this scripture has been fulfilled in your hearing." On that George Caird wrote a classic and sufficient comment: "He has not merely read the scripture; as King's messenger he has turned it into a royal proclamation of release."[11] The great Jubilee has begun!

The answer of Jesus to John the Baptist's question whether he was truly the "Coming One," or whether Israel had to look for another (Matthew 11:5/Luke 11:20), is an equally unambiguous expression of our Lord's consciousness of being the bearer of the kingdom of God. The essential part of his answer to John reflects Isaiah 35:5–6, though filled out with other aspects of his ministry (namely the healing of lepers, raising the dead, and preaching the good news to the poor, which echoes Isaiah 61:1). It is noteworthy that this passage follows on a terrible description of the day of the Lord in Isaiah 34, which begins with an account of a destructive theophany in the heavens and against all nations on the earth, but in reality is specifically directed against Edom, which is to suffer a like judgment as Sodom and Gomorrah. This description of a fearful theophany is followed (in chapter 35) by one in which nature is transformed and bursts into joy and fruitfulness at the Lord's coming in his kingdom. That is the time when:

> the eyes of the blind shall be opened,
> the ears of the deaf unsealed,
> the lame shall leap like a deer,
> and the tongues of the dumb sing for joy.

By citing this passage it is as though Jesus was saying to John, "Do not confine yourself to the prophetic descriptions of the day of the Lord; contemplate also the prophets' descriptions of the salvation of the kingdom of God, for it was to accomplish this very thing that I was sent, and my works attest its fulfillment."

---

[10] This interpretation is maintained by C. Westermann, *Jesaja 40–66* (Das Alte Testament Deutsch; Göttingen: Vandenhoeck & Ruprecht, 1966) 292.

[11] G. B. Caird, *St. Luke* (Pelican Gospel Commentaries; London: Penguin, 1963) 86.

It so happens that one of the most enigmatic utterances in which Jesus relates his mission to the kingdom of God is set by Matthew in the context of a tribute of Jesus to John the Baptist (11:12–13; Luke has it in a different context, 16:16). The two versions of Matthew and Luke are extraordinarily different. Matthew's reads:

> From the days of John the Baptist until now the kingdom of heaven suffers violence, and violent men are ravaging it.
> For all the prophets and the law prophesied until John.

Luke's rendering of the saying is as follows:

> The law and the prophets were until John;
> from that time the kingdom of God is being proclaimed,
> and everyone is forcibly trying to enter it.

The difficulty is compounded by the ambiguity of the terms used in the Greek Gospels. They reflect a corresponding ambiguity in the language of Jesus. "The kingdom of God *biazetai*"—that term can reflect a favorable or hostile meaning, and it can have an active or a passive meaning: that results in different possibilities:

> the kingdom of God is powerfully active;

> the kingdom of God is being violently opposed.

Those concerned are *biastai*—either "violently pressing into it," i.e., seeking at all costs to enter it, or "violently opposed to it." Matthew and Luke probably give different translations of a single statement of Jesus. On investigating the possibilities (and they have been widely discussed), I came to the conclusion that Jesus was making a play on a single word that in Hebrew and in Aramaic was relatively common (the former *pāras,* the latter *pᵉras*). Its basic meaning was to "break through," such as breaking through a city wall that was being attacked; it was applied to the "breaking out" of God in violent acts of judgment, as also the violent acts of men, but then in a gentler way to breaking over the limits, hence to spread and make known news, and even the pressure of persuasion on people. The first and fundamental meaning controlled Matthew's version, the second made Luke's rendering possible. On the basis of the former it would appear that Jesus stated:

> The law and the prophets were until (the days of) John;
> from that time on the kingdom of heaven

has been powerfully breaking into the world,
and powerful opponents are powerfully working against it.

Jesus here appears to represent John the Baptist as a bridge between the old and the new ages; John has been silenced by enemies, but he made a unique contribution to the service of God's kingdom, and through Jesus the kingdom has made a breach into the world, and it is irresistibly forging ahead. It is a remarkable saying, alike in its consciousness of Jesus as the spearhead of the kingdom of God, successfully breaking through despite all opposition, but aware that the opposition was relentlessly continuing and would have dire results in the time ahead.[12]

One further important utterance of Jesus, in harmony with his proclamation of the kingdom as present in his ministry, is his answer to the Pharisees who asked when the kingdom of God was coming. He replied: "The kingdom of God does not come with observation" (Luke 17:20). This term "observation," found only here in the New Testament, was used generally of doctors and scientists observing signs and symptoms, whether of the body or material elements or the movement of planets and stars. The latter was important to Jews for determining the times of festivals, but great store was set on signs on earth and in the heavens for determining the time of the coming of the Messiah and God's kingdom. The calculations in the latter chapters of the book of Daniel were pondered by the Pharisees, particularly in the first century of our era as the Roman war loomed ahead; A.D. 70 was reckoned as a favored date, and when it came, but no Messiah or kingdom, there were great heart-searchings as to why there was only destruction but no deliverance.[13] It is unlikely that there was no such eager speculation in the time of Jesus. He plainly rejected all such apocalyptic calculations. The "signs" alluded to in the parable of the Fig Tree in Mark 13:28–29 are of a different order—they do not allow a calculation of the date of the kingdom's coming.

---

[12] For a fuller discussion of the saying and justification of this interpretation, see Beasley-Murray, *Jesus and the Kingdom of God*, 91–96.

[13] On the late Jewish eagerness to calculate the time of the end see my earlier *Jesus and the Future* (London: Macmillan, 1954) 175–76, and the excursus 30, "Vorzeichen und Berechnung der Tage des Messias," in H. L. Strack and P. Billerbeck, *Kommentar zum Neuen Testament aus Talmud und Midrasch* (6 vols.; Munich: Beck, 1922–1961) 2.977–1015.

Luke 17:21a continues with words ("Look here! Or there!") which in Mark 13:21 are said of the Messiah to counter a Jewish view that the messiah will be born and raised as a man, and none will know him until he be revealed in a secret place; it is possible that Luke, or his source, has joined the phrase to this saying. In that case Jesus followed the negative statement, "The kingdom of God does not come with observation," immediately by "The kingdom of God is within—your grasp!" The common translation "within you" is hardly to be received, for the kingdom of God is not a purely interior reality but the saving sovereignty of God that embraces all of life. "Among you" is a possible, but rare meaning. In the remains of ordinary people's letters, preserved in the Egyptian papyri, the contemporary use of "within you" as signifying "within your reach or grasp" is seen.[14] This interpretation was known to Cyril of Alexandria, who understood Luke 17:21 as meaning: The kingdom of God "is in the scope of your choices, and it lies in your power to receive it."[15] The Pharisees were therefore counseled by Jesus not to be unduly concerned about the date of the coming of God's kingdom in the future; it was present already, since he, the Messiah, was present with them, and the gift of the kingdom was open to them as soon as they received the word of the kingdom which he offered.[16]

To this point we have been concentrating on the sayings of Jesus that show him as the inaugurator of the kingdom of God. But they speak of the initiation of the kingdom which has a future. That is inherent in the summary of the proclamation of Jesus in

---

[14] C. H. Roberts first brought this to light in his article "The Kingdom of Heaven (Lk. xvii.21)," *Harvard Theological Review* 41 (1948) 5ff. It was accepted, and further examples of the usage supplied by A. Rustow, "ἐντὸς ὑμῶν ἐστιν: Zur Deutung von Lukas 17, 20–21," *ZNW* 51 (1960) 197–224.

[15] *"en tais hymeterais proairesesi kai en exousia keitai to labein autēn,"* *Explanatio in Lucae evangelium,* section 368, Migne, PG 72, 840–41. H. J. Cadbury draws attention to Cyril's interpretation in a brief article, "The Kingdom of God and Ourselves," *Christian Century* 69 (1950) 172–73.

[16] The interpretation of v. 21 as relating to the future appearance of the kingdom of God, implying "The kingdom of God does not come with observation . . . for the kingdom will appear among you all of a sudden," is implausible, since it can have that signification only by adding the all-important phrase that is not there. It is most likely that Luke himself conjoined vv. 20–21 with vv. 22–37, thereby providing a conspectus of Jesus' teaching on the kingdom of God. See R. Otto, *Kingdom of God and Son of Man* (London: Lutterworth, 1943) 135, and the excellent discussion by J. A. Fitzmyer, *The Gospel according to Luke X–XXIV* (2 vols.; Anchor Bible 28A; New York: Doubleday, 1985) 2.1161–62.

Mark 1:15. We saw that the statement "the kingdom of God has drawn near" in its context means that the kingdom has entered into our history and presses on to its ultimate future glory. A. M. Ambrozic, in an intensive investigation of the passage, stressed this feature:

> The present kingdom is hidden and is still waiting to become manifest and unfold all its eschatological powers. The tension between its present hiddenness and its future glory is in the very flesh and blood of the Second Gospel.[17]

It was in the very flesh and blood of Jesus also, as is evident above all in his parables. The future of the kingdom of God, however, is manifest in many of his non-parabolic utterances. We shall consider two of the most important examples, namely, the Beatitudes of the Sermon on the Mount, and the prayer that he taught his disciples.

Preachers are generally aware that the Sermon is a compilation of sayings of Jesus brought together for the instruction of converts. They are less commonly aware that the Beatitudes in Matthew 5 also have been gathered together by the evangelist. That follows from the fact that whereas Matthew has nine of them, Luke (in 6:20–23) has only four. Of these the last one clearly belongs to the latter part of the ministry of Jesus, when association with him entailed the likelihood of opposition such as he suffered. The first three of Luke's are reminiscent of the passage on which Jesus preached in the synagogue of Nazareth, Isaiah 61:1–2, together with the closely related Isaiah 58:6, which Luke reports Jesus as enclosing within the citation of Isaiah 61:1. Since Isaiah 58:7 mentions sharing bread with the hungry, it is likely that the three beatitudes on the poor, the hungry, and the sorrowful were originally uttered together by Jesus, and Matthew added to them others known to have been spoken by him.

The thorny issue as to whether Jesus declared the Beatitudes in the third person ("Blessed are the poor . . . for *theirs* is the kingdom . . . ") or in the second person ("Blessed . . . for *yours* is the kingdom . . . ") is still controverted. The last beatitude in both Matthew and Luke is in the second person, but that is directed explicitly to followers of Jesus who are to share his suffering. Jaques Dupont has examined the Beatitudes more minutely than

---

[17] A. M. Ambrozic, *The Hidden Kingdom,* (CBQMS 2; Washington: Catholic Biblical Association of America, 1972) 24.

any other person.[18] He declares that beatitudes are generally spoken in the third person, and in this respect Matthew has probably correctly reported Jesus. Moreover Luke does not actually relate the first three beatitudes in the second person, but has a mixed construction: "Blessed (are) the poor, for yours is the kingdom. . . . " There is no verb in the first clause. Having examined hundreds of beatitudes, Dupont has found no such mixed construction in any of them. It appears that Luke has sought to bring the first three beatitudes into line with the last one.

More important is the content of these blessings. The first feature to be noticed is the meaning of the term usually translated "Blessed." The Greek word *makarios* is the common or garden adjective "happy." But it renders a Hebrew word which is not an adjective, but an interjection that introduces an exclamation, so we should translate each beatitude as beginning, "Oh the happiness of . . . !" It makes most of the beatitudes quite startling when one considers who are pronounced so happy. But the "happiness" is due to the latter clause of each beatitude: they all relate to the future kingdom of glory, as is evident when one lists them:

Theirs is the kingdom of heaven.
They shall be comforted.
They shall inherit the earth.
They shall be filled.
They shall obtain mercy.
They shall see God.
They shall be called sons of God.
Great is their reward in heaven.

The third, sixth, and last beatitudes determine the interpretation of the rest: "they shall inherit the earth . . . they shall see God . . . great is their reward in heaven. . . . " These undoubtedly refer to the consummation of the kingdom, and therefore so do the rest. The first, like the third, is a declaration concerning the inheritance of the kingdom, precisely as Mark 10:14 ("Let the little children come to me . . . the kingdom of God belongs to such," literally "is theirs," cf. v. 15: "whoever does not receive the kingdom of God as a little child *will never enter it*"). Interestingly, a number of early authorities for the text place Matthew 5:5 immediately before v. 4, so that verses 3 and 5 are juxtaposed:

---

[18] See his three compendious works on the Beatitudes, J. Dupont, *Les Béatitudes* (3 vols.; Paris: Gabalda, 1969–1973).

Oh the happiness of the poor (in a spiritual sense),
for theirs is the kingdom of heaven!
Oh the happiness of the meek,
for they shall inherit the earth!

The effect is striking. Some scholars consider that Matthew himself so ordered these sayings (the *Jerusalem Bible* and its French predecessor follow this ordering). Whether that be so or not, the two statements are closely bound, for the second echoes Psalm 37:11, which declares that the "poor" (Hebrew *anawim*) will inherit the land. The Hebrew noun comes from a verb meaning to be bowed down, afflicted, and so the noun covers the meanings poor, afflicted, humble, meek; in Isaiah 61:1 the same term appears in the first sense. In view of the fact that the Hebrew term *erets* (used in Psalm 37:11) means both land and earth, it is plain that the two beatitudes relate to the same class of people and promise the same gift—the kingdom of God! But the first one has the consolation of Isaiah 61:1 in view and the second Psalm 37. The seer of Revelation describes the descent of the city of God from heaven to earth, but few scholars have acknowledged that Jesus may have done likewise. J. Schniewind is one of the few; he observed that Jesus offered hope for the earth, and hope for a new world through the promise of resurrection.[19]

The fourth beatitude (Matthew 5:6) has in view the image of the feast of the kingdom, in which the hunger of the people will be "satisfied" with food and drink (for the figure cf. Isaiah 25:6-8; Luke 22:15-18, 28-30). The "merciful" will have mercy shown them—not by people, but by God in the future judgment. The "pure in heart" (cf. Psalm 24:4) will "see God"; set between vv. 7 and 9 this could refer to seeing "God on my side," as in Job 19:26-27, again in the judgment, although it certainly extends its reference to life in the eternal kingdom of God (Revelation 22:3-5). The peacemakers will be called "children (literally sons) of God," i.e., they will be owned by God as his children. There may be a reminiscence here of Hosea 1:10, which relates to the future kingdom:

It will no longer be said to them,
"you are not my people";
they will be called Children of the Living God. (REB)

---

[19] J. Schniewind, *Das Evangelium nach Matthäus* (Neue Testament Deutsch; Göttingen: Vandenhoeck & Ruprecht, 1964) 42–43.

(Cf. also the significant change of tenses in Romans 8:14–17, 23–24.)

Matthew 5:10 with its present tense ("theirs is the kingdom of heaven"), like the first beatitude, has in view the inheritance of the future kingdom. So also the more complex final beatitude, "Your reward is great in heaven." Dupont quotes the Targum on Numbers 23:23 to illustrate its meaning: "Happy are you righteous! What a good recompense is prepared for you with your Father who is in the heavens in the world which is coming!"[20]

That the Beatitudes as a whole refer to present happiness in view of the future coming of the kingdom of God seems to be established. But who are these "happy" people? Here is a further difference between the sayings in Matthew and in Luke. The latter speaks simply of "the poor . . . the hungry . . . those who weep now." Matthew adds to this description: "The poor *in a spiritual sense* . . . those who hunger and thirst *for righteousness* . . . those who mourn." Has Matthew interpreted the sayings of Jesus or has Luke secularized them? I would agree with the majority that the former is true, but I believe that Matthew had reason to do so, notably in his understanding of "the poor." The first and the third beatitudes have similar content, and clearly hark back to Isaiah 61:1–2 and Psalm 37:11. In those two passages the people in view are not the proletariat in a Marxist sense, but *God's poor* who look to him because they have no other resource. Isaiah 61 is consolation addressed to the oppressed people of God, and of them it is said, "They will be called trees of righteousness, planted by the Lord for his adornment" (v. 3); "You will be called priests of the Lord and be named ministers of our God" (v. 6). Psalm 37 is addressed to those who "trust in the Lord . . . delight in the Lord . . . commit their way to the Lord . . . wait quietly for the Lord"; these are the righteous, contrasted with evildoers throughout the psalm. The fact is that for centuries in Israel authentic religion was maintained by the poor, and to them prophets and apocalyptic seers gave hope and encouragement to persist in their faith.

Admittedly the addition in Matthew 5:6, "those who hunger and thirst *for righteousness*" appears to make the beatitude refer purely to yearning in a spiritual sense, which could hardly have been the intention of the original saying. But the rendering of the REB should be observed:

---

[20] Dupont, *Les Béatitudes,* 2.42–43, 348.

Blessed are those who hunger and thirst *to see right prevail*; they shall be satisfied. (REB)

Here "righteousness" is understood in relation to God's gift of his kingdom, which will replace the tyranny and oppression of evil rulers with justice and peace. If that be a correct interpretation, it makes the beatitude harmonious with the others, especially the first, even if it stretches the meaning of "those who hunger"; but at least it holds in prospect the feast of the kingdom for such!

It will be seen that the first four beatitudes are really "gospel": to those who have nothing, and in the eyes of the world are nothing, the greatest gift of God is promised, to which none can attain by their own efforts, however wealthy, powerful, and intelligent they may be. The second group of four have an ethical slant, in that they characterize people who seek to reproduce in their own lives the nature of God (mercy, holiness, creation of peace, righteousness). The last one is addressed to disciples of Jesus for their comfort, in a time when they are liable to persecution precisely because of their attachment to him. When they are so cruelly slandered they are to "exult and be glad"—Luke uses the term "leap in a dance"! That command undoubtedly runs counter to ordinary human reaction to such circumstances. The reason for the joy is equally beyond the outlook of the irreligious: disciples of Jesus are to take seriously the prospect of life in the consummated kingdom of God and the privilege of sharing the destiny of the prophets.

The so-called Lord's Prayer, taught by Jesus to his disciples, is recorded by Matthew and Luke, but in different contexts. Luke states that it was given in response to the request of one of his disciples to teach them to pray as John the Baptist taught his disciples (11:1–4); Matthew has placed it in the midst of instruction on how to carry out typically Jewish religious observances (6:1–18). Luke presumably has preserved the original context. Luke's version of the prayer is considerably shorter than Matthew's, but in later texts (reflected in the King James Version) it was filled out from Matthew's version. It is commonly believed that Luke's rendering accords more with the original length of the prayer, and that Matthew's version has been amplified by certain clauses or expressions known to have been used by Jesus himself in his prayers. We cannot, of course, be certain of this issue, for the originality of Luke in the first half of the prayer is contested by some scholars who have most closely studied the prayer. The additions are held to include the phrase "who are in heaven" (after "Father"), "your will be done," "as in heaven, so on earth," and the final doxology, "For yours is the kingdom and the power and the glory for ever." (The last is absent from our earliest manuscripts.)

In any case we should not deny the authenticity of the additional phrases and clauses reproduced in Matthew's version of the prayer. The expression "who are in heaven," coming after "Father," is closely paralleled in Matthew 11:25 ("I thank you, Father, Lord of heaven and earth"). "Your will be done" is the heart of Jesus' prayer in Gethsemane (Mark 14:36); but it is unlikely that that petition, with its agonizing connotation in that setting, was taken straight from there and incorporated into the Lord's Prayer. Curiously, the wording of the Gethsemane prayer in Matthew (26:42) shows the reverse phenomenon, since it has been accommodated to his version of the Lord's Prayer, and the meaning of "your will be done" is different in the two passages (see our comment on it below). If it was not original to the prayer taught by Jesus, the petition will have been used by him in a context of prayer for the kingdom. The language of the final doxology is reminiscent of that of David's prayer in 1 Chronicles 29:11, but since there is no mention of the name of Jesus in it, which Christians would be prone to add, the doxology could well echo the prayer language of Jesus himself.

Of one thing we may be sure: Matthew and Luke were not responsible for the wording of the prayer they reproduced; on the contrary they will have recorded it as it was handed on to them in the churches they served. Of this we may be confident for one extraordinary reason: in both cases the prayer retroverts naturally into Aramaic, and when that is done *both versions manifest rhythm and rhyme.* That is a highly unusual double feature, since Jewish poetry typically had the former but not the latter. They are, however, found together in the most important prayer of the Jews, known variously as the Tefillah, the Amidah, or the Eighteen Benedictions, a prayer that was not only used in every synagogue service but also was said by every observant Jew three times a day and has remained in use to the present time.[21]

---

[21] This feature of the Lord's Prayer has been fully demonstrated by K. G. Kuhn in *Achtzehngebet und Vaterunser und der Reim* (Tübingen: Mohr, 1950), especially 30–33.

We must therefore briefly consider the relation of the Lord's Prayer to the prayers of the Jews of his day. The affinity of the Prayer to the ancient doxology known as the Kaddish, which concluded synagogue services, is widely recognized. It reads:

> Magnified and sanctified be his great name
> in the world which he has created according to his will.
> May he establish his kingdom
> in your lifetime and in your days
> and in the lifetime of all the house of Israel,
> even speedily and at a near time.

Both clauses of this doxology express in different language the one desire for the kingdom of God to appear in the near future. It is an indication of the intensity of the hope of the kingdom which the Jews had in the time of Jesus.

The Eighteen Benedictions also illustrate, though with less intensity than the Kaddish, the extent to which the coming of the kingdom of God filled the horizon of the Jews in their prayers. They are very long; most of them (other than the first three and the last) consist of petitions that issue into benedictions. It is believed that in the time of Jesus there were twelve of them, the first three and last three being added later, along with the benedictions which end each prayer. Even so, the time taken to recite the prayer three times daily (coinciding with the time of the offering of the temple sacrifices) was considerable, and in due course an abbreviated twelve in twelve lines was authorized for Jews slow in speech. The contrast in length between the original Benedictions and the prayer taught by Jesus is striking, especially in the Aramaic form of the Lord's Prayer, which in the Lukan version takes barely half a minute to speak. Even so, the prayers share one important feature: in both cases the structure is twofold, one half relating to the coming of the kingdom of God and the other to human needs; but whereas the Eighteen Benedictions puts the needs of the people prior to prayer for the kingdom, Jesus reverses the order and sets concern for the kingdom of God first. Clearly, Jesus has applied to prayer the maxim of Matthew 6:33 and Luke 12:31, "Seek first the kingdom of God, and the rest will be yours as well"; significantly, this latter saying occurs in the context of anxiety for life's basic needs of food, drink, and clothes.

The first word in the Lord's Prayer is not only fundamental but revolutionary: "Father." It represents the Aramaic term *Abba*. (Luke has the term "Father" alone; Matthew's "Our Father" is a legitimate rendering of *Abba* and is more obviously suitable for a congregation.) The understanding of God as Father of their nation goes back to early Israelite history, but it would seem that while the Jewish people recognized God as their Father, they never addressed him in their prayers as *Abba*. J. Jeremias, with his research students, investigated Jewish literature to find out if this really was the case; after completing the task he concluded, "There is no analogy at all in the whole literature of Jewish prayer for God being addressed as *Abba*."[22] Doubtless this was motivated by reverence for God, for *Abba* was, and still is, used by little children in addressing their fathers. That Jesus constantly used it in his own prayers is an indication of his awareness of his relation to God; this usage he extended to his followers inasmuch as they received the message of the kingdom he brought from God. So this usage differs from the legitimate deduction that human beings are children of the God who created them and cares for them; to receive the message of the kingdom of God present in and with Jesus is to experience the manifold grace of the kingdom in the here and now.

The first half of the prayer that follows contains three parallel petitions for the kingdom of God to come, with an added phrase which governs all three:

> Your name be hallowed,
> your kingdom come,
> your will be done,
>   as in heaven, so on earth.

A few scholars have viewed the first clause as a little benediction, after the manner of Jewish rabbis, who regularly added a clause like "Blessed be he" after mentioning the name of God.[23] This was not a habit that Jesus followed. The example of the Kaddish indicates that the clause rather is likely to be a prayer for *the sanctification of the name of God through the revelation of his sovereign rule*. That is confirmed by a remarkable passage in Ezekiel 36:16–32, which emphasizes God's intention of redeeming Israel from its exile for the sake of his name among the nations:

---

[22] See the essay of Jeremias, "Abba," in *The Prayers of Jesus* (SBT, 2d series, vol. 6; London: SCM, 1967) 11–65 (the citation is from p. 57).
[23] So Martin Dibelius, *Jesus* (Philadelphia: Fortress, 1949) 120. Bultmann acknowledges the possibility of so interpreting it in *Jesus and the Word* (New York: Scribners, 1934) 181.

> It is not for your sake, you Israelites, that I am about to act, but for
> the sake of my holy name, which you have profaned among the
> nations to which you came. . . . And the nations will know that I am
> the Lord, says the Lord God, when through you I display my holiness
> before their eyes. (36:22–23, NRSV, adapted)

In the description of the cleansing and spiritual renewal of Israel
and the material blessings of the kingdom of God that the nation
will receive, Ezekiel states that its purpose will be that the nations
may acknowledge the holiness and glory of the God of Israel. Far
from that being a joyous day of redemption Ezekiel declares:

> You will recall your wicked conduct and evil deeds, and you will
> loathe yourselves because of your wrongdoing and your abomina-
> tions. . . . So feel the shame and disgrace of your ways, people of
> Israel. (36:31–32, REB)

Extraordinary consolation! But "Hallowed be your name" in the
prayer taught by Jesus is clearly a plea that God will so act for the
creation of salvation and righteousness in the world as to reveal
his holiness and glory.

The petition "Your kingdom come" is a summary prayer for
the fulfillment of God's promises made known through the Old
Testament prophets, as well as the yearnings of the Jews, who for
long years had experienced more than their share of oppression
from Gentile super-powers. It embraces the revelation of God's
glory (Isaiah 40:1–11), universal recognition of his sovereignty
(Isaiah 26:1–15), universal establishment of justice and peace
(Isaiah 2; 4; 11; 32), and the conquest of death, with the abolition
of all humanity's sadness (Isaiah 25:8). Naturally this can come
about only through God's saving action. "Your kingdom come" is
virtually a prayer for God himself to come and bring to pass his
purpose in creating this world.

That that may be accomplished is precisely the meaning of
the third petition, "Your will be done." It is perhaps inevitable, in
view of our knowledge of God's will enshrined in the Ten Commandments, to assume that this petition is directed to the replace-
ment of the wickedness of this world by a universal obedience to
God's laws, notably as interpreted by Jesus in the Sermon on the
Mount. That certainly lies within the scope of the prayer, but less
as its meaning than the result of its intention. For in the context
of the Prayer of Jesus it is a request that God will fulfill the
purpose for which he created the world, and that has in view not
only obedience to God but active love for God and for all his

children, a reconciliation that creates the kind of fellowship between God and man that we envisage in the Trinity, and which entails the unity of all so united with God in Christ by the Spirit. Such is the intent of the prayer of Jesus in John 17:20–23.

The expression "as in heaven, so on earth" governs all three petitions for the coming of the kingdom. It is a reminder of the sovereign limitation of the kingdom brought in the ministry, death and resurrection of Jesus, for the rule of God in heaven is assumed to be absolute, whereas it can be so on earth only in the final revelation of God's sovereignty. The brevity of the prayer of Jesus does not allow an explanation of how that will come to pass, but the rest of his teaching shows that it will happen through the action of God in him through whom the kingdom was inaugurated. H. Traub expressed the significance of the phrase in a very insightful manner:

> Through the saving event in Jesus Christ heaven and earth acquire a new relation to one another, expressed in the formula "as in heaven—so on earth." In the first instance this can serve to denote an embracing of heaven and earth. . . . It also implies a new interrelation of heaven and earth effected by God's saving action. . . . The formula "as in heaven, so on earth" expresses the new participation of heaven in earth which in the saving work of Jesus Christ has replaced the division of heaven and earth.[24]

The interpretation of the second half of the Prayer and its relation to its first half now falls to be considered:

> Give to us today our bread for the coming day,
> and forgive us our debts,
> as we have forgiven our debtors;
> and do not bring us into temptation,
> but deliver us from the evil one.

I am under the impression that most Christians think of these petitions as without relation to the prayer for the coming of the kingdom of God. By contrast some scholars see them in closest relation, due especially to the influence of J. Jeremias. He drew attention to Jerome's report that the Aramaic *Gospel of the Nazarenes* translated the term generally rendered "daily" (*epiousios*) by "tomorrow" (Aramaic *mahar*). Jeremias held that that meant God's tomorrow, namely the kingdom of God; hence it was a prayer for God to grant today the bread of the kingdom, the bread

---

[24] H. Traub, "οὐρανός," *TDNT* 5.517–19.

of life.[25] That led him further to relate the forgiveness asked for to the impending day of judgment, and to interpret the "temptation" as denoting the final tribulation of history, when the danger of apostasy will be a real one; accordingly he understood the latter to mean, "Preserve us from falling away, from apostasy."[26]

Undoubtedly this interpretation is attractive, but it appears to me to be unnatural. The whole ministry of Jesus was conditioned by his consciousness of being sent to initiate the kingdom of God that should finally cover the earth, and his life and works showed the nature of that sovereignty, namely God's love in action on behalf of people in need (the "poor in spirit"). The feeding of the multitude in the wilderness showed Jesus' concern for hungry people and the divine sovereignty in action to meet it; Mark 2:5–12 shows that forgiveness of present sins is integral to the saving sovereignty; and in the exorcisms of Jesus present deliverance from the power of Satan is a clear manifestation of the kingdom of God. The petitions in the second half of the Lord's Prayer therefore are best understood as expressing the dependence upon God of those who already live under the saving sovereignty of God, and are looking for its perfection in the fulfillment of the first half of the prayer.

As to details: If "bread for the coming day" is a correct translation, then it relates to the day that stretches ahead, and is a morning prayer. W. Foerster, however, in an intensive examination of this clause, has argued that in view of the use of the term "today" a further reference to time is needless; he considers that the petition conveys the simple meaning, "The bread which we need (for a day), give us today."[27] It is instructive to compare this with the ninth of the Eighteen Benedictions:

> Bless for us, O Lord, our God, this year for our welfare, with every kind of the produce thereof.[28]

That prayer is a perfectly normal one for people to pray, but the disciple of Jesus is encouraged to live one day at a time and to

---

[25] Jeremias, *The Prayers of Jesus*, 102.

[26] Ibid., 102–6. Note that the NRSV renders the clause "Do not bring us to the time of trial."

[27] W. Foerster, "ἐπιούσιος" *TDNT* 2.590–99.

[28] In the so-called Abbreviated 18 (i.e., a shortened version of the Eighteen Benedictions—for those slow of speech) the corresponding prayer for food reads, "Fatten us in the pastures of your land."

look to God to supply daily needs. Such a prayer is in harmony with the spirit of Matthew 6:25–34.

The prayer for forgiveness of sins (pictured as "debts" owed to God) assumes that the person praying has forgiven any who have sinned against him or her. We recall that this is prayer of one who has accepted Jesus' message of the kingdom and has already learned the meaning of grace. But it is entirely one with such a passage as Matthew 5:23–24 and the parable of the unmerciful servant (Matthew 18:23–35), and it is reinforced by the only comment on the Lord's Prayer given by Jesus in 6:14–15.

The final petition, "Do not bring us into temptation," appears to ask that God should not lead us to *succumb* to temptation, but behind it lies a causative use of the Semitic verb, in this context having the force, "*Cause us not to succumb* to temptation."[29] The clause that follows suggests that the source of temptation is "the evil one" (rather than "evil" considered as impersonal or material). The thought is developed by Paul in 1 Corinthians 10:13.

THE SOVEREIGN FATHERHOOD OF GOD

Our Lord's teaching on the fatherhood of God is second only in importance to his revelation of the kingdom of God, and is integral to it.

That God was king, all Jews passionately believed. If his right to rule was denied by the nations in this age, he yet overruled their evil in his sovereign providence, and the covenant people of God looked for him shortly to exercise that sovereignty in a universal judgment and in the establishment of his kingdom.

That God was father the Jews also affirmed, especially in his relation to the nation as a whole. Moses' message to Pharaoh stipulated that just as Pharaoh had a son, so Israel was God's son (Exodus 4:22–23). Israel's king was viewed as the representative son of God (Psalm 2:7; 2 Samuel 7:14), which naturally led to seeing the king-messiah as the son of God.[30] The term was applied

---

[29] So I. H. Marshall, *Commentary on Luke* (NIGTC; Grand Rapids: Eerdmans, 1978) 461, after J. Carmignac, *Recherches sur le "Notre Père"* (Paris: Letouzey & Ane, 1969) 236–304, 437–45.

[30] So 2 Samuel 7:14 came to be interpreted. For the Qumran literature see 4QFlor 1:6–7, 1QSa 2:11ff., and the references to the Son of God in the Daniel apocryphon in Cave 4. H. Braun stated that this understanding of the Messiah

to specially worthy Israelites, notably the "righteous" (Sirach 4:10; Wisdom 2:28), and to charismatic workers and mystics.[31] The majority of Jews, however, will hardly have included themselves in such favored company. The transcendence of God had so impressed itself on them that they did not find it easy to effect a genuine synthesis between it and the concept of his immanence. To this difficulty the doctrine of the *Bath Qol* (literally "daughter of a voice") gives curious expression. To a nation which scrupulously endeavored to order its life in accordance with the Holy Scriptures, the concept of revelation was of primary importance. But if God is exalted in the heaven of heavens, how is it possible for him to speak to humankind today? The answer given was that he does not do so—directly. But while too remote in his majesty to speak with human beings face to face, he can yet direct his voice to them; what people then hear of God's speech is the "daughter of a voice," i.e., an echo. Accordingly when a rabbi heard a voice from heaven it was said that he had heard a *Bath Qol*.

In such an environment it was scarcely possible for the fatherhood of God to become a vibrant religious doctrine. That it became central in the understanding of Jesus was due on the one hand to his perfect balance in his concept of the transcendence and immanence of God, but still more to the intensity of his experience of God, which intellectual concepts cannot of themselves create. T. W. Manson, in his lectures to students in Manchester, tabulated the Gospel texts in which Jesus refers to God as Father: Mark has 4, Luke 6, Matthew 17, John 107. Of Mark's 4 references, 3 refer to God as the Father of Jesus (8:38, 13:32, 14:36) and 1 to his disciples (11:25); of John's 107 references, over half relate to God as the Father of Jesus. Manson commented, "When Jesus speaks of God as his Father he is not just stating a matter of fact; he is drawing the veil from something that to him is absolutely sacred."[32] We drew attention above to the significance of Jesus addressing God as *Abba*. In his latest work Jeremias made the following statement:

---

was not unique to the Qumran group but was "simply Jewish," *Q und das Neues Testament* (Tübingen: Mohr, 1966) 76.

[31] So D. Flusser, *Jesus* (New York: Herder & Herder, 1969) 93–94; G. Vermes, *Jesus the Jew* (New York: Macmillan, 1974) 206–10; M. Hengel, *The Son of God* (Philadelphia: Fortress, 1976) 42–43.

[32] T. W. Manson, *On Paul and John* (ed. M. Black; London: SCM, 1963) 129.

> The complete novelty and uniqueness of *Abba* as an address to God in the prayers of Jesus shows that it expresses the heart of Jesus' relationship to God. . . . *Abba as a form of address to God expresses the ultimate mystery of the mission of Jesus.*[33]

If that insight is true, and we believe that it is, it supplies the supreme clue to Jesus' consciousness of his messianic mission and of the message he was called to proclaim. Like Jeremias, the Catholic scholar Schillebeeckx also finds in the "Abba experience" of Jesus the secret of his life, "the soul, source and ground of Jesus' message, praxis and ministry as a whole."[34] Note those terms, "message, praxis, ministry": the communication of the message of God as Father, and his ministry to enable others to enter into that relationship, were linked with his message of the kingdom of God as the very center of Jesus' mission.

Reflection will show that this understanding on the part of Jesus of his relationship to the Father must have existed prior to his embarking on his ministry to Israel and will have been rooted in his earlier years in Nazareth (cf. Luke 2:49–50). It explains how he came to perceive his messianic calling, and how he came to interpret it through bringing together the figures of the Son of David–Son of God Messiah of Psalm 2; 2 Samuel 7; and Isaiah 9 and 11; the Servant of the Lord in Isaiah 40–55; the Son of Man in Daniel 7; the Righteous Sufferer of the Psalms; and the prophet like Moses of Deuteronomy 18:15, 18, to whom the Servant of the Lord in Isaiah 49; 50; 53 also approximates.

The intensity of the Abba relationship of Jesus will have deepened his understanding of the Messiah as Son of God, as also of the interrelationship of these quasi–messianic figures. This latter feature applies especially to the relationship between the Son of God and the Son of Man of Daniel 7. An example of this relationship in the teaching of Jesus appears in Mark 8:38:

> Whoever is ashamed of me and of my words in this adulterous and sinful generation, *the Son of Man will also be ashamed of him when he comes in the glory of his Father* with the holy angels.

The clear implication of this statement is that for Jesus the Son of Man is the Son of God. It is noteworthy that in the Fourth Gospel the Son (of God) and Son of Man are frequently used interchange-

---

[33] Jeremias, *New Testament Theology,* 67–68.
[34] E. Schillebeeckx, *Jesus: An Experiment in Christology* (New York: Crossroad, 1989) 266.

ably (see e.g., John 3:14–16 and 5:25–27), although it is plain that the expression "the Son" is the fundamental feature in John's Christology. That, too, accords with the *Abba* experience of Jesus; i.e., his experience of a unique filial relationship with God.

In Judaism, sonship entails both likeness and the duty of obedience to one's father. This applies to Israel as God's son, for to be set in such a relation to God and to be appointed for service to God go together in Israel's history, as Exodus 19:4–6 illustrates. For Jesus also the consciousness of God-relatedness was accompanied by a sense of vocation and representation, as is illustrated in the complementary sayings of Matthew 11:27 and Mark 13:32; the former speaks of the Son's vocation to reveal the Father, the latter a limitation of the Son's knowledge regarding the time of his coming to complete the establishment of the Father's kingdom. Above all, his service includes suffering in order that the kingdom of God may be salvation for the world (Mark 8:31; 9:31; 10:45), but it includes his role of perfecting the kingdom (e.g., Mark 14:62) in fulfillment of the portrayal in Isaiah 52:13–15 of the suffering and exaltation of the Lord's Servant.

All this illustrates the enormous privilege and stupendous implications for life in Jesus' teaching his disciples to address God as Abba in the prayer he taught them. "When you pray say Abba," reports Luke (11:2). That includes not only repeating the prayer, but using it as a model prayer. Those who receive his message of the kingdom are always to remember that they are accepted by God as their "dear Father" in virtue of their relation to his Son and inclusion in the saving sovereignty he brought.

It is remarkable how closely the sayings of Jesus that illustrate the care and compassion of the Father to his children relate to the latter clauses of the Lord's Prayer, despite their brevity. The petition for bread for the day is illuminated by the questions and observations in Matthew 7:9–11:

> Would any of you offer his son a stone when he asks for bread, or a snake when he asks for a fish? If you, bad as you are, know how to give good things to your children, how much more will your heavenly Father give good things to those who ask him! (REB)

So also the principle of prayer for forgiveness as we forgive those who sin against us is expressed by Jesus in Mark 11:25:

> When you stand praying, if you have a grievance against anyone, forgive him, so that your Father in heaven may forgive you the wrongs you have done. (REB)

The rationale for that is set forth vividly in the parable of the unforgiving servant in Matthew 18:23–35.

The prayer for God's enabling us to withstand temptation and for deliverance from the evil one does not have a precise equivalent in a statement of Jesus relating to the Father's care for his children; but the Father's compassion for them, as expressed in Matthew 18:12–14, may be said to lie behind it, as also the ministry of deliverance seen in Jesus' exorcisms and concluded with his redemptive death, as hinted in Luke 23:53 and clearly stated in John 12:31–32.[35]

All this is bound up with the relationship of disciples to Jesus the Son. Naturally there are limits to their inclusion in the unique relation of the Son to the Father. We who are believers in Jesus are not one with the Father as the Son is, nor are we able to take away the sin of the world as he did, but he is our representative with the Father, and we are his representatives in the world. Accordingly we share his mission to the whole world, and are called to carry it out in the same spirit of love and compassion as he did, even to readiness to sacrifice and suffer as he (cf. Mark 8:34; 10:42–45). But that leads on to a consideration of the church and discipleship, and before we do that we must reflect on the teaching of Jesus about his task in making the kingdom of God the saving sovereignty of the Father for the world.

THE REDEMPTION BY THE CHRIST-SON

In contrast to the frequency with which sayings of Jesus in the Gospels concern his proclamation of the kingdom of God, relatively few refer to his suffering and death. This difference between the Gospels and the rest of the New Testament has often been commented on: Jesus proclaimed the kingdom of God, the apostolic church proclaimed the crucified and risen redeemer. The difference, however, is rooted in the necessities of history. In the nature of things it was simply impossible for Jesus to go about the land of Israel proclaiming his impending death and resurrection and their relation to the kingdom of God.

Nevertheless, there is a problem involved in this difference which has been strangely neglected in discussions through the

---

[35] On the relationship between the Lord's Prayer and the disciples' life see T. W. Manson, *The Teaching of Jesus* (Cambridge: Cambridge University Press, 1943) 114–15.

centuries about the atoning work of Christ. The Gospels show that Jesus declared that the promise of the kingdom of God was in process of fulfillment, in anticipation of its future manifestation in power and glory. Yet those same Gospels make it clear that Jesus was also deeply burdened by his destiny to suffer and die for the redemption of the world. How did he relate the two aspects of his calling?

Albert Schweitzer, who maintained that Jesus consistently proclaimed the coming of the kingdom in the near future, believed that Jesus came to see that the tribulation prior to the kingdom's manifestation must be borne by him. This was what Jesus revealed to his disciples at Caesarea Philippi: "He must suffer for others . . . that the kingdom might come."[36] Whether Jesus related his suffering of death to the apocalyptic tribulation prior to the kingdom is debatable, but there is little doubt that according to the apostolic gospel Jesus' death and resurrection were at the center of his service for the coming of the kingdom of God. This is the intent of Paul's citation of the kerygma in 1 Corinthians 15:3–4, and the same point is expressed with particular clarity in Colossians 1:13–14. On the other hand, C. H. Dodd, with his concept of realized eschatology, posed the question: if Jesus preached that the kingdom had arrived, how could he represent that the kingdom would come through his death? He suggested that Jesus saw his death as falling *within* the kingdom of God; judgment and salvation do not go before the kingdom of God, but are actions which reveal God working in sovereign power to overcome "the kingdom of the enemy," to remove sin and make his righteousness and life triumphant; they are therefore evidences of the kingdom of God, not anticipations of it.[37]

It appears to me that these two views are not so much opposed as complementary, in that they embody two very important facets of our Lord's redemptive work: first, the kingdom of God, which is his saving sovereignty, was truly revealed in the words and deeds of Jesus in his ministry; secondly, the revelation of the kingdom of salvation reached its climax in his death and resurrection on behalf of the world; and the two elements form one unbroken process. We may therefore affirm: Jesus is the mediator of the kingdom of God in the totality of his action on

---

[36] A. Schweitzer, *The Quest of the Historical Jesus* (2d ed.; London: A. & C. Black, 1911) 387.

[37] See the discussion in Dodd, *Parables of the Kingdom*, 75–80.

behalf of humanity, which embraces his ministry, his death and resurrection, his sending of the Holy Spirit, and his coming in power and glory at the end of the age.

Having already considered sayings of Jesus that show the kingdom in action in his ministry, we shall briefly examine some cardinal utterances of his which appear to link his death and resurrection with the coming of the kingdom of God.

The first three Gospels give prominence to three statements of Jesus which predict his forthcoming suffering, death, and resurrection (Mark 8:31; 9:31; 10:32ff.).[38] The question has often been raised whether these predictions were actually uttered on three different occasions, or whether they are three different versions of one prophecy. Judging from the reaction of the disciples to Mark 8:31 (a perfectly comprehensible one), Jesus will have found it necessary to repeat his instruction on this theme. Mark 9:30–32 is significant in this respect:

> They went on from there and passed through Galilee. He did not want anyone to know it; for he was teaching his disciples, saying to them, "The Son of Man is to be handed over into the hands of men, and they will put him to death. . . . " But they did not understand what he was saying and were afraid to ask him. (NRSV, adapted)

A similar statement prefaces the third prediction in 10:32. This last is more detailed than the other two, and could well have been amplified in the light of events; but the fact that Jesus gave warning in less specific terms of what lay ahead of him is not to be denied.

Mark 8:31 is typical of the others, and reads:

> He began to teach them that the Son of Man must suffer greatly, and be rejected by the elders and chief priests and lawyers, and be put to death, and after three days rise.

There is an echo here of Psalm 118:22:

> The stone that the builders rejected
> has become the chief cornerstone.
> This is the Lord's doing;
> it is marvelous in our eyes. (NRSV)

---

[38] For a very full treatment of the so-called "predictions of the passion" see H. F. Bayer, *Jesus' Predictions of Vindication and Resurrection* (WUNT 2; Tübingen: Mohr, 1986); more briefly in Beasley-Murray, *Jesus and the Kingdom of God*, 237–47.

Mark 9:31 speaks of the Son of Man being "handed over." There is a tendency for English translations to render that word as "betrayed," but it occurs frequently in Mark's passion narrative in an identical sense: Jesus is "handed over" to the Jewish leaders (14:10, 41), they "handed him over" to Pilate (15:1), and he "handed him over" to the soldiers for crucifixion (15:15); in the primitive kerygma, however, Jesus was "handed over" for our trespasses (Romans 4:25), i.e., by the Father, who "did not spare his Son but "handed him over for us all" (Romans 8:32). If this thought was present in the mind of Jesus when he uttered Mark 9:31, he will have been conscious of the content of Isaiah 53, especially vv. 6, 10–12; in view of the contemporary Jewish emphasis on Genesis 22 (the account of Abraham's attempt to sacrifice Isaac) he may even had had that incident in mind also. However much moderns may hesitate to accept that Jesus believed it to be the will of his Father that he should so die, it would appear that the rest of our Lord's instruction on this theme, together with the agony of Gethsemane, leave no ground for doubting it; in which case the verb "is to be handed over" must be interpreted as a "divine passive," i.e., an action attributed to God, whose name is not mentioned out of reverence.

This conviction was in harmony with certain fundamental elements of the Old Testament revelation, to which Jesus would have been sensitive.

The figure of the righteous person who suffers at the hands of the unrighteous is frequently met in the Psalms; people who are in distress, often falsely accused and threatened with death, identify themselves with it and pray for deliverance; on finding it they offer thanksgiving to God, often accompanied by a vow. The simplest example of the phenomenon is Psalm 34:19:

> Many are the afflictions of the righteous man, but the Lord rescues him out of them all.

Psalms 7, 22, 26, 56, 57, 59, and 69, of which the most frequently cited are the second and the last, expound and apply this pattern. There are many echoes of these psalms in the narratives of the Lord's sufferings and death in the Gospels, pointing to the fulfillment of the pattern in Jesus, including his vindication in resurrection.[39]

---

[39] This point has been demonstrated by J. Gnilka, "Die Verhandlungen vor dem Synhedrion und vor Pilatus nach Markus 14:3–15:5," in Evangelisch-

It is now acknowledged that the Servant of the Lord, whose sufferings and vindication are most fully set forth in Isaiah 52:13–53:12, is the supreme example of the Righteous Sufferer. What is written of him anticipates most clearly the substance of our Lord's prophecies of his passion. In Isaiah 53:11 the subject of the song is actually called "the righteous one, my servant"; yet he is rejected by his contemporaries (vv. 3–4), suffers at their hands (vv. 7–8), is put to death unjustly (vv. 7–9), but will be vindicated and exalted (52:13–15; 53:10–12). The entire song is marked by the dual motif of affliction by men (vv. 3, 7–9) and by God (vv. 6, 10). But a new note is introduced: the affliction he bears is to expiate the sins of the unrighteous (vv. 4–6, 8, 10–12), and so the Servant will see light, find satisfaction, and make many righteous (vv. 10–11).

Another strand in the passion predictions appears to be the rejected prophet who is vindicated by the Lord. Isaiah was told that his prophetic ministry would be largely in vain (6:9–13), but he became an honored counselor of the king. By contrast Elijah, Micaiah, and Jeremiah were persecuted, and Uriah and Zechariah son of Jehoiada were put to death (Jeremiah 26:20–24 and 2 Chronicles 24:21). Later tradition maintained that Isaiah, Jeremiah, Ezekiel, Amos, and Micah were all slain. Jeremias affirmed that in the time of Jesus "martyrdom was considered an integral part of the prophetic office."[40] Jesus himself appears to have anticipated suffering the fate of the rejected prophets, as is seen in his response when told of Herod's desire to kill him: "It is unthinkable for a prophet to meet his death anywhere but in Jerusalem" (Luke 13:33); he quoted the "wisdom of God," which told of the killing of prophets and righteous men throughout Jewish history, and the judgment that would fall on "this generation," which would consummate the same process by its rejection of God's final messenger (Luke 20:49–51); and in his lament over Jerusalem he called it "the city which murders the prophets and stones the messengers sent to it" (Matthew 23:37–39).

Finally, the concept of the martyr for God's cause was widespread in the era of Jesus. When Antiochus Epiphanes in the second century B.C. attempted to force Israel to adopt the paganism of the Hellenistic world, large numbers of Jews preferred to

---

Katholischer Kommentar zum Neuen Testament: *Vorarbeiten*, Heft 2 (Neukirchen-Vluyn: Neukirchener Verlag, 1970), especially 11–12.

[40] J. Jeremias, "παῖς θεοῦ," *TDNT* 5.714.

suffer torture and death rather than give up the faith of their fathers. A celebrated story of a widow who had seven sons, all of whom were martyred for their faith, is recounted in the books of the Maccabees in the Apocrypha. The significant thing about the narratives is the meaning they attached to the martyrs' deaths. The last of the seven is reported to have told the king:

> I, like my brothers, surrender my body of life for the laws of our fathers. . . . With me and my brothers may the Almighty's anger, which has justly fallen on all our race, be ended! (2 Maccabees 7:37–38)

In 4 Maccabees 6:28–29 Eleazar the priest is said to have prayed for his people when he was about to be killed:

> Make my blood their purification, and take my soul to ransom their souls.

There is no question of Jesus directly borrowing from this narrative its interpretation of a redemptive death and applying it to himself; we are not certain of its date, and in any case this motif is already reflected in Isaiah 53; but it is important as witness to a belief that had become increasingly pervasive among Jews in this period, helped no doubt through further reflection on the scriptures by reason of their own experience of suffering.

One feature in contemporary Jewish faith was undoubtedly quickened by the persecution they endured: suffering and death for God's cause had as its reward resurrection for the kingdom of God. So the book of Daniel teaches (12:2–3) and most apocalyptic literature after it. The like applies to the other categories of biblical faith we have reviewed: the Righteous Sufferer is delivered by God for life in his presence (see especially Wisdom 2:10–5:23); the Servant of the Lord is raised and exalted after his death (Isaiah 52:13–15; 53:10–12); and the rejected prophet is vindicated by God, as are the martyrs, who are promised a place at the right hand of God.[41] It is, accordingly, in harmony with these elements of contemporary Judaism that each of Jesus' predictions of the passion concludes with a declaration that he will rise from death. It is also in harmony with the message of the kingdom of God which Jesus preached and which determined the

---

[41] In the *Apocalypse of Elijah* it is written of the martyrs: "The Lord says, I shall place them at my right hand, they will render thanks for the others; they will conquer the Son of Iniquity, they will see the destruction of the heaven and of the earth, they will receive the thrones of glory and crowns," 4:27–29.

mode of his ministry, for if he saw in his death the climax of his mission to inaugurate the kingdom of God he must have looked beyond death to its future completion. (We have yet to consider Jesus' teaching on his *parousia,* his coming again.)

The reference to resurrection "after three days" is not an indication of "prophecy after the event," as has often been claimed. "After three days" is peculiar to Mark's version of the passion predictions; Matthew and Luke in each case accommodate it to the formula of the resurrection in the kerygma, "on the third day." There is no difference in meaning. "Three days" in Jewish parlance, however, represented a short time.[42] In view of the frequency of the expression in significant contexts in the Hebrew Bible the Jews saw it as proof of the divine overruling of history. Hence the statement in the midrash on Genesis 42:17, "The Holy One, blessed be he, never leaves the righteous in distress more than three days." The principle is explicitly said to embrace the "third day of resurrection," referred to in Hosea 6:1–2:

> Come, let us return to the Lord . . .
> After two days he will revive us;
> on the third day he will raise us up,
> that we may live before him. (NRSV)[43]

To say the least, that is a significant precedent for the resurrection of the Messiah on the third day. But it also gives pause for thought: if Jesus spoke so plainly about his resurrection on the third day following his impending death, how was it that his disciples were so totally unprepared for it? The very use of the expression "three days" in connection with the resurrection in Hosea 6 provides a clue to the answer, for there the resurrection of the nation is in mind. Needless to say, that event was still awaited and lay in the unknown future, despite the prophet's

---

[42] An example of its use by Jesus is seen in Luke 13:31–33.

[43] The principle is fully illustrated in the *Midrash Rabbah* on Genesis 22:4 ("On the third day Abraham lifted up his eyes and saw the place afar off," i.e., the place of sacrifice and deliverance), where it is defined as "the third day of Abraham," Genesis 42:18 as "the third day of the tribal ancestors," Exodus 19:16 as "the third day of revelation," Joshua 2:16 as "the third day of the spies," Jonah 2:1 as "the third day of Jonah," Ezra 8:32 as "the third day of the return from Exile," Hosea 6:2 "the third day of the resurrection," Esther 5:1 "the third day of Esther." Most of these passages relate to deliverances of various kinds. For the full text see *Midrash Rabbah* (10 vols.; trans. and ed. H. Freedman and M. Simon; London: Soncino, 1939) 1.491.

mention of "the third day." The shock administered by Jesus to the disciples after they had confessed him to be the Messiah—that he was to be rejected by Israel's leaders, suffer greatly, and be put to death—was in no way removed by the reference to his resurrection after three days, for in their understanding that would not take place until the day when all were raised. Meanwhile all their hopes and dreams of Jesus as God's emperor of the world and themselves as his associates were dashed to the ground; the consolation offered by Jesus that on the last day, at some unknown time in the future when Jesus was dead, everything would be changed, was cold comfort. It was colder still when it all happened, and Jesus was arrested, condemned, crucified, and buried. What a shock was theirs when Jesus' words about the third day proved true!

One more observation on the passion predictions must be made. The subject of them all is "the Son of Man." That was Jesus' favorite way of referring to himself when speaking of his mission. It echoed Daniel 7:13, where "one like a son of man" came on the clouds of heaven and received from God the kingdom, which replaced the kingdoms of the world symbolized by beasts. Since apparently the expression "son of man" could also be a way of referring to oneself it was distinctly ambiguous and therefore suited Jesus well in making statements about his messianic role. The Son of Man in the predictions of the passion was able to represent the Righteous Sufferer whom God delivers, the Servant of the Lord who dies and rises for the sake of sinful humanity, the prophet of the end who completes the ministry of the prophets who preceded him, and the supreme martyr for the cause of God, which is his kingdom. The link in Daniel 7:13f. between the "one like a son of man" and the kingdom of God is evident in these passion predictions: the humiliation, suffering, death, and resurrection of the Son of Man complete his service whereby the kingdom of God comes for humanity.

A saying of Jesus in the spirit of the passion predictions, but more explicitly stating the reason for his death, is the well known Mark 10:45:

> The Son of Man came not to be served but to serve,
> and to give his life a ransom for the many.

It was spoken in the context of dispute between the disciples as to precedence in the kingdom of God. Luke has a similar saying, also in a context of dispute as to who is greatest, but he sets it in the Last Supper (22:27):

> I am in the midst of you as one who serves.

It has been suggested that both sayings were independent in the period of oral tradition, and that Mark conjoined the second clause to the first, thus:

> I am in the midst of you as one who serves.
> The Son of Man came to give his life a ransom for many.[44]

That is, of course, purely speculative, but there is increasing consensus that both sayings were linked with the Last Supper. Léon-Dufour views Luke 22:27 as an interpretation of the action of Jesus at the Supper that sees his blood as given on behalf of others; Mark reflects a dogmatic concentration and Luke a liturgical situation, but both versions of the saying deal with service in an absolute sense; in both sayings "we are in the presence of an understanding of the sacrifice of Jesus as service."[45]

It could be that an original saying lies behind its two versions:

> The Son of Man . . .
> who serves,
> and gives his life
> a ransom for many.

That would form a perfect basis for the version of the saying reproduced in 1 Timothy 2:5–6:

> (There is one Mediator between God and man)
> the man Christ Jesus,
> who gave himself
> a ransom for all.

In what sense, however, is the life of Jesus given as "a ransom for many"? The Greek term for ransom *(lytron)* commonly meant "money paid as a means of release," especially as payment for the release of prisoners of war, slaves, or debtors. It frequently translates the Old Testament term *kopher,* "the price of a life."

---

[44] So H. Schürmann, *Jesu Abschiedsrede, Lk 22.21–38* (Münster: Aschendorff, 1957) 96.

[45] X. Léon-Dufour, "Jésus devant sa mort à la lumière des textes de l'institution eucharistique et des discourses d'adieu," in *Jésus aux origines de la christologie* (ed. J. Dupont; Leuven: Gembloux, 1975) 165.

Morna Hooker considers that the chief link here is with the redemption of Israel from Egyptian slavery at the exodus and the hope for a second exodus for the kingdom of God.[46] That is certainly included in the meaning of the ransom, but the additional phrase "for the many" indicates that something more is in mind, i.e., a substitutionary action on behalf of the many. In this respect Isaiah 53 comes to mind, especially the last stanza, which is closely parallel to Mark 10:45:

> When you make his life an offering for sin (*'asham*) . . .
>   (Isaiah 53:10)
> He bore the sin of many. . . . (Isaiah 53:12, NRSV)

Jeremias affirmed that Mark 10:45 "relates word for word to Isaiah 53:10f., and indeed to the Hebrew text."[47] It is difficult to deny that, but we recall also the prayer of Eleazar in 4 Maccabees 6:29, "Make my blood their purification, and take my soul to ransom their souls." The thought is the same, except for one aspect: Eleazar's prayer has in view a ransom for his own people, whereas in Isaiah 53:12 and Mark 10:45 the ransom is "for the many," i.e., "for all" (as in 1 Timothy 2:6). The Son of Man thus gives his life as a redemptive sacrifice that the kingdom of God may be opened for humankind in its totality.

The sayings of Jesus at the Last Supper are burdened with the same meaning. Whether or not the meal was a Passover celebration or an anticipated Passover, it undeniably was filled with Passover associations and anticipated that meal to which the Passover in the time of Jesus pointed, the feast of the kingdom of God. Mark 14:25 sets at the end of the meal the statement of Jesus' anticipation of the feast; Luke reports that Jesus referred to it twice, at the beginning of the meal and at its end (Luke 22:15–18). It is likely that the latter passage is an independent report of the Supper set within the Passover context, while vv. 19–20 reproduce a tradition drawn up for the guidance of the churches in their celebrations of the Lord's Supper.[48]

Jesus added two unique features to the usual recitation of the significance of the meal. Before handing round the loaf at the beginning of the meal he broke it and said, "This is my body"

---

[46] M. Hooker, *The Son of Man in Mark* (London: SPCK, 1967) 144.

[47] Jeremias, *New Testament Theology*, 299.

[48] So H. Schürmann, *Der Einsetzungsbericht Lk. 22.19–20* (Münster: Aschendorff, 1955) 133–50.

(Mark 14:22). After the meal was finished he took the cup, and handing it round to the disciples he said, "This is my blood of the covenant" (Mark 14:24). These actions were a double parable of the sacrifice that he was about to make. The words "my blood of the covenant" ("new covenant," Luke and Paul) recall two Old Testament statements: Exodus 24:8, when Moses at the exodus dashed sacrificial blood upon the people and said, "Look, the blood of the covenant"; and Jeremiah 31:31, announcing the making of a new covenant, when Israel will be transformed to become the people of the kingdom of God. Both aspects constitute the new covenant in the blood of Jesus—on the one hand forgiveness of sins, and on the other hand spiritual renewal of the redeemed and the (re)constitution of a people for the kingdom of God. This interpretation is underscored in a statement which Luke alone has preserved (22:29–30):

> I covenant with you, as my Father covenanted with me, a kingdom, so that you may eat and drink at my table in my kingdom, and you will sit on thrones judging the twelve tribes of Israel.[49]

The last clause is a reminiscence of Matthew 19:28, brought to the essential saying in v. 29 either in the early tradition or by Matthew; it clearly relates to the apostles by virtue of their unique association with Jesus. Verse 29, however, is an essential part of the new covenant with the people of God represented by the apostles. The forgiveness and the renewal are present realities consequent on the death and resurrection of the redeemer, whereas the eating and drinking with him "in a new way in the kingdom of God" (Mark 14:25) is a sure and certain promise of participating in the feast of the kingdom at the end of the age. What was promised to the disciples as they ate the bread and drank the wine is pledged to all who in faith eat bread and drink wine at the Lord's Supper.

What more, then, is there to say about this topic? Has not the redemption of the Christ-Son been completed in his death and resurrection? The cry from the cross, "It is finished" (John 19:30), is often so interpreted, as though the death of Jesus alone has achieved all that is meant by redemption in the Bible. The

---

[49]The Greek verb *diatithemai* is regularly used with the cognate noun *diathēkē* for making or establishing a covenant, and it should be so understood here. See R. Otto, *Kingdom of God and Son of Man*, 292, and A. Schlatter, *Das Evangelium des Lukas* (2d ed.; Stuttgart: Calwer, 1960) 424.

representation in the Fourth Gospel of the unity of the death and resurrection of Christ comes close to that notion, but it is better to understand the shout of Jesus as signifying the completion and accomplishment of the task assigned to him in his earthly life, namely the inauguration of the saving sovereignty of God for all humanity, whereby its gifts are available to all who receive him and his message from God. There is, however, one great feature of the kingdom of God that remains to be accomplished, and it is implied in the use of the term "inauguration" of Jesus' service of the kingdom: its *universality,* in the twofold sense of the total subjugation of everything that opposes God, and therefore the execution of judgment, and the extension of the new creation over all existence, implied by Paul in 2 Corinthians 5:17 and described by the prophet John in Revelation 21:9–22:5, namely, resurrection to life in the kingdom of God that leaves no room for death. In the entire New Testament—Gospels, Acts, Letters, book of Revelation—that is the awaited work of the Christ-Son in his future coming.

My understanding of the teaching of Jesus as to this aspect of his task has been set forth in fullness elsewhere,[50] and here I can only summarize. But one statement requires to be made at once: the future coming of Christ should never be treated in isolation, but always in relation to the revelation of the kingdom of God in his incarnate life. This is the supreme difference between the gospel of Jesus and Jewish apocalyptic generally: in his life, death and resurrection the kingdom of God came into the midst of humankind, it is operative in the present by his Spirit, and it is to be consummated by him at his appearing. That is the intent of the ancient liturgical confession of the church, "Christ died, Christ rose, Christ will come again." We must see how that confession relates to the teaching of Jesus.

A good place to begin this review is the so-called Q Apocalypse of Luke 17:22–37, which Matthew mainly sets after his reproduction of the eschatological discourse of Mark 13 (Matthew 24). It commences with an isolated saying of Jesus, "Days will

---

[50] See especially Beasley-Murray, *Jesus and the Kingdom of God.* The earlier work, *Jesus and the Future* (London: Macmillan, 1954), with its companion volume *A Commentary on Mark Thirteen* (Macmillan, 1957), have been replaced by *Jesus and the Last Days* (Peabody, Mass.: Hendrickson, 1993). Note also the *Commentary on Revelation* in the New Century Bible (London: Oliphants, 1974), now a paperback (Grand Rapids: Eerdmans, 1981).

come when you will greatly desire to see one of the days of the Son of Man, and you will not see it" (v. 22). The interpretation of this saying is conditioned by the later sayings of the passage, v. 24, "so will the Son of Man be in his day," v. 26, "the days of the Son of Man," and v. 30, "the day when the Son of Man is revealed." Matthew replaces these varying expressions with, "So will be the coming (parousia) of the Son of Man" (24:27, 37, 39). The plural of Luke 17:26 is probably due to the immediately preceding phrase, "the days of Noah," and may also be influenced by the common rabbinic expression "the days of the Messiah." At all events the statement of v. 22 appears to be a warning of hard times ahead for the disciples, when they will yearn for the coming of their Lord, but they must continue to endure whatever suffering has come their way.

In contrast to Jewish claims that the Messiah is in a secret location (v. 23) the appearance of the Messiah will be publicly, universally, and suddenly revealed (v. 24). The reference to the necessity of the Messiah to suffer and be rejected by "this generation" (v. 25) is likely to be an abbreviation of the first passion prediction, inserted by Luke here to remind readers that as the Christ had first to suffer before entering on his glory so must his disciples (cf. Luke 24:26, 44).

The comparison of the appearing of the Son of Man with the onset of Noah's flood and the overthrow of Sodom in Lot's day (vv. 26–30) is of interest: the generation of Noah and the people of Sodom in Lot's day were notorious sinners on whom judgment fell; yet not a word of their exceptional evil occurs in this passage, only their complete preoccupation with the affairs of this world, so that they were utterly unprepared for the judgment that fell. That is the point of comparison with the "day when the Son of Man is revealed": it will be wholly unexpected for those who live only for this world.

Verses 31, 32, 33 look like isolated sayings brought to this place either in an early source or by Luke himself. Verse 31 is set by Mark in the context of warning about the "abomination of desolation" (13:15f.), and there relates to the necessity of flight before an advancing army (underscored in 13:17–18). Luke's application of the saying to the coming of the Lord can only be in a referred sense, such as sitting loose to the things of this world in the light of his coming.

The implicit warning conveyed in the comparisons with Noah's flood and Sodom's destruction is continued in the more domestic scenes of the separation at the Lord's coming of a husband and wife in bed (v. 34) and of two women grinding corn in a mill (v. 35). Matthew adds the picture of two men working on a farm (24:40), but omits that of two in a bed together. The illustrations are vivid, showing how the separation on the last day could affect the closest of human ties.

Luke concludes with a question asked by Jesus' disciples: "Where will this happen, Master?" The answer is enigmatic: "Where the corpse is, there the vultures will gather" (v. 37). Matthew places this saying immediately after the comparison of the Lord's coming with a lightning flash (24:28), hence he will have had in mind the significance of this saying for the revelation of the Son of Man and the suddenness of his coming; that accords with the fact that vultures quickly appear where there is a corpse. But the element of judgment that runs through these Q sayings is also apparent, so that the answer to "Where, Lord?" is "Everywhere." "The universality of the coming of the Lord corresponds to the universality of the judgment of the world."[51] The judgment, of course, is both positive and negative, hence one is "taken," i.e., for the joys of the kingdom, the other "left," i.e., outside the banquet hall where the feast of the kingdom takes place (cf. Matthew 22:13f.; 25:30).

An even longer discourse on "last things" is contained in Mark 13, with parallels in Matthew 24 and Luke 21. It is generally conceded that Matthew has largely reproduced Mark's discourse, but that Luke, while using the same procedure, has had access to another source.[52] Certainly the material of the discourse was in circulation in the churches prior to the composition of the Gospels, as parallels in the letters of Paul, especially 1 and 2 Thessalonians, show.[53] Some of this diverse material had probably

---

[51] J. Zmijewski, *Die Eschatologiereden des Lukas-Evangeliums* (Bonn: P. Hanstein, 1972) 515–16.

[52] The issue is complex. V. Taylor thought that Luke acted as he had in his composition of the passion narrative, viz., that he gave non-Markan material preference and fitted into it Markan extracts (*Behind the Third Gospel* [Oxford: Oxford University Press, 1926] 125). I would think the reverse process more likely. Compare the discussions of the issue by Marshall, *Gospel of Luke,* 753–57 and Fitzmyer, *Gospel according to Luke,* 2.1324–29.

[53] See the references compiled in Beasley-Murray, *Jesus and the Kingdom of God,* 412 n. 54, and D. Wenham, "Paul and the Synoptic Apocalypse" in *Gospel Perspectives: Studies of History and Tradition in the Four Gospels* (ed. R. T. France and D. Wenham; Sheffield: JSOT Press) 2.345–75.

already been grouped in catechetical collections of Jesus' sayings; Mark himself gave it its present shape.[54]

The discourse begins with a prophecy of Jesus about the temple: "Not a stone will be left on a stone, every one will be thrown down" (v. 2). To the disciples the prophecy was all but unbelievable; on the one hand the stones of the walls were immense, but more important, the temple had barely been completed, and like all Jews who looked for the kingdom of God they would have assumed that this temple would become its center in the world. Jesus, however, had strong precedent for his prediction in statements of Old Testament prophets as to the judgment of God upon the temple and city of Jerusalem, e.g., Micah 3:12; Jeremiah 7:11; Ezekiel 9–11 (cf. also the denunciation by Amos of the temple in Bethel, 9:1). Moreover, Jesus is recorded elsewhere as declaring the judgment that threatened Israel, Jerusalem, and the temple, e.g., Luke 13:1–5, 34–35; 23:28–31; but above all Luke 19:44:

> They will bring you to the ground . . .
> and not leave you one stone standing on another. (REB)

This statement relates to the city, whereas Mark 13:2 relates to the temple; but the one could not be destroyed apart from the other, and both were inseparable as the center of the nation's life; consequently, similar language is used of the destruction of both. The rejection of God's Messiah and his kingdom occasions a rejection by God of the place that served as the sign of his presence with his people, and therefore judgment—a veritable "day of the Lord" on Israel, its city, and its temple.

The question of the disciples in vv. 3–4 is wholly comprehensible:

> When will these things be,
> and what will be the sign when all these things will happen?

It is assumed that the destruction of the temple could not take place alone, but must be part of the end of the age ("these things," "all these things"). It is commonly suggested that Mark has related the first clause to the destruction of the temple and the second to the coming of Christ, in view of the actual content of the discourse. It is simpler, however, to take the two clauses as strictly

---

[54] For an elaboration and justification of this statement see Beasley-Murray, *Jesus and the Last Days*, 350–76.

parallel. The language of the second clause echoes Daniel 12:6–7, as that of v. 19 echoes Daniel 12:1: a day of the Lord on Jerusalem is in view. But Mark knows that that is to be followed by a greater day, that of the coming of the Lord to the world of nations.

Verses 5–23 form the first major section of the discourse, the greater part of which may be summarized under the term "Tribulations," i.e., for the nations (vv. 7–8), for the church (vv. 9–13), for Israel (vv. 14–20), preceded and followed by warnings against false prophets and false messiahs (vv. 5–6, 21–23). These warnings embrace the signs for which the disciples asked but go beyond, in that they herald both the destruction of Jerusalem and the coming of the Lord. In all likelihood they were so placed by Mark because false prophets and messiahs were active at the time of writing and were creating confusion. The Roman-Jewish war was then taking place, and the Jews, including Jewish Christians, were looking for the Messiah to deliver Jerusalem and its people; it was urgently necessary for the followers of Jesus not to be led astray.

Wars, earthquakes, and famines (vv. 7–8) are standing elements in prophetic and apocalyptic descriptions of the end of the age. In the Old Testament they are not so much signs of the end as elements of God's judgments in a (or the) day of the Lord (cf. Ezekiel 14:21–23). Here they are spoken of as signs of what is to happen among the nations, but not of an end immediately impending: "the end is not yet . . . these things are the beginning of the birth-pangs." These signs evidently characterize the whole time between the Lord's death and his coming.

The description of tribulation to be experienced by the church (vv. 9–13) hints of the reason for it: believers are going to suffer persecution at the hands of their own rulers and pagan governors and kings. Why? " For witness to them" (v. 9). On the one hand, the obedient witness to the world of Jew and Gentile will cause their arrest, but on the other hand, when they are brought before courts they are to use these opportunities to witness as the Holy Spirit gives them utterance (v. 11). These two statements are a continuous sentence in the source common to Matthew and Luke (i.e., Q—see Matthew 10:17–20/Luke 12:11–12). The command to preach the gospel to all the nations "first" (Mark 13:10) will have been inserted by Mark at this point to make it plain that the church's mission is the church's great priority and that it must be completed before the end comes. This is why Christians must be deaf to false announcements of the end:

they have a task to fulfill before it comes. The book of Acts provides a commentary on this passage.

Israel's tribulation, described in vv. 14–20, begins with the prime answer to the disciples' question in v. 3, both as to time and sign: "When you see the abomination of desolation . . ." This expression is mentioned three times in Daniel (9:27; 11:31; 12:11), of which the most important is the first. In the Old Testament an "abomination" is something abominable to God, often an idol. "Desolation" may be interpreted of horror or destruction. First Maccabees gives the clue to what Daniel means by this cryptogram. It tells how the Greek emperor Antiochus Epiphanes, after conquering Egypt, entered Jerusalem and plundered its temple. Later an official of his attacked the Jews, plundered Jerusalem and set it ablaze. He then ordered the Jews to give up their religion and adopt the religion of the empire. On the altar of the temple he placed a smaller altar on which was an image of Zeus made in the likeness of Antiochus, and on that altar he offered "swine and other unclean beasts." The author of 1 Maccabees calls this "the abomination of desolation" (1:54). The name entails a typical Jewish play on words. *Zeus Olympios* could be rendered in Hebrew *Baal Shamayim,* i.e., "Lord of Heaven"; the Jews replaced *Baal* by *Shiqqutz,* "an abomination," *Shamayim* by *Shomem,* i.e., "that desolates." So "lord of heaven" became "an abomination that desolates"—not, however, simply of the spirit, but an abomination that brings about destruction. Such is the meaning of Daniel 9:26–27:

> the troops of the prince who is to come shall destroy the city and the sanctuary. Its end shall come with a flood, and to the end there shall be war. Desolations are decreed. He shall make a strong covenant with many for one week, and for half of the week he shall make sacrifice and offering cease; and in their place shall be an abomination that desolates, until the decreed end is poured out upon the desolator. (NRSV)[55]

---

[55] It is important to recognize that the "abomination" not only appalls, but also devastates and destroys. Through adopting the first meaning only many scholars have claimed that the discourse gives no answer to the question of the disciples in vv. 3–4, and therefore that it has no reference to the prophecy of v. 2. On the contrary, vv. 14–20 speak directly to the issue: the abomination will bring about the destruction of the city and temple. On this see Beasley-Murray, *Jesus and the Last Days,* 408–11. For a thorough examination of the problem see D. Ford, *The Abomination of Desolation in Biblical Eschatology* (Washington, D.C.: University Press of America, 1979).

The crisis precipitated by Antiochus was never forgotten by the Jews, and for an understandable reason: the Maccabee brothers revolted against the emperor and under their leadership defeated army after army sent against them. Three years to the day after Antiochus' desecration of the temple they cleansed the temple of its defilement and offered sacrifices according to the law. They decreed that ever after a festival be held annually to remember the blasphemy and the deliverance, and it is celebrated to this day—*Hanukkah*, the Festival of Lights. Jesus himself will have joined in the celebration every year. He saw an equivalence of Antiochus' attack on the Jewish people as the means of God's judgment upon them. Precisely what *he* had in mind we cannot tell, but it is enough to know that he looked for a further fulfillment of the prophecy of Daniel 9. Luke does not use the wording "abomination of desolation"; he interprets it for his Gentile readers as "Jerusalem surrounded by armies," and in this he was heading in the right direction, for only the Roman forces could achieve the destruction of Jerusalem. This explains the language that follows Mark 13:14. When the abomination is seen, then *flight from Jerusalem* is the answer (vv. 15–16). Alas for pregnant women and nursing mothers—they cannot run (v. 17)! Pray that it may not happen in winter, when rains fill up the wadis and make rivers impassable (v. 18). The suffering of the nation will be unprecedented (v. 19). The language of v. 19 is proverbial; it echoes descriptions of the plagues of Egypt (see Exodus 9:18; 10:14) and the eschatological tribulation in Daniel 12:1; yet in adding that the like "never will be" again the statement shows that another time will follow this day of the Lord—time enough for Israel to repent, as suggested in v. 20.

There is, accordingly, an unspecified distance between Jerusalem's tribulation and the high point of the discourse, vv. 24–27, the coming of Christ. The language is highly pictorial—it alludes to Isaiah 13:10; 34:4, and Joel 2:10; 4:15–16, but it reflects typical Old Testament depictions of the coming of God on the day of the Lord (cf., e.g., Amos 9:5; Micah 1:4; Habakkuk 3:6–11; Nahum 1:5). There is no question of portraying through this imagery the breakup of the universe; the intention rather is to represent the coming of the Lord as the intervention of God for the salvation of the world. In other words it is a *theophany of the Christ*. Incidentally, the "word of the Lord" on which the classic description of the coming of Christ in 1 Thessalonians 4:14–17 is based is none other than this passage.

The final section of the discourse, vv. 28–37, deals with the times of the events described in the foregoing discourse. The parable of the fig tree in vv. 28–29 compares the appearance of the fig tree's leaves as pointing to the nearness of summer with events that show the nearness of the coming of the Lord or the kingdom of God. The language is ambiguous: it denotes either that "*he* is near" or "*it* is near"; the use of the figure of the door suggests that the former interpretation is in view (as in James 5:8–9). But what are "these things" that show that the Lord is "at the door"? If the parable is independent, originally from another context, as is highly likely, we cannot well know, but it is evident that the sign of the abomination of desolation is neither immediately in view, nor the wars and rumors of wars, for these do not indicate the immediacy of the end (vv. 7–8). Nevertheless those factors in history through which God works out his purpose for the nations are likely to be included, perhaps above all the fulfillment of the church's mission through suffering. The whole period between Easter and the Lord's coming is "kingdom of God time," in which events in the world, the church, and Israel are to be viewed as signs of the coming of God's kingdom.

Verses 30–32 are three isolated sayings that make specific statements about "times." Verse 30 declares that "all these things" will happen in the contemporary generation.[56] Since the statement follows the description of the coming of the Son of Man in vv. 24–27 it is often thought to cover that as well as the preceding sign; at one time I could see no way out of that conclusion. When, however, it is recognized that Mark has brought together sayings from various sources, spoken on various occasions, the issue is changed. The discourse opens with the Lord's prediction of the destruction of the temple, which appears to be effected by the abomination of desolation. The Q source contains a closely related saying to that of v. 30, which explicitly relates to the judgment of God on "this generation"; it is placed by Matthew just before Jesus' prediction of the temple's ruin: "All these things shall come on this generation" (Matthew 23:36; Luke 11:50–51 is even more emphatic). So striking a statement will certainly have been

---

[56] Although the Greek term *genea* can mean birth, progeny, or race, in the Greek Old Testament it frequently translates the Hebrew term *dor*, meaning age or generation in the sense of contemporaries. In our Lord's teaching "this generation" always denotes his contemporaries and carries an implicit criticism. See the article by F. Büchsel ("γενεά, κτλ," *TDNT* 1.663).

repeated in the church as the Lord's word about Jerusalem, and Mark reserved it for this suitable point. Then to show that it does not refer to the coming of Christ he placed almost next to it a saying that clearly does relate to the latter, viz. v. 32: "Of that day or hour nobody knows, nor the angels, nor the Son, but the Father only." One is reminded of the similar statement of the risen Lord recorded in Acts 1:7: "It is not for you to know the times and seasons which the Father has set in his own authority." But Mark 13:32 goes further: the Son willingly leaves the times in the Father's hands, for the mark of the Son is to maintain obedience to the Father. How much more should it be the mark of followers of the Son to renounce all pretense to knowledge of the day! For all attempts to announce the date of the Lord's coming prove to be erroneous and manifest a spirit of pride and disobedience to the Father.

In light of the unknowability of the day or hour the discourse ends with a call for vigilance (vv. 33–37). Every sentence in the conclusion emphasizes a single appeal: *Keep on the alert!* While attention has often been called to echoes of various parables of Jesus in the passage (the Watching Servants, Luke 12:35–38; the Burglar, Matthew 24:42–44; the Good and Bad Servants, Matthew 24:45–51; the Talents/Pounds, Matthew 25:14–30/Luke 19:12–27), it is evident that vv. 34–36 constitute a genuine parable in its own right, a variant of Luke's parable of the Watching Servants, 12:35–38. The element of preparedness for the return of the master of the house has been linked with the theme of authority to work, which is the primary feature of the Talents or Pounds parable. Thus *watchfulness* has been strengthened by the motive of *faithfulness*. Precisely that conjunction of concepts has been embodied in the three parables of Matthew 25, and rightly so. Preparedness for the end includes serving the Lord till the end.

One final saying of Jesus as to his future return that we must consider is his answer to the high priest's question at his trial, "Are you the Messiah, the Son of the Blessed One?" Jesus replied (Mark 14:62):

> I am; and you will see the Son of Man sitting at the right hand of the Power, and coming with the clouds of heaven. (NRSV, adapted)

The statement has been vigorously controverted, above all through claims that the trial scene in which it is set (Mark 14:55–64) is unhistorical, a fiction created by Christians to set the blame for the crucifixion of Jesus on the Jews. Since the appalling persecution of Jews throughout history, culminating in the Holocaust, was based in no small measure on the Christian depiction of Jews as "murderers of God," it is not surprising that contemporary Christian and Jewish scholars have been eager to remove any vestige of a historical basis for such hateful rhetoric. And yet sound historical judgment must transcend ideological concerns, however noble; and the claims that the Gospel accounts of the Jewish trial of Jesus are fictitious have been answered in detail by capable scholars, to whose works the reader is referred.[57]

This is the only utterance of Jesus in which he publicly and plainly states that he is the Messiah, and it is wholly due to the unique circumstances. Not surprisingly he adds words to explain in what sense he is Messiah, and in so doing he cites two important Old Testament passages: Daniel 7:13–14 tells of one like a son of man coming with the clouds of heaven to the Ancient of Days, and "to him was given dominion, glory, and kingship"; Psalm 110:1 declares:

> The Lord says to my Lord,
>   "Sit at my right hand,
>   until I make your enemies your footstool." (NRSV)

The conjunction of the two passages goes far beyond the ordinary concept of the Davidic Messiah. Jesus identifies himself with the Son of Man who is to "come" as the exalted Lord at God's right hand and to rule the kingdom as God's representative. It is, of course, a future exaltation which Jesus has in view, i.e., future to the time of speaking, but it is not one that proceeds step by step—first resurrection, then later coming in glory, as from the post-resurrection Christian point of view we sometimes assume. The language is controlled by the Danielic vision: the Son of Man is to come in theophanic glory to be revealed as the one who is set at God's right hand, and so exercises God-given authority to judge and to rule.

---

[57] See especially J. Blinzler, *Der Prozess Jesu* (4th ed.; Regensburg: Pustet, 1969); the 2d edition was translated into English as *The Trial of Jesus* (Westminster, Md.: Newman, 1959). A. N. Sherwin-White, *Roman Society and Roman Law in the New Testament* (Oxford: Oxford University Press, 1963), and idem, "The Trial of Christ" in *Historicity and Chronology in the New Testament* (Theological Collections 6; London: SPCK, 1965); *The Trial of Jesus: Cambridge Studies in Honour of C. F. D. Moule* (ed. E. Bammel; London: SCM, 1970); D. R. Catchpole, *The Trial of Jesus* (Leiden: Brill, 1971).

Two points should be noted regarding this utterance. Some of the sayings about the future appearance of the Son of Man give the impression of distinguishing between him and Jesus. A notable example of this is Luke 12:8–9:

> Whoever confesses me before men, the Son of Man will
> confess before the angels of God;
> and whoever denies me before men
> will be denied before the angels of God.

If one did not know the sayings of Jesus about the Son of Man who forgives sins, has nowhere to lay his head, is to suffer many things from the Jewish authorities and be put to death and rise from the dead, etc., one could be excused for thinking that in Luke 12:8 the Son of Man is another than Jesus. But the same phenomenon is present in Mark 14:62: "I am (the Messiah), and you will see the Son of Man sitting at the right hand of God . . ."; only in this case it is transparently clear that the Son of Man is the Messiah that Jesus claims to be. The apparent distinction is due to the fact that virtually all the sayings relating to the coming of Jesus have the Son of Man as subject, since they all (including Luke 12:8) are rooted in the vision of Daniel 7.

The second point to observe is that Jesus is making this confession of his messianic status when on trial; in so doing he knows that he will die for it, but he does not hesitate to declare it. Plainly it is one with his earlier declarations that the Son of Man will be rejected by the Jewish authorities, suffer and die, and be raised from death. It is the climax of those sayings, since it shows beyond contradiction that the mission of Jesus is to bring into being the kingdom of God in its totality, and that his service for the kingdom is a single process—through his ministry, death and resurrection, exaltation to the Father's right hand, and coming as Lord of the kingdom at the end of the age.

One last issue must be raised about this saying: it has become common among New Testament scholars to interpret it not of the coming of Jesus *from* heaven at the end of the age, but as his ascent *to* heaven after his death, on the ground that in Daniel 7:13 the one like a son of man rides on the clouds to God in heaven, and so receives from him dominion. This is believed to be supported by the version in Matthew 26:64, "From now on you will see the Son of Man . . . ," and in Luke 22:69, "From now on the Son of Man will be seated at the right hand of the power of God" (in Greek the two phrases "from now on" are different). The interpretation is not new, but was advocated as long ago as 1864 by Timothy Colani and has had its advocates to the present day.[58] Nevertheless I am convinced that it is mistaken. The vision of Daniel 7 is an adaptation of the ancient myth of a battle between the monster of the sea and the storm god of heaven, who rode on the storm clouds to confront and defeat the sea monster; it became a kind of cartoon in Israel to represent the defeat of oppressive political powers by the God of heaven (so in Daniel 7 the four kingdoms are beasts from the sea). It has been pointed out that nowhere in the Old Testament or later Jewish literature are clouds mentioned as means of movement in the heavenly spheres, but only of theophanies to earth.[59] That applies to Daniel 7, for in vv. 21–22 it is said that the anti-God tyrant wrought his mischief "until *the Ancient in Years came;* then judgment was given for the saints." So the session of the heavenly court to judge the rebellious power that vaunted itself against heaven was depicted in vision as on earth, where the violent ruler raged against God and his people; therefore the one like a son of man of necessity came on the clouds to the Ancient in Years on earth.[60] G. Vermes, a notable Jewish scholar deeply interested in Jesus and the Gospels, affirmed:

> Although Daniel 7:13 could have provided an excellent scriptural basis for the construction of Christian belief in the resurrection of Jesus, and even more so for his ascension, there is no evidence of its direct use in any other context but that of an earthward journey at the *Parousia* (i.e., coming).[61]

As to the variations of Matthew and Luke, W. Trilling paraphrased the former as, "From now, from this hour on, since you utter the judgment, you will experience the Son of Man only in glory and prepared for judgment (over you)."[62] Luke 22:69

---

[58] T. Colani, *Jésus Christ et les croyances messianiques de son temps* (2d ed.; Strasbourg: Traettel and Wurtz, 1864). Many scholars in the twentieth century have agreed with Colani, notably T. F. Glasson, "The Reply to Caiaphas (Mk 14:62)," *NTS* 7 (1960) 91; J. A. T. Robinson, *Jesus and His Coming* (London: SCM, 1957) 45; Jeremias, *New Testament Theology,* 273–74.

[59] So K. H. Muller, "Der Menschensohn im Danielzyklus" in *Jesus und der Menschensohn: Für Anton Vögtle* (ed. R. Pesch and R. Schnackenburg; Freiburg: Herder, 1975) 45.

[60] So Dalman, *Words of Jesus,* 241 n. 2, and H. H. Rowley, *Relevance of Apocalyptic* (2d ed.; New York: Harper, 1946) 30 n. 1.

[61] Vermes, *Jesus the Jew,* 187.

[62] Trilling, *Das wahre Israel,* 86.

undoubtedly emphasizes the exaltation of Christ, but in view of the many sayings Luke preserved as to the coming of Christ, it is likely that he intended the coming to be understood as "the revelation of that which in 22:69 applies 'from now on.'"[63]

For the believer there is immense encouragement and challenge in the doctrine of Christ's coming. It conveys the assurance that the Lord who introduced the kingdom of God to humankind through his life, death, and resurrection will complete the purpose for which creation was made. The challenge lies in the call to live and serve in the manner of him who so brought the kingdom and will complete it at his coming.

THE NATURE OF DISCIPLESHIP

The term "disciple" is so frequently used among Christians, it comes as a surprise to discover that in the Bible it is found only in the four Gospels and Acts, apart from a solitary appearance in the Old Testament (Isaiah 8:16, of the prophet's disciples); it does not occur at all in the rest of the New Testament. That is sufficient to make us realize that it must denote a special relationship between Jesus and his followers. The word "special," indeed, is to be emphasized, for the Gospels show that people did not decide to become disciples of Jesus; he always took the initiative and invited them to become such. Reviewing the evidence K. H. Rengstorf stated:

> The relation between Jesus and his disciples is always presented in the tradition as unique. It is wholly personal, whether as the relation of Jesus to the disciples or as that of the disciples to Jesus. The factor on which the whole emphasis lies is exclusively the person of Jesus. As it is he who finally decides whether a man enters into discipleship, so it is he who gives form and content to the relationship of his disciples.[64]

A disciple's commitment to Jesus is but a response to Jesus' commitment to a disciple; priority of choice on his part goes with his prior commitment to the disciple. That should be borne in mind when one considers the radical demands of Jesus for the disciple to put him first in life. Consider, for example, Matthew 10:37:

---

[63] J. Zmijewski, *Die Eschatologiereden des Lukas-Evangeliums,* 248–49.
[64] K. H. Rengstorf, "μανθάνω," *TDNT* 4.445.

> Whoever loves father or mother more than me is not worthy of me;
> and whoever loves son or daughter more than me is not worthy of
> me. (NRSV)

That appears to be a paraphrase of the original saying for those
who are deemed not to understand Semitic idiom, for in Luke
14:26 the saying reads:

> If anyone comes to me and does not hate his father and mother, and
> wife and children, and brothers and sisters, indeed his own life, he
> cannot be my disciple.

While the Matthaean version may well give the sense of Jesus'
words, I. H. Marshall points out that the Hebrew term for hate
(sane) also has the meaning of "leave aside, abandon," and this
could be the intended meaning: "The thought is, therefore, not of
psychological hate, but of renunciation."[65] In that case the disciple is asked to do what Jesus himself did—leave all for the sake
of the kingdom of God. The power of Jesus to draw men and
women after him is seen in that, despite such demands, the
number of his disciples grew greatly, as is seen in such passages
as Matthew 12:15; Luke 6:17; 19:37; John 6:60. Clearly there were
many more disciples than the twelve apostles!

According to Mark there was at least one occasion (there
could have been more) when Jesus gave a general invitation to
people to become his disciples. It occurred after he had made
known to the Twelve the necessity of his impending death:

> If anyone would come after me, let him renounce himself, and take
> up his cross, and follow me. (Mark 8:34)

In light of that utterance it is strange how "following Jesus" has
popularly come to mean following his *example,* as though it were
a call to take home a copy of the Sermon on the Mount and do
one's best with it. On the contrary, it meant what Jesus always had
in view when inviting people to become disciples, namely to live
with him, learn from him, and serve with him. The Lord was on
his way to Jerusalem to fulfill a destiny—death on a cross. He was
giving warning that anyone who wished to belong to his group
must be prepared for the same fate. Shouldering a cross beam to
a place of crucifixion was a familiar enough sight to Jesus' hearers.
The picture suggested was that of a procession of men and women
carrying the instruments of their death, with Jesus at their head.

---

[65] *Commentary on Luke,* 592, after O. Michel, "μισέω," *TDNT* 4.690–91.

It was a call to total renunciation of the world, of home, kith and kin, and life itself, a staking of everything on the ability of Jesus to redeem from death and give one a share in the kingdom of God. It is a frightening picture. It puts the issues of the gospel with a starkness that modern man faces only in a milieu which imposes suffering and death as the price for being a Christian. Such was the situation in which the first gospel, that of Mark, was composed; the cross was replaced by the stake and the lions, but the issue was the same as Jesus set before his would-be followers.

For most of us in the Western world it is highly improbable that we shall ever be called on to face lions, or the stake, or any such instruments of death, as the price for being disciples of Jesus. Yet the latter half of the twentieth century has seen multitudes of Christians in the third world compelled to yield all in their following of Christ. At the moment of my writing this is still happening. The fundamental issue is inescapable. Not even modern people can serve both God and mammon, though they think they can. The ethic of Jesus is irreconcilable with that of Vanity Fair. The disciple of the twenty-first century, no less than the first-century Christian, is called to surrender all if he would win the pearl of great price. The reward of the kingdom outshines in glory anything that God could demand of us, but demand remains for those who would have it.

When this aspect of the Christian faith is slurred over by preachers the church becomes soft and finds itself too weak to resist either the deceitfulness of riches or the attacks of opponents. It is not always easy for the proclaimer of the word to give this necessary element of the gospel its rightful place. Everyone in a public position knows the temptation to be a "crowd-pleaser." The danger therefore must ever be watched of esteeming the praise of men above that of God, and of hesitating to declare truths which are unpalatable. Even to formulate the temptation is sufficient to condemn the idea in our minds with indignation—as though *we* would fall prey to it! Yet the preacher, like his hearers, is flesh and blood; if the devil thought it worthwhile to tempt Jesus to take an easy road to popularity, we may be sure that we are not immune to the possibility! The surest way of avoiding it is to see that we tread the Savior's path ourselves; then we shall not simply *point* the way to others, but *invite* them to join us, and that is always a more appealing invitation.

The secret of the matter, which makes this way a privilege rather than a cost, is that Jesus invites us to follow along with him, i.e., to walk with him in the way he takes. Our reward is to enjoy his company—a privilege of the modern as of the ancient disciple. The call of the earthly Jesus to follow him puts in pre-resurrection terms the affirmation of the risen Lord in Revelation 3:20: "I stand at the door and knock; if anyone listens to my voice and opens the door I will come in. . . . " Those who accompany the Lord to Calvary are the ones who know what it is to be risen with him, for there is no other path to the fellowship of the resurrection than that which traverses Golgotha (cf. Philippians 3:10); but the further side is "joy unspeakable and full of glory" (1 Peter 1:8).

There is, of course, a more tranquil side of discipleship. It is expressed in the invitation of Jesus in Matthew 11:28–30:

> Come to me, all you that are weary and are carrying heavy burdens, and I will give you rest. Take my yoke upon you, and learn from me, for I am gentle and humble in heart, and you will find rest for your souls. For my yoke is easy, and my burden is light. (NRSV)

Jesus is not here addressing men and women worn out through physical labor. He has in mind people weary in their search for the peace of God, burdened by the prescriptions of those who think that they know the way to it but who do not heed his castigations of teachers of the law who "bind heavy burdens and grievous to be borne and lay them on people's shoulders, but will not stir a finger to move them" (Matthew 23:4). To such Jesus offers rest, the relief that comes when we know that at last we are in touch with reality, and that God in his compassion has received us. With this thirst quenched and this rest enjoyed the service of God is welcome, for it is labor for the kingdom, and it can never be in vain. To a restless, toiling, and anxious age like ours, this is a balm that truly heals. It is a joyous privilege to make it known.

THE FAMILY OF GOD

We began the foregoing section on discipleship by pointing out that in the New Testament the term "disciple" appears only in the Gospels and Acts, not at all in the Letters and the book of Revelation. Here the precise opposite is true: the term "church" is very frequent in the Letters and the Revelation, but is rare in the Gospels. In fact it does not appear in Mark, Luke, and John; it occurs in two passages only in Matthew, but one of them does not count! Matthew 18:15–17 tells how to deal with a "brother" who has sinned against another; if attempts at reconciliation fail then one must "tell it to the church." But reflection will lead to the realization that Jesus did not form churches during his ministry; he is here speaking of procedures to be adopted in a synagogue; the principle enunciated, however, came to be recognized as applicable to Christian groups. The sole occasion when Jesus used the name "church" is his statement to Peter in Matthew 16:18, "I will build my church." Its meaning we have already considered, but the very fact that this is the only reference on the lips of Jesus to his church has led a number of scholars to question its authenticity. They have maintained that Jesus had no intention of forming a church within or even separate from his nation; he preached the kingdom of God to his people, and looked for them to respond to it, but the end result was the emergence in history of the Christian church.[66]

This argument overlooks the possibility that an idea or object may be present in the mind of a person under a variety of terms. The term "church" no more occurs in the Fourth Gospel than it does in Mark or Luke, but the concept is present under a variety of images, e.g., that of Christ the shepherd of his flock, drawn not alone from Israel but from all nations (John 10:11–16); Christ the door into the pastures of the kingdom of God for his sheep (10:9–10); Christ the true vine, and his followers who are its branches (15:1–10); Christ the bridegroom and the church his bride (3:29); and various ways of representing Christ's community as the fellowship of those who are one with the Father and in him (above all 17:20–23) and who are sent to continue his mission (20:21). Similar illustrations could be given from the Synoptic Gospels.

Robert Newton Flew, a Methodist New Testament scholar, tackled this problem, motivated by the conviction that there is a great deal of evidence in the Synoptic Gospels to show that the formation of a community, the church, was an essential part of the intention of Jesus in his ministry. Leaving aside the controverted passage about Peter in Matthew 16:17–19, he summarized the evidence under five heads:

i. *The kingdom of God presupposes a people of the kingdom.* Jesus' proclamation of the kingdom was directed to the reconstituting of Israel, and so become the object of the

---

[66] So most notably A. Harnack, *The Constitution and Law of the Church* (New York: G. P. Putnam, 1910).

rule of God and its instrument in the world. The call to repent was an essential part of the proclamation. This entailed the creation of a remnant, the "little flock" to whom the kingdom was promised (Luke 12:32) and for whom made the new covenant was made at the Last Supper (Luke 22:20, 29).

ii. *The concept of messiahship,* especially in the form in which Jesus used it, implies the gathering of a new community. Our Lord called twelve men to be his associates—note the symbolic number; the first purpose of his choice was that they should be with him (Mark 3:14). Confession or denial of him would be the crucial factor of entry into or exclusion from the kingdom of God (Luke 12:8–9).

iii. *The word or gospel which Jesus proclaimed* was regarded as constitutive of the new community (cf. Mark 4:11–12; Matthew 11:25–26, 27, 28–30).

iv. *The ethical teaching of Jesus* can be understood aright only as directed to this nucleus of the new Israel and as involving a promise of God's power to enable disciples to live out the teaching, thus pointing forward to the gift of the Spirit promised for the last days (cf. Mark 9:23; 10:27; 11:23–24; Luke 10:19; 12:11–12).

v. *The mission of the new community* is revealed when Jesus sends forth his disciples (Mark 6:7–13; Matthew 10:40; Mark 13:10). It becomes explicit, and is seen to be integral to the church's existence in the resurrection commission (so especially Matthew 28:19; Luke 24:46–47; John 20:21).[67]

This evidence has sufficient cumulative force to convince most of those who have read it that Jesus in his ministry sought to gather a people who would both rejoice to receive the kingdom of God and its powers and also accept the task of being its instruments in the world, so sharing the mission that Jesus himself had accepted from the Father. In such a context as this, Matthew 16:17–19 fits perfectly. It is worth noting that the Jewish leaders themselves played a part in Jesus' formation of the rem-

---

[67] This summarizes R. N. Flew, *Jesus and His Church* (2d ed.; London: Epworth, 1943) 35–88.

nant, in that, according to Mark 3:6, they made it impossible for Jesus to continue ministry in the synagogues. The decision to seek the death of Jesus concludes a series of episodes narrated by Mark consisting of controversies between Jesus and the Jewish leaders; there is no intention to suggest that they all happened in the earliest days of Jesus' ministry. F. C. Burkitt pointed out that Mark 3:6 apparently closes the ministry of Jesus in the synagogues; henceforth Jesus labors to form a remnant which will receive the message of the kingdom, a church which will be "Israel made new in the remnant."[68]

That very perceptive definition of the church is entirely harmonious with Paul's discussion of Israel and the church in Romans 9–11.

There is a different aspect of the church, however, which is commonly overlooked, but which is characteristic of Jesus' teaching as to his own relation to the Father and that to which he invited his followers. He depicted the church as God's family. It finds expression in a somewhat heated discussion after the "rich young ruler" departs from Jesus in real grief (Mark 10:29–30). Jesus declares:

> There is no one who has left house, or brothers or sisters, or mother or father, or children, or lands for my sake and for the sake of the gospel, who will not receive a hundredfold now in this age—houses, brothers and sisters, mothers and children, and lands, with persecutions—and in the age to come eternal life.

When the second-century opponent of the church, Celsus, read that, he made great sport of it. If a person should leave one house for Christ's sake, apparently, he gained a hundred in return, for one mother another hundred, for two or three children two or three hundred! "This is a crazy idea," said he! It is, in fact, an interesting example of the difficulty of understanding the word of God and the church of God from a spectator's viewpoint. To a Christian who has experienced the pain of family division for Christ's sake, the compensating grace of the fellowship of Christ's people is a most precious reality. In the earliest Jewish communities (as not infrequently now) division of this kind was most bitter, as our Lord said it would be (cf. Mark 13:12–13). In Roman society it was often no better, and it is so to this day in many

---

[68] See *The Gospel History and its Transmission* (5th ed.; Edinburgh: T. & T. Clark, 1906) 79–82.

anti-Christian societies. In all such circumstances the loving so-
licitude of brothers and sisters in Christ, yes, and of fathers and
mothers too, was a foretaste of the life of the family in heaven. So
real was the family spirit in the early church that it became the
example for family life in contemporary society, where frequently
it was little known. It could hardly have been anticipated a
generation ago that the like is rapidly becoming standard in the
Western world also. The churches are freshly realizing that they
have an urgent task to recall the secularized societies of our time
to the fundamental values of family life, to see that they are
preserved among their members, and to embody them in their
own fellowships. Reconciliation and redemption are rapidly gaining fresh significance, to be experienced and proclaimed.

Kingdom of God and church are not identical, as for centuries has been assumed, but they are correlatives, certainly in this
age. We may fittingly bring to a conclusion this study of the
teaching of Jesus by a citation from one who labored long to
define their relationship, namely Gerhard Gloege:

> The Church has neither to "spread" the news of the divine sovereignty
> in the world—that would be too little—nor to "build" the divine
> sovereignty—that would be too much, and to make God himself the
> creation of man. The Church's task rather is to carry the divine
> sovereignty into the world by the word of reconciliation through
> Christ, to make effective the divine powers as powers of the new age
> now breaking in, and to make the world ready for the onset of the
> sovereignly working God.[69]

---

[69] G. Gloege, *Reich Gottes und Kirche im Neuen Testament* (Gütersloh:
C. Bertelsmann, 1929) 424.

5

THE GOSPEL IN THE

PARABLES OF JESUS

If the question were asked what things were best known about the life of Jesus, a few outstanding facts would almost certainly find mention. Thanks to the makers of Christmas cards, most people in countries where Christianity has been long established know that Jesus was born in a stable, and the widespread symbol of the cross or crucifix results in their knowing that he died on a cross. People also know that Jesus was reputed to have performed a lot of miracles, and that he told many parables. This last item is almost as well known as the rest. It is difficult to picture Jesus addressing the crowds of his day without calling to mind some of his celebrated stories. They were his most characteristic mode of utterance. Since they were largely addressed to crowds, rather than to his disciples, a modern preacher should be able to find a wealth of material here for proclaiming the gospel. He need have no fear that the passing of the years may have diminished their interest and relevance. One of the notable features of our Lord's parables is their evident relation to the environment of his hearers, coupled with their perennial relevance to people of all times and places. They illustrate the assertion of the fourth evangelist, "He knew what was in everyone" (John 2:25). Hugh Martin described a common reaction to the reading of these parables as, "How like So-and-So!" and then, if we are honest, "How like me!" Martin added: "Boys still visit the far country and find its dainties turn to husks. Rich fools—and poor ones too—still think that money is all that matters. Men and nations still fall among thieves."[1] These significant stories of our Lord seem to abide for ever.

Why did Jesus use parables so frequently in his discourse? Not only because he was a born storyteller; more importantly, parables were a long-standing element of the heritage of his people. This is the more readily grasped when we bear in mind that the Hebrew term for a parable, *mashal*, has a more complex meaning than its counterpart in English. The noun is derived from a verb with the same spelling which means "to be like." The application of *mashal*, however, is unexpectedly wide. It can denote (1) a proverb, (2) a byword, (3) a riddle, (4) a fable, and finally (5) a parable. We give some examples of these, particularly from the Old Testament.

The book of Proverbs, as the title suggests, is a collection of wise sayings which are associated especially with Solomon, though other names also occur in the book as authors and collectors of proverbs. It is known that in the ancient world, particularly in the Orient, the formulation and assembling of proverbs was a common pastime. Frequently proverbs are expressed in couplets which entail a comparison, as the following examples from the book of Proverbs illustrate:

> Hope deferred makes the heart sick; a wish come true is a tree of life. (13:12, REB)

> A straightforward answer is as good as a kiss of friendship. (24:26, REB)

> Like a muddied spring or a polluted well is a righteous man who gives way to a wicked one. (25:26, REB)

> The whip for a horse, the bridle for a donkey, the rod for the back of a fool! (26:3, REB)

The term *mashal* is sometimes applied to the nation Israel, particularly where their fate becomes a fearful example to the

---

[1] H. Martin, *The Parables of the Gospels and their Meaning for Today* (London: SCM, 1937) 14.

nations about them. Such appears in the following warning to Solomon of the result of his or his sons' turning away from the Lord:

> Israel will become a byword *(mashal)* and an object-lesson among all peoples. (1 Kings 9:7, REB)

The psalmist laments that this has come to pass through the humiliating defeats suffered by the nation:

> You have made us a byword among the nations, and the peoples toss their heads at us. (Psalm 44:14, REB)

In a similar strain cf. Deuteronomy 28:37; Jeremiah 24:9; Ezekiel 14:8.

Since proverbs and the fates of individuals and nations are sometimes difficult to understand, it is comprehensible that *mashal* can have the meaning of "riddle." The most famous example of this in the Old Testament is the *"mashal"* that Samson proposed to Philistines in Judges 14:14, inspired by his killing a lion and later eating honey from bees that had swarmed in the lion's mouth:

> Out of the eater came something to eat;
> out of the strong came something sweet. (REB)

That riddle completely stymied the Philistines! The significance of this riddle element in the *mashal* will become evident later.

At a very early date in history the comparison, such as is seen in proverbs, became extended to a story with a salutary meaning. The first such kind of story was the fable.[2] Normally fables were not intended to convey religious lessons but wisdom relating to life generally. Very often they spoke about animals or plants, attributing to them human characteristics. There are a few fables in the Old Testament. One is told by Jotham, the son of Gideon, after his brother Abimelech has persuaded the men of Schechem to kill all his other brothers so that he may reign as king alone:

> Once upon a time the trees set out to anoint a king over them. They said to the olive tree: "Be king over us." But the olive tree answered:

---

[2] B. H. Young, in *Jesus and His Jewish Parables: Rediscovering the Roots of Jesus' Teaching* (New York: Paulist, 1989) 238, cites Schwartzbaum for the antiquity of the fable: "It should be pointed out that some of the antecedents of the so-called Aesopic fables are to be found in a highly developed tradition from the ancient Near East (Mesopotamian, Egyptian, etc.)."

"What, leave my rich oil by which gods and men are honoured, to go and hold sway over the trees?"

So the trees said to the fig tree: "Then will you come and be king over us?" But the fig tree answered: "What, leave my good fruit and all its sweetness, to go and hold sway over the trees?"

So the trees said to the vine: "Then will you come and be king over us?" But the vine answered, "What, leave my new wine which gladdens gods and men, to go and hold sway over the trees?"

Then all the trees said to the thorn bush: "Will you come and be king over us?" The thorn answered: "If you really mean to anoint me as your king, then come under the protection of my shadow; if not, fire will come out of the thorn and burn up the cedars of Lebanon." (Judges 9:8–15, REB)

An application of the fable is added by Jotham. The same is true of the single-sentence fable told by Jehoash, king of Israel, to Amaziah, king of Judah, when the latter challenged him to battle:

A thistle in Lebanon sent to a cedar in Lebanon to say: "Give your daughter in marriage to my son"; but a wild beast in Lebanon, passing by, trampled down the thistle. (2 Kings 14:9, REB)

There are no fables in the Gospels, but they were used at times by certain of the rabbis. When a fable is formulated to convey a religious lesson it easily shades into a parable. R. Meir, a noted disciple of R. Akiba, is said to have had a collection of three hundred fox "parables," though only a few of them have survived. Apparently, in this predilection of his he followed the example of his master Akiba.[3]

And so we come to the parable proper. In the Old Testament these are most frequently associated with the prophets. We call to mind especially Nathan's parable told to David after the latter had committed adultery with Bath-Sheba and had sent her husband to his death in battle. When David heard Nathan's story of the rich man who seized a poor man's only ewe-lamb and slaughtered it for a guest to eat, David was enraged and declared that the rich man deserved to die; whereupon Nathan said, "You are the man!" (2 Samuel 1:1–7). That effectively illustrates an important function of the parable, namely to drive home a lesson and evoke a response from those to whom it is directed.

Significantly, Old Testament prophets frequently conveyed their messages through parables. The prophecies of Balaam are

---

[3] See Young, *Jesus and His Jewish Parables*, 78–79, where one of Akiba's fox fables is cited.

actually called "parables" in the Greek version of Numbers 23–24. Isaiah's famous "Song of the Vineyard" is a prophecy of judgment in two parts, first the brief story (5:1–2) and then the lesson it is intended to teach (vv. 3–7). It is, however, Ezekiel above all who employs parables and allegories in the proclamation of his message to Israel. We have in mind the allegories of the two sisters in chapters 16 and 23, and his lengthy parable on God as the shepherd of his people in ch. 34, which inspired Jesus' parable of the shepherd who left the ninety-nine sheep in the fold to seek the one lost sheep (Luke 15:3–7) and the discourse on the good shepherd in John 10. Further, the prophets not only spoke parables but sometimes acted them out. Isaiah 20 tells of the prophet walking about naked and barefoot for three years as a prophetic sign of the conquest and shaming of the Egyptians and Ethiopians by Assyria, thereby demonstrating to Hezekiah and his court the uselessness of looking to Egypt and Ethiopia for help. Hosea is told to marry Gomer, whose faithlessness as a prostitute depicts Israel's faithlessness to God, and Hosea's faithfulness to her mirrors the enduring love of God to his people (Hosea 1–3). For a year Ezekiel acts out the siege of Jerusalem and its effects on the populace (ch. 4), and he is commanded not to mourn the death of his wife, a prophetic sign of the impending desolation of the nation (24:15–24). Not all these actions were immediately understood by those who saw them, any more than the spoken prophecies were—a reminder of the link between riddle and parable contained in the term *mashal*. To this Ezekiel himself refers when recounting the parabolic prophecy of 20:45–49:

> This word of the Lord came to me: "O man, turn and face toward the south and utter your words towards it; prophesy to the scrubland of the Negeb. Say to it: Listen to the word of the Lord. The Lord God says: I am about to kindle a fire in you, and it will consume all the wood, green and dry alike. Its fiery flame will not be put out, but from the Negeb northwards everyone will be scorched by it. Everyone will see that it is I, the Lord, who have set it ablaze; it will not be put out." "Ah Lord God," I cried, "they are always saying of me, 'He deals only in figures of speech.'" (REB)

The *New Jerusalem Bible* translates that last sentence, "Lord Yahweh, they say of me, 'He does nothing but speak in riddles!'"

It is likely that this acknowledged relationship of riddle and parable made it natural for explanations frequently to be added to parables. Such explanations, in fact, became standard in rabbinic parables that were constructed to explain features in the law (the Torah). Clemens Thoma went so far as to say:

> All rabbinic parables have a bipartite structure composed of narrative (*mashal* proper) and normative instruction (*nimshal*, i.e., interpretation).[4]

Thoma offers an instructive example that occurs in various Talmudic tractates, entitled "The Parable of the Two Luminaries." It was formulated to explain the significance of the statement, "This month will be for you," which occurs at the beginning of instructions relating to the celebration of the Passover (Exodus 12:2):

> "This month . . . " You calculate by it, but the people of the world do not calculate by it. Rabbi Lewi in the name of Rabbi Yose bar Le'ay (said): Usually the great calculates by the great and the small by the small. Esau (= Rome), who is great, calculates by the sun, which is great. Jacob, who is small, calculates by the moon, which is small. Rabbi Nahman said: This is a good sign: Just as the great rules the day and not the night, so wicked Esau rules in this world and not in the world to come. Just as the small rules during the day and at night, so Jacob rules in this world and in the world to come.

There follows this parable and explanation:

Mashal	*Nimshal*
Rabbi Nahman said:	So:
As long as the light	As long as the light
of the great	of wicked Esau
shines in the world	shines in the world,
the light	the light
of the small	of Jacob
is not noticed.	is not noticed.
When the light	When the light
of the great	of wicked Esau
has set,	has set,
the light	the light
of the small	of Jacob
will be noticed.	will be noticed.
	"Arise, give light,
	for your light will come"
	(Isaiah 60:1).[5]

---

[4]C. Thoma, "Literary and Theological Aspects of the Rabbinic Parables," in *Parable and Story in Judaism and Christianity* (ed. Clemens Thoma and Michael Wyschogrod; New York: Paulist, 1989) 27.

[5]The parable is in *Pesiq. Rab Kah.* 5.14 with parallels in *Gen. Rab.* 6.3; *Pesiq. R.* 15; *Yalq. Ber.* 8; *Yalq. Jes.* 500. See Thoma, "Literary and Theological Aspects," 32.

B. H. Young cites David Flusser's belief that this literary form of rabbinic parables was preceded by an earlier "classic" type of parable, more in the style of popular anecdotes and story illustrations. Flusser has sought to show that in Jewish tradition parabolic teaching is the combining of known motifs, so that one who has mastered the art of using parables draws from a repository of illustrative expressions and word pictures to communicate a particular message; accordingly, "Jesus' parables on the one hand, and the rabbinic parables on the other, contain similar illustrative motifs which show a continuity of expression in parabolic teaching."[6] This leads to the conviction that, despite the later date of the Talmudic tractates, there was a continuity of parabolic tradition from the Old Testament, maintained in popular form by Israel's teachers to the era of rabbinic literature, and in that movement Jesus himself participated and was a master of it.[7] I see nothing offensive or revolutionary in the position that he who claimed to have come not to destroy but to fulfill the law and the prophets (Matthew 5:17) used current forms of speech in proclaiming their fulfillment.

Admittedly some modern students of the form and purpose of the parables of Jesus would find that unacceptable. Perhaps the most attractive recent alternative mode of viewing the Gospel parables sees them as aesthetic constructions. Dan Via has persuasively set forth this approach to the parables. He rejects the notion that the parables should be interpreted in the light of their situation in the ministry of Jesus, on the ground that the non-biographical nature of the Gospels does not allow it. In any case, he urges, it is not the situation of Jesus which interprets the parables but the parables which interpret his situation. Via claims that just as an author of an artistic work, whether in the sphere of literature, painting, music, drama, says more than he knows he is saying, so a parable by its metaphorical nature has a power independent of its historical context to open new possibilities for those who hear or read it. He therefore views the parables of Jesus as independent of time and of life setting; their intention is not to provide information but to lead to decision for new life. Their subject matter is none other than a new understanding of existence.[8]

---

[6] Cited by Young, *Jesus and his Jewish Parables,* 34, 38.

[7] So ibid., 108–9, 319–20.

[8] D. Via, *The Parables: Their Literary and Existential Dimension* (Philadelphia: Fortress, 1967), especially 21–38.

Clearly there is truth in this approach to the parables of Jesus. We cannot pinpoint the precise historical situation of each parable; and without doubt a fundamental element of their intention is to challenge the attitudes of their hearers (and readers). But an important part of their purpose is to convey and illuminate the revelation Jesus came to bring, a purpose which is bound up with Israel's history and his mission, and we have no right to cut off Jesus from his people.[9] The fundamental context of the parables of Jesus is indicated by the fundamental content of his non-parabolic teaching, and that, as we have seen, is the coming of the kingdom of God—inaugurated through his earthly ministry and climaxed by death and resurrection, maintained in his post-resurrection ministry and pressing on to the revelation of the kingdom at his coming again. The controlling motif is the same in all forms of his teaching.

This is exemplified above all in Mark 4:11-12, which in the REB reads thus:

> To you the secret of the kingdom of God has been given; but to those who are outside, everything comes by way of parables, so that (as scripture says) they may look and look, but see nothing; they may listen and listen, but understand nothing; otherwise they might turn to God and be forgiven.

What is the "secret of the kingdom of God" which Jesus says has been given to the disciples? Daniel 2 provides the clue, for in that chapter the term "secret" appears no less than eight times with reference to Nebuchadnezzar's vision of the kingdom of God that is destined to replace the kingdoms of this world (see especially vv. 44-47). There is widespread agreement among scholars that in Mark 4:11 the secret of the kingdom of God is its breaking into the world in and through the ministry of Jesus; this is the knowledge that has been given to the disciples of Jesus. What of those "outside," i.e., not within the circle of his followers? The REB rendering is typical of modern English translations: "Everything comes by way of parables" (NIV has, "Everything is said in parables"). But that is not the literal meaning of the statement, which should read, "Everything happens in parables." Clearly that relates not to words only but also, and especially, to events. The whole

---

[9] On this Amos Wilder cites Maxime Hermaniuk, *La Parabole évangélique* (Paris: Desclée de Brouwer, 1947) 287-88: "The Christ preaching in parables appears as one who reveals mysteries, and not as one who instructs the multitudes" (A. N. Wilder, *Early Christian Rhetoric* [London: SCM, 1964] 80).

ministry of Jesus in word and action occurs "in parables," in the twofold sense of being both parabolic and enigmatic—it happens "in riddles"! The key to the ministry of Jesus is the recognition that in and through him, by word and deed, the promise of the kingdom of God is in process of fulfillment.

So far as the majority in Israel and its rulers are concerned, the declaration to Isaiah on the outcome of his ministry is finding a fresh fulfillment in the ministry of the Messiah: the people are blind and deaf to the revelation through him. Since the scriptures bind divine predestination and human responsibility, the saying expresses the judgment of God on the nation that rejects its Messiah—but not final judgment, for the covenant remains (cf. Matthew 23:39; Romans 11:25–29).

A majority of recent scholars believe that Mark 4:11–12 was an independent saying in the earliest tradition but was set by Mark in its present context to relate it to the spoken parables of Jesus. His justification for that procedure will have been the insight that whoever possesses the "secret of the kingdom" has the clue to the parables that Jesus uttered. Mark did not mean that Jesus used parables to prevent people from understanding his message. He knew, however, that while many of them are transparent in their meaning, some of them share the riddle-like quality of parables in Jewish tradition and so demand reflection.[10] Insofar as the truism "there are none so blind as those who will not see" applies to Jesus' contemporaries who heard and rejected the message of his parables, the previous paragraph's comment on their attitude to his ministry applies here also.

A brief word on the relation of parable to allegory should be given before we proceed to the exposition of the Gospel parables. An allegory is a story contrived in such a way as to make every detail in it bear a figurative meaning, whereas a parable has a much more limited aim. The most famous example of a Christian allegory is John Bunyan's *Pilgrim's Progress.* Largely through the influence of the Alexandrian scholar Origen, who taught in the first half of the third century, our Lord's parables have been

---

[10] J. Schniewind insisted that Jesus' parables are simple: "children and simple people understand them immediately," *Das Evangelium nach Markus* (Göttingen: Vandenhoeck & Ruprecht, 1937) 75. But that follows his exposition of the parable of the Sower, which he believed to teach that "the normal result of the Word of God is failure," an interpretation rejected by almost all scholars!

viewed as allegories throughout the history of the church; elaboration on the supposed meaning of every detail in them frequently resulted in a complete misunderstanding of their original intention. In reaction to this, A. Jülicher, in his pioneer work on the parables of Jesus, labored to rescue them from their traditional treatment as allegories and insisted that each parable was fashioned by Jesus to teach a single lesson.[11] Granting the grievous loss of authentic understanding of Jesus' parables through unbridled allegorization, many now realize that Jülicher went too far in claiming that the parables have one point only. He overlooked the importance of the Old Testament parabolic tradition for interpreting the parables of Jesus. In this respect John Drury was right:

> Ezekiel was a man who virtually lived historical allegory, lived parabolically. . . . He provides a much better point of departure for the historical investigation of parables than Aristotle or the prejudices of critics to whom allegory is an embarrassment.[12]

If a parable commonly has a primary lesson, it is evident that various parables of Jesus also have genuine secondary features of some importance, such as that of the Prodigal Son, which could as well be entitled "The Two Lost Sons." Scholars increasingly acknowledge that allegorical elements in parables of Jesus are not necessarily inauthentic.[13]

Finally we must give thought to the classification of the Gospel parables. Claus Westermann, in his very significant work *The Parables of Jesus in the Light of the Old Testament*,[14] urged the desirability of assigning the parables to groups so as to determine their connection with the message and ministry of Jesus. He suggested a five-fold division and briefly reviewed the parables in its light.[15] The classification appears to me sound—not dissimilar

---

[11] For an extensive demonstration of the misunderstanding of the parables of Jesus by those who treated them as allegories see A. Jülicher, *Die Gleichnisreden Jesu* (2d ed.; Tübingen: Mohr, 1910), especially 1.203–322.

[12] J. Drury, *The Parables in the Gospels: History and Allegory* (New York: Crossroad, 1985) 19–20.

[13] On this issue cf. the statement by Madeleine Boucher: "Since every similitude and parable has both a literal and metaphorical meaning, every simile or parable is allegorical," "The Parables," in *New Testament Message* (ed. W. Harrington and D. Senior; Wilmington, Del.: M. Glazier, 1981) 29.

[14] C. Westermann, *The Parables of Jesus* (Edinburgh: T. & T. Clark, 1990).

[15] The suggested division is: (1) stories involving sudden change (parables of proclamation); (2) parables of growth; (3) announcements of judgment

to that which I used in exposition of the parables in *Jesus and the Kingdom of God.* I have therefore adapted and simplified it, and reworded it thus:

A. *Parables of proclamation:*
    1. Parables of the advent of the kingdom of God.
    2. Parables of growth.
    3. Parables of judgment.
B. *Parables of action in relation to the kingdom of God:*
    1. Action commensurate with the presence of the kingdom of God.
    2. Action in light of the future of the kingdom of God.

We shall examine the major parables of Jesus under this grouping.

A. PARABLES OF PROCLAMATION

1. Parables of the Advent of the Kingdom of God

i. The Strong Man Bound: Mark 3:27;
Matthew 11:29; Luke 11:22

All three synoptic evangelists report this one-sentence parable as part of Jesus' answer to the allegation of Jerusalem lawyers that his exorcisms were due to an alliance between him and Satan: "He drives out demons by the prince of demons" (Mark 3:23). On the contrary, replied Jesus:

> No one can break into a strong man's house and make off with his goods unless he has first tied up the strong man; then he can ransack the house. (REB)

The "goods" with which the Strong Man has filled his house are self-evidently victims whom he has overpowered and seized. But one stronger than he has overcome *him* and rendered him helpless to prevent the release of his victims. Jesus thereby represents himself not as an ally of the devil but as victor over him. The picture recalls Isaiah 49:24–25, wherein the "captives of the mighty and the prey of the tyrant" will be rescued by the Lord,

---

in a parable; (4) A: instruction for present action, B: instruction for future action (ibid., 284).

and in that day all flesh will know that he is the redeemer, the Mighty One of Jacob. This suggests that Jesus in the parable declares that he is the one through whom God acts to accomplish that redeeming purpose. His opponents are right in assuming that he casts out demons by a superhuman power, but they have wrongly identified the power. Hence both Matthew and Luke (surely rightly) set the Q saying in immediate association with the parable:

> If it is by the finger (Matthew "spirit") of God that I drive out the demons, then be sure that the kingdom of God has come upon you. (Matthew 12:28; Luke 11:20)[16]

Strictly speaking, the parable assumes that it is by virtue of Jesus' prior conquest of the devil that he has power to release his victims (note the wording, "unless he has *first* tied up the strong man . . . "). If we are intended so to interpret it, that event in all probability is to be understood as the temptation of Jesus, particularly in view of Mark's strong language, "The Spirit *drove him out* into the wilderness . . . " to confront Satan (1:12–13).[17] R. Guelich doubted that we should press the language in this manner, but agreed that the parable and its context reflect the eschatological defeat of Satan as seen in the exorcisms of Jesus.[18] That is of first importance. The New Testament frequently associates the defeat of Satan and the decisive entry into history of the kingdom of God with the death and resurrection of Jesus, and understandably so, since that dual redemptive act was the climax of the redeeming ministry of Jesus; but this early parable of Jesus indi-

---

[16] For first-century Jews the alternate expressions "Spirit of God" and "finger of God" would have similar meaning but different associations. Throughout his book Ezekiel attributed his visions to "the hand of the Lord" (i.e., the Spirit of God) being upon him (see Ezekiel 1:3; 3:14, 22; 8:1; 33:22; 37:1; 40:1). But the exodus narrative reached a critical point when the Egyptian magicians, unable any longer to imitate the plagues initiated through Moses, had to confess, "This is the finger of God" (Exodus 8:19). The appropriateness of the latter expression in the Gospel context is clear. Contrary to the common belief, however, that Luke's version is original on the ground that he would never exclude a reference to the Spirit, one could equally hold that Matthew's interest in the exodus would have led him to retain "finger of God" had it been in the Q source. For an example of Luke redacting out a reference to the Spirit, cf. Mark 13:11/Luke 12:11–12 with Luke 21:15/Acts 6:11.

[17] Such is the view of A. Schlatter, *Der Evangelist Matthäus*, 99; Jeremias, *Parables of Jesus*, 122–23; J. M. Robinson, *The Problem of History in Mark* (London: SCM, 1937) 30–31; E. Best, *The Temptation and the Passion* (Cambridge: Cambridge University Press, 1965) 12–13.

[18] Guelich, *Mark 1–8:26*, 176–77.

cates that the whole ministry of Jesus, from its beginning to its end, had redemptive power, since in him the kingdom of God was a liberating and emancipating force. Such was the content of his message in the synagogue of Nazareth (Luke 4:16–21).

ii. The Bridegroom and his Friends: Mark 2:19–20; Matthew 9:15; Luke 5:34–35

Here is another brief parable that is highly significant for the understanding of Jesus and his role in the kingdom of God.

The context is that of fasting: disciples of John the Baptist and Pharisees were observing a fast, and either they or observers asked Jesus why his disciples were not doing likewise. He replied:

> The friends of the bridegroom cannot fast while the bridegroom is with them, can they? As long as they have the bridegroom with them they cannot fast. But days will come when the bridegroom is taken away from them, and then they will fast in that day. (Mark 2:19–20)

Some scholars have wished to limit the parable solely to the question in v. 19a and view the two sentences that follow as a later construction to justify the reintroduction of fasting in the church.[19] Others object to that notion, since not only is there no difference of viewpoint between the question and the answer in vv. 19a and 19b, but also between vv. 19 and 20.[20] The question of 19a is certainly startling, but it is highly unlikely that it circulated in the early communities on its own. We take it that Mark found the whole paragraph of vv. 18–22 in the collection of controversies recorded in 2:1–3:6, without thereby suggesting that it belonged to the early ministry of Jesus.

The law prescribed only one day for compulsory fasting, the day of Atonement (Leviticus 16:29–31). After the destruction of Jerusalem and the transportation of Jews to Babylonia in 586 B.C. four additional fast days, scattered through the fourth, fifth, seventh, and tenth months, were observed to remember the tragic event (Zechariah 8:19). It was typical of the Pharisees to go beyond the requirements of the law; in the time of Jesus they

---

[19] So, e.g., Jülicher, *Die Gleichnisreden Jesu*, 187; Lohmeyer, *Das Evangelium des Markus*, 59; Dodd, *Parables of the Kingdom*, 116 n. 22; J. Jeremias, "νύμφη, νυμφίος," *TDNT* 4.1103; W. G. Kümmel, *Promise and Fulfillment* (London: SCM, 1957) 76.

[20] See J. Wellhausen, *Das Evangelium Marci* (Berlin: G. Reimer, 1903) 18–19. He argues that the whole passage was written later.

fasted twice a week (Luke 18:12). By the end of the first century some elements at least of the church were doing the same. In the *Didache (Teaching of the Twelve Apostles)* it is written:

> Let not your fastings be with the hypocrites, for they fast on the second and fifth day of the week, but you keep your fast on the fourth and on the preparation (i.e., sixth) day.

It was not so with Jesus. He compared his situation with that of a bridegroom and his wedding guests. In that setting, fasting is unthinkable. Paul Billerbeck observed, "The chief duty of the friends and wedding guests of the bridegroom was to contribute as much as possible to the delight of the bridal pair during the wedding celebration."[21] But what sort of a wedding is this? It would appear that Jesus is combining two Old Testament expectations into one: the "feast of the kingdom" that celebrates the beginning of the kingdom of God (Isaiah 25:6–10), and the marriage of God to his people Israel (Hosea 2:19; Isaiah 54:4–10, especially v. 5: "Your husband is your maker, his name is the Lord of Hosts"; also Isaiah 62:4–5; Ezekiel 16:7–8). To avoid the application to Jesus of the figure of God as husband of his people Jeremias proposed that the phrase "while the bridegroom is with them" is equivalent to "during the wedding festival,"[22] adding elsewhere that "in all later Jewish literature there is no instance of an application of the allegory of the bridegroom to the Messiah."[23] That, however, is an unsatisfactory exegesis of the words of Jesus; by it Jeremias turned a statement about relationships into one about an impersonal event. Jesus was affirming that there was no question of his disciples fasting, since the bridegroom was with them and, as everyone knows, *the bridegroom's friends cannot fast in his presence.* Zechariah 8:19 has already been cited in connection with the four additional fast days of Israel; in reality it is a promise of their abolition in the time when God brings his kingdom:

> Thus says the Lord of hosts: The fast of the fourth month, and the fast of the fifth, and the fast of the seventh, and the fast of the tenth, shall be seasons of joy and gladness, and cheerful festivals for the house of Judah. (NRSV)

---

[21] Strack-Billerbeck, *Kommentar zum NT,* 1.500–501.
[22] Jeremias, *Parables of Jesus,* 117.
[23] Jeremias, *TDNT* 1.1102.

So also the parable of Jesus proclaims that the time of feasting instead of fasting has arrived, for the Bridegroom-Messiah is with his people in the kingdom of God!

What, however, are we to make of v. 20? "Days will come when the bridegroom will be taken from them, and then they will fast on that day." It is conceivable that the statement merely refers to the time when the bridegroom leaves his friends because the wedding is over, and regulations regarding fasting are again in force. J. B. Muddiman has called attention to Joel 2:16, a call for a fast in view of the imminence of a day of the Lord, the seriousness of which is expressed in the words:

> bid the bridegroom leave his wedding-chamber
> and the bride her bower (REB),

for the threatened present is no time for feasting. Muddiman considers that the parable of Jesus was inspired by Joel's prophecy, but subsequently the active verb in the parable "leave" was replaced by the passive "be removed, taken away," through reminiscence of Isaiah 53:8, "by a perversion of justice *he was taken away.*"[24] That is an ingenious solution of a longstanding problem, but while it is admittedly possible, it is more likely that the allusion to Isaiah 53:8 was original to the parable. It is not without significance that the parallel text at Matthew 9:15 reads, "The friends of the bridegroom cannot *mourn* while he is with them, can they?" Fasting is an accompaniment of mourning; the time for that will be when the bridegroom has been taken away and put to death. For the first hearers of the parable, that will doubtless have been mystifying, but what Jew will object to a parable containing a riddle?

Further, how long is the "mourning" (= fasting) to go on? The church in due course concluded that it should continue until the Lord's return. That, however, is a strange concomitant of the Easter joy that is celebrated every Lord's Day! John 16:16–22 has an interesting exposition of this theme:

> Amen, amen I tell you, you will weep and make lamentation, but the world will be glad; you will be plunged into anguish, but your anguish will be turned into joy. When a woman is in labor she has anguish, because her hour has come; but when the child is born she no longer remembers the anguish because of the joy that a human

---

[24] Muddiman, "Jesus and Fasting, Mk ii.18–22" in *Jésus aux origines de la Christologie* (ed. J. Dupont; Leuven: Gembloux, 1975) 276–78.

being has been born in the world. You, too, now have anguish; but I shall see you again, and your heart will be gladdened, and your gladness no one will take from you.

That is an accurate reflection of the joy of the disciples in the presence of their Lord, as the book of Acts clearly shows. The dying and the rising of the Bridegroom has led to his restoration to his friends, and the festivity of the kingdom of God is to be shared with the multitude of believers. But it is not to be forgotten when it began—with the Bridegroom's association with repentant sinners!

iii. The Great Feast: Matthew 22:1–14; Luke 14:14–24

Here we have two very different stories with a common theme, that of a man with great resources issuing invitations to people to a feast; in Matthew the man is a king who invited people to attend the marriage banquet of his son, in Luke he is simply described as "a certain man." Either Jesus himself embodied a single notion in two different parables, or a parable of his came to be related in two different forms. The latter solution is commonly adopted, on the not unreasonable assumption that Matthew's variant was due to his conjoining the parable with another that told of a man attending a marriage feast without a wedding garment, and the introduction to the second parable was made to serve the first one. The violent treatment of the king's servants by some of the invited in Matthew 22:5–6, leading to the king's fury and burning of their city, even if they were traditional elements, echo features of Matthew's version of the parable of the Wicked Husbandmen (Matthew 21:35–36); we may take it, therefore, that Matthew himself was led to bring together the two parables. Despite the differences, the fundamental symbol embodied in the two versions of the parable is the same: the celebration of the advent of the kingdom of God in a great feast, as in Isaiah 25:6–9; but Matthew's adaptation makes it closer to the parable of the Bridegroom and his Friends which we have just considered.

The striking feature of the parable is the emphasis on the one hand that the feast is now ready (Luke 14:17), and on the other hand the rejection of the call by the invited. The image of the great feast in Isaiah 25 is of the celebration in the kingdom of God at the end of the age; here, however, the meal is prepared and the guests are called to participate in it *now*. The picture is one with the proclamation of the presence of the kingdom in Jesus' non-parabolic teaching, and with that of the Bridegroom rejoicing with his friends. The spurning of the invitation is one with the Gospels' account of the rejection of Jesus' call by the Jewish leaders, especially by the Pharisees and teachers of the law and the people who listened to them.

The host/king therefore sent his servant(s) into the streets and lanes of the town to invite all whom they found to the feast. Luke adds that after that had been done there was still room at the tables, whereupon the giver of the feast told them to go out yet again and compel people to come in (Luke 14:23). Most frequently that second sending is interpreted of the later mission to the Gentiles in which Luke is so interested (cf. volume 2 of his work!); but it is conceivable that it relates to that aspect of the ministry of Jesus which is directed not alone to the poor of Israel but also to the outcasts of his people, the "tax collectors and sinners," those despised and neglected by the religious majority. To them was extended the privilege of experiencing the grace of the kingdom of God which is salvation.

But the final sentence of Luke's narration of the parable tells of the host's wrath: "I tell you, not one of those who were invited shall taste my banquet" (v. 24). That is not only an exclusion from the salvation of the kingdom in the present, but a threat of exclusion from the feast of the kingdom in the future, for the kingdom which Jesus brings into the present is always that which belongs to God's future. To reject the kingdom in the present therefore is to face exclusion from it in the future. As Eta Linnemann quaintly put it, "Anyone who is not willing to be summoned to the first course does not get to taste the meal proper."[25]

This note of warning comes to expression in the additional parable added by Matthew in 22:11–14. The king enters the dining hall and moves among the guests. He sees one who is not wearing a wedding garment, and he asks him how it is that he came to the feast so clothed. From this it has often been assumed that it was customary in those times to provide guests with a wedding garment, but there is no evidence of such a custom in the time of Jesus. A hint of what is meant is provided in a parable of Johanan ben Zakkai, composed in the period when Matthew and Luke wrote.

---

[25] E. Linnemann, *Jesus of the Parables* (New York: Harper & Row, 1966) 91.

> A king summoned his servants to a banquet without appointing a time. The wise dressed themselves and sat at the door of the palace, for they said, "Is anything lacking in a royal palace?" The fools went about their work, saying, "Can there be a banquet without preparations?" Suddenly the king desired the presence of his servants; the wise entered adorned, while the fools entered *soiled*. The former ate and drank, the latter stood and watched.[26]

It is evident from that parable that a wedding garment is not one that is kept for special occasions, but simply one that is clean. The "fools" entered the palace with dirty clothes and disqualified themselves from participating in the feast. In the parable of Jesus the offending guest, when questioned by the king, attempted no explanation; he knew that he was attending the feast in an unfit condition, and thereby had insulted the king and the occasion; accordingly he was ejected from the hall as a guilty man.

The conclusion of v. 13 employs a picture associated with the last judgment in Matthew (cf. 8:12, also regarding exclusion from the feast of the kingdom in the last day; 13:42; 24:51; 25:30). The parable is one with those utterances of Jesus in which distinctions of time are set aside, when people are confronted with the ultimate issues of grace and judgment, and decision is demanded in relation to those issues. But the point of emphasis in the parable is not that of future judgment but of present joy. The feast of the kingdom is a party for the nations to celebrate the coming of the kingdom of God, when life triumphs over death, tears of sadness are wiped away by the Lord himself, injustice is removed and peace reigns; hence the people cry, "Let us rejoice and exult in his deliverance" (Isaiah 25:6–9). The Christ has actualized that happiness in the present and bestows now the first installment of its fullness in the future. It is the privilege of believers to experience those realities now.

iv. The Hidden Treasure and the Pearl: Matthew 13:44–46

These two parables are often regarded as "twins," i.e., as having come down together in the Gospel tradition, but this is doubtful. Whereas none of the other four Gospels report them, versions of both occur in the *Gospel of Thomas* but widely separated (logia 109 and 76). Since, however, they convey the same basic message, Matthew was clearly led aright in bringing them together.

---

[26] Cited by Young, *Jesus and His Jewish Parables*, 103.

As to the Hidden Treasure, Jesus presumably had in mind a jar containing silver coins or jewels.[27] If Belgium was earlier called the cockpit of Europe because of the many foreign armies marching through the land, Palestine in ancient times occupied a similar position between the powers of east and west; in the minds of the populace burying money in the ground was the safest procedure for this reason alone, to say nothing of safeguarding it against thieves breaking into their houses. Inevitably, however, people sometimes forgot where valuables were hidden; it was therefore quite possible that a laborer should accidentally discover treasure as in the parable. The same thing continues to happen from time to time in Britain in the discovery of valuables and coins buried in the ground from Roman times on. In the latter case treasure trove has to be surrendered—it belongs to the state; in ancient Palestine that was not the case; it belonged to the person who owned the field.[28] The workman therefore would not have been condemned for hastily reburying the treasure and buying the field.

The situation in the second parable is quite different. Unlike the poor laborer who accidentally discovers treasure in the course of his work, this one concerns a merchant seeking pearls—presumably a jeweler. Anyone seeking to buy pearls had to be wealthy, for they were greatly sought after and very costly. Jeremias states that Julius Caesar presented to the mother of Brutus, who later murdered him, a pearl worth six million sesterces, in today's values about a million pounds. Cleopatra is reputed to have possessed a pearl worth a hundred million sesterces, i.e., about sixteen million pounds.[29] The pearl that the merchant in the parable found is stated to have been "very expensive"; if that statement relates to the value of the pearl in comparison with other pearls, then it is represented as unimaginably expensive so far as the hearers of Jesus were concerned, and it is assumed that the merchant purchased it not to sell but to keep for himself.

---

[27] So Jeremias, *Parables of Jesus*, 198.

[28] This caused the possibility of arguments between a seller and buyer of land, but the rabbinic parable recorded in *Song Rab.* 4.12 (see Jeremias, *Parables of Jesus*, 32) assumes the right of the buyer to retain the treasure. For Jewish discussions of this see Strack-Billerbeck, *Kommentar zum NT*, 1.674.

[29] Jeremias, *Parables of Jesus*, 200—making due allowance for the escalation of prices since Jeremias wrote in 1962!

The common feature of the two parables is plainly the tremendous worth of that which the two contrasting persons found and their joy in finding it. The information that both had to sell all that they possessed in order to buy the costly items is perhaps intended to enhance the value of what they had discovered, rather than to emphasize the cost of discipleship, as is usually assumed in expositions of these parables. The treasure and the pearl both symbolize the kingdom of God; the blessings that are associated with that are beyond the imagination of human beings to realize, and certainly beyond the resources of the wealthiest to purchase. No wonder the individuals in the two parables are overjoyed at the opportunity of possessing what they have found and are ready to sell everything to secure it.

But observe the point of emphasis: by their actions *the two men not only found treasures, they made them their own.* This is not primarily a picture of the hope of participating in the kingdom of God at the end of the age; these two persons gained it! The future has come into the present, and people are able to receive the promised salvation of the end time now, for the one who related the stories has brought it. Such is the perspective of these parables. They do not state that the Christ is in process of bringing the kingdom of God to humankind, and that in order to open it for all humanity he must give himself for the sin of the world and rise from death for the life of the world. The essential point is the reality of God's saving action in the world in and through Jesus, and the joy of sharing in it as people welcome his word, believe it, and follow him. The unstated implication of the parables is a call to receive the revelation they contain and so know the joy of which they speak.

v. The Lost Sheep, The Lost Coin, The Lost Son: Luke 15:1–32

These three parables have been brought together by Luke because on the one hand they are linked by a common theme, and on the other hand they constitute a powerful answer to Pharisees who criticized Jesus for his association with people who in their eyes were reprobate and an abomination to God (cf. John 7:49).

Luke's introduction to the three parables in vv. 1–2 is a generalization of a concrete situation which he has already recorded in 5:27–32, and which he derived from Mark 2:13–17. Jesus invited the tax collector Levi (= Matthew) to join his group of disciples, whereupon Levi arranged a reception for him at which "a great crowd of tax collectors and others reclined at table with him" (5:29). The Pharisees and teachers of the law who saw it were shocked that Jesus would not only mix with such people but actually eat and drink with them, thereby incurring their uncleanness. Luke recalls this in 15:1–2 and in v. 3 represents Jesus as answering the criticism of the Pharisees with the parable of the Lost Sheep; by adding the other two parables Luke greatly strengthens the defense of Jesus. One must admit that the opening clause of the Lost Sheep parable, reminiscent of an introduction to similes often used by Jesus (cf. e.g., Matthew 7:9–11; 12:11f.; Luke 11:5–8; 17:7–10) has in view farmers who have the care of flocks of sheep; even if any Pharisees owned farms they would not act as shepherds looking for lost sheep—they despised a shepherd's calling; on the other hand, neither can we imagine Jesus addressing a meeting of farmers! It will have been a mixed audience to whom he spoke the parable, and at least some Pharisees would have been present. The context in which Matthew has reproduced the parable (18:12–13) is a collection of instructions concerning the care of the church and concludes with an affirmation of God's care for his own, with the implication that such should be the attitude of the church's leaders. There is no indication of the original context of the parable in Matthew.

A hundred sheep would be a fair size flock for ordinary Palestinian farmers. It was customary to count the sheep each evening when gathering them into a sheepfold; the parable assumes that on discovering that one was missing, the owner left the ninety-nine in the care of another shepherd and went in search of the lost. Having found it he lifted it joyfully on his shoulders, carried it home, and bade his friends and neighbors "Rejoice with me! I have found my lost sheep!" Such is the joy of heaven over one sinner who repents (v. 10).

A corresponding situation in the life of a woman is depicted in the next parable concerning one who possesses only ten drachmas and loses one of them. It has been suggested that the coins may have belonged to the woman's headdress, or what was left of her dowry, or her savings. In any case, she must have been a very poor woman, and she could ill afford to lose one-tenth of her resources. She therefore lights a lamp (the house being windowless), sweeps the floor and searches and searches—till she finds the missing coin! Then she too calls her friends and bids them share her joy: "I have found the coin I had lost." The same lesson is drawn as with the previous parable, namely heaven's happiness over one repentant sinner.

The point of both these parables is well stated by Eta Linnemann: "Finding creates boundless joy."[30] J. D. Crossan agrees with the maxim, but regards the joy as that of man and not of God. He rejects Luke's association of the parables with the Pharisees' criticism of Jesus' table fellowship with sinners and holds that the church has been led astray by the identification of Jesus with the Good Shepherd of John 10:11. In Crossan's view the application of "I am the Good Shepherd" to the parable of the Lost Sheep should lead to a parallel affirmation regarding the second parable, namely that God or Jesus is "the Good Housewife." He therefore equates the joy of finding with the joy of discovery in the parables of the Treasure and the Pearl.[31] The interpretation of these parables in terms of the joy of *discovery* is interesting, but they speak of *recovery* rather than discovery, and include God as well as persons. It is Ezekiel 34 which provides the inspiration of Luke 15 and John 10; in that discourse God is the shepherd who seeks and restores the sheep who are lost, and he promises to send another David who will do the like work. In the parable of the Lost Sheep, Jesus sets forth primarily the pattern of the Father's work, and implies that what God does he himself does, namely seeks and saves the lost. If the Pharisees shared the Father's compassion they would be doing the same, and in that case they would approve of the efforts of Jesus to bring home the lost rather than be disgusted by them. In the labors of Jesus, the Lord God is seeking and finding and rejoicing over the lost; in him therefore the saving sovereignty of God is at work where the religious leaders of his day are blind to it.

The story of the Prodigal Son is a double parable. Which half of it is the more important? Most assume that the first is, whereas some scholars favor the second, on the ground that in a two-point parable the accent usually falls on the second half (cf. the story of the Rich Man and Lazarus in Luke 16:19–31, where the emphasis undoubtedly falls on its conclusion). Here, however, it is a case of both/and rather than either/or. Both parts of the parable convey a message of importance, alike for those who first heard it and for subsequent generations.

---

[30] Linnemann, *Jesus of the Parables,* 66.
[31] J. D. Crossan, *In Parables* (New York: Harper & Row, 1973) 38.

While we inevitably concentrate attention on the two sons, we are not to forget that "the waiting father," as Thielicke characterized him, is to the fore throughout the narrative. Having granted the younger son his wish to have his share of the inheritance and leave home, the father waits for his return—and for the scandalized elder brother to join in welcoming back his younger brother. The parable still generally retains the title "The Prodigal Son," though some, wishing to recognize its connection with the two previous parables, are now calling it "The Lost Son," or even "The Lost Sons," in light of the second half of the parable. It is, however, clear that the dominating feature of the parable is really the father's steadfast love, hence Jeremias wished it to entitle it, "The Parable of the Father's Love."[32] J. A. Fitzmyer rightly said that on the lips of Jesus it stressed

> the boundless, unconditioned love of the father, who not only welcomes back with love his (repentant) son who has wronged him, but will not even allow the attitude of the ever faithful elder son to deter him from expressing that love and acceptance of the younger son, "who was dead and has come back to life."[33]

Fitzmyer further points out the relationship between this parable and the two previous ones that stress the joy of finding that which was lost. The parable of the Father's love has a virtually identical conclusion in its two parts, vv. 24 and 32, "he was lost and has been found." There is, however, a significant difference: v. 24 says, "This *my son* was . . . lost and is found," while v. 32 reads, "This *your brother* was . . . lost and is found"; and it becomes plain that in Luke's context the elder son represents the grumbling Scribes and Pharisees.[34]

The parable offers an interesting contrast between the two brothers, in that both were self-centered, but in different ways. The younger brother was concerned above all to rid himself of the restrictions of an inhibited home life and to enjoy the freedom of the world outside, more precisely the world beyond the limitations of his own country, and this he did with abandon. The older brother by contrast "asked for nothing, desired nothing, enjoyed nothing. He devoted himself dutifully to his father's service . . . yet he himself was the center of his every thought, so that he was

---

[32] Jeremias, *Parables of Jesus*, 128.
[33] Fitzmyer, *Gospel according to Luke*, 2.1085.
[34] Ibid.

incapable of entering sympathetically into his father's joys and sorrows."[35] But both brothers suffered in accordance with their differing ways of sinning.

The younger brother will speedily have experienced the readiness of friends to join in revelry at his expense, and their departure when his resources were spent. He plunged from the heights to the depths, for nothing could be lower in a Jewish mind than becoming a swineherd in the employment of a Gentile master. A rabbi in later years said, "Cursed be the man who raises pigs, and cursed be the man who teaches his son Greek wisdom!"[36] It took the experience of humiliation and hunger to bring him to his senses. Then he realized that to be a day laborer in his father's house was preferable to what he was enduring. So he swallowed his pride and set out for home, with a speech formulated in his mind for his father. But he was not allowed to give it: his father saw him from a distance, ran to meet him, and smothered his words in a loving embrace and kisses. For the first time the prodigal understood how deeply his father loved him, and what real celebration was: the best robe, the signet ring, shoes for the feet, the fatted calf, music and dancing with those he loved! There was no question of his being allowed to be a servant, on the contrary he entered into an experience of sonship such as he had never known before. G. Quell suggested that the appeal to return to the Lord in Jeremiah 31:18–20 may well have been the inspiration of (this section of) the parable.[37] In the REB it reads:

> I listened intently;
> Ephraim was rocking in his grief:
> "I was like a calf unbroken to the yoke;
> you disciplined me, and I accepted your discipline.
> Bring me back and let me return,
> for you are the Lord my God.
> Though I broke away I have repented:
> now that I am submissive I beat my breast;
> in shame and remorse
> I reproach myself for the sins of my youth."
>
> Is Ephraim still so dear a son to me,
> a child in whom I so delight

---

[35] Caird, *Saint Luke,* 182.

[36] *B. Qam.* 826, cited by Manson, *Sayings of Jesus,* 288.

[37] G. Quell, "πατήρ," *TDNT* 5.973.

that, as often as I speak against him,
I must think of him again?
Therefore my heart yearns for him;
I am filled with tenderness towards him.

The anger of the elder brother is vividly described in the second half of the parable. He would not enter the house and share in the rejoicing at the return and restoration of his brother. T. W. Manson observed, "His real annoyance is not for what he has not had, but for what his brother has got . . . It is the veal that sticks in his gullet, not the goat's flesh!"[38] So the father had to go out to him, even as he had gone out to his younger son, but this time to listen to the bitter complaint and try to mollify it. The remarkable thing about this meeting is the gentle way the father answers him. Not a word of criticism is uttered, but a patient expression of love equal to that which was shown to the younger brother: "My son, you are always with me, and everything I have is yours. How could we fail to celebrate this happy day?" In the story these words are literally true: the younger son had received his share of the inheritance, and now everything that the father has belongs to his eldest son. But Jesus is telling a parable, and it is difficult not to see in the elder son a reflection of the Pharisees and teachers of the law, and their attitude to the riff-raff of society with whom Jesus is willing to share meals. One might have expected Jesus to give a spirited reply to their criticisms, as indeed we see him doing on other occasions in the Gospels (e.g., Mark 3:22–30; 12:38–40; Matthew 23). In the words of the father to the elder son, however, we see an extraordinarily generous acknowledgment of the relation of the Pharisees to God. Adolf Schlatter saw in v. 31 a statement of the wonder of their being God's children that cannot be advanced, an unqualified affirmation of the father's fellowship which gives to his son participation in everything the father has. "It is significant that John [the author of the Fourth Gospel] had no stronger formula to describe Jesus' sonship of God: 'You are always with me, and everything that is mine is yours.'" Schlatter went on to assert that there is no representation of Pharisaism in the New Testament which so completely comes to terms with its purposes and claims as this; precisely for this reason, however, through making plain to the Pharisees the glory of their sonship to God, condemnation meets

---

[38] Manson, *Sayings of Jesus,* 290.

them most severely in their rejection of God's other children and Jesus' acceptance of them.[39]

The parable comes to an unexpected end in that it does not tell whether the older brother relented and joined in the celebration. That has the result of setting the hearers of the parable in the same position, namely, of having to decide whether they were willing to accept "God's other children" and enter into the spirit of the party. On this Jeremias commented:

> So Jesus does not yet pronounce sentence; he still has hope of moving them to abandon their resistance to the gospel, he still hopes that they will recognize how their self-righteousness and lovelessness separate them from God, and that they may come to experience the great joy which the good news brings (v. 32a).[40]

This parable accordingly is a parable of the kingdom, no less than the Lost Sheep and the Lost Coin. The sovereignty of love dominates the whole. If God's kingdom signifies God's sovereign action, so too sovereign love is seen in action which forgives and restores to relationship with God those who had forfeited fellowship with him. The righteous who are scandalized by this are called on to recognize the nature of God as a merciful and compassionate Father, for they too need that mercy and compassion. Let them take the message seriously: he is ready to grant it to them.

2. Parables of Growth

Most Jewish people in Biblical times lived in rural communities, growing their own food and rearing their animals on small farms. Naturally they had their towns in which varied crafts flourished, but in the parables of Jesus he drew his pictures largely from the agricultural life of his people. This is particularly seen in his frequent use of the symbol of harvest. It is, of course, often found in the Old Testament. In the books of the prophets, harvest is predominantly an image of the end of the age and symbolizes especially the judgment of the day of the Lord, as in Hosea 6:11; Jeremiah 51:33; Joel 3:13; Isaiah 27:12–13. But since the day of the Lord leads on to the kingdom of God, the passage last cited also relates to the "gathering" of the scattered Israelites to their own land for the kingdom.

---

[39] Schlatter, *Das Evangelium des Lukas*, 356–57.
[40] Jeremias, *Parables of Jesus*, 132.

In the well-known Q saying of Jesus, Matthew 9:37–38/ Luke 10:2, the harvest becomes a positive symbol for the mission of Jesus and his disciples:

> The harvest is plentiful, but the laborers are few; therefore ask the Lord of the harvest to send out laborers into his harvest. (NRSV)

In this statement the harvest is not awaited in the future but is present—it is "plentiful," and the disciples are told to pray that more laborers will be sent to gather it in. Matthew and Luke make this an introduction to the sending of the disciples (Luke, of the seventy-two) to the villages and towns of Israel, so that the disciples become part of the answer to their own prayers.

Some exegetes interpret the saying strictly in the light of the judgment aspect of the harvest image, so that the sending of the disciples is seen as a proclamation of judgment and a call for repentance.[41] This, however, is unlikely. Fitzmyer rightly urges that in the Gospel of Luke this harvest is "a figure for the season when the mature preaching of the kingdom takes place. The time has come for its widespread announcement and the great numbers that will accept the message." The further instruction to pray that more workers be sent into the harvest implies that "the work of Jesus and the mission of his disciples are under the providence of God himself, who is creating a new phase of salvific preaching and will be the judge of it on a given 'day.' "[42] The same application of the harvest image is seen yet more clearly in John 4:35–38.

This use of the time-honored symbol of harvest places the mission of Jesus and his followers in a context that affirms the present fulfillment of God's promise. W. D. Davies speaks for a majority of recent scholars in affirming:

> The mission of the twelve and of the post-Easter church belongs to the latter days. It is not simply a prelude to the end but itself part of the complex of events that make up the end. This means that the evangelist and his community perceived their own time as eschatological time.[43]

---

[41] So, e.g., P. Bonnard, *L'Evangile selon St. Matthieu* (2d ed.; Neuchâtel: Delachaux et Niestle, 1970) 143; D. Hill, *Gospel of Matthew* (New Century Bible Commentaries; London: Oliphants, 1972) 182.

[42] *Gospel according to Luke,* 2.846. See further F. Hauck, "θερίζω, θερισμός," *TDNT* 3.132–33.

[43] W. D. Davies and D. C. Allison, *A Critical and Exegetical Commentary on the Gospel according to Saint Matthew* (ICC; Edinburgh: T. & T. Clark, 1991) 2.149.

Naturally this holds good above all for Jesus himself in his own ministry.

None saw this more clearly than C. H. Dodd, but he drew from the figure an application not commonly held today. He was persuaded, with regard both to the saying, "The harvest is plentiful . . . ," and to the parables of Jesus which portray sowing and reaping, that the picture assumes not that Jesus is the sower and the reaper, but that he is the reaper of an earlier sowing. Such, in his view, is the clear implication of John 4:37–38, although that saying applies primarily to the disciples and later church ("others have toiled, and you have entered into the results of their toil"). On this Dodd comments:

> If we then ask, Who sowed the seed? we may answer, The sowing is that initial act of God which is prior to all human activity, the 'prevenient grace' which is the condition of anything good happening among men. The stages of growth however are visible. We know that Jesus regarded his work as the fulfillment of the work of the prophets, and that he saw in the success of John the Baptist a sign that the power of God was at work. Thus the parable (of the seed) would suggest that the crisis which has now arrived is the climax of a long process which prepared the way for it.[44]

This interpretation is very plausible, particularly in its emphasis on the activity of God and on that of John the Baptist, whom Jesus saw as the last of the prophets, and in whom the preparation for the kingdom of God came to its end.[45] This latter consideration is emphasized in the tribute of Jesus to John, Matthew 11:12–13 (cf. Luke 16:16), which may be rendered:

> From the day of John the Baptist until now the kingdom of God is powerfully making its way (in the world), and powerful individuals are attacking it. For all the prophets and the law prophesied until John.[46]

The saying is often interpreted as though Jesus saw two periods in God's saving history: law-prophets-John, which then gave place to his own ministry. It is more likely, however, that he distinguished three: law and prophets, climaxing in John's work; the ministry of John, which served to introduce the eschatological period; the ministry of Jesus himself, in which the kingdom of God operates

---

[44] Dodd, *Parables of the Kingdom,* 179–80.

[45] Cf. also John 5:31–40, wherein the testimony of the Father to Jesus through John the Baptist, the works of Jesus, and the scriptures are cited.

[46] See Beasley-Murray, *Jesus and the Kingdom of God,* 91–96.

in power.[47] It suggests that John the Baptist forms the bridge between the old order and the new in such a fashion as to belong to both. If that is correct the work of the prophets belonged to an order which can be thought of as preparing the ground for the sowing of the seed which should result in the harvest of the kingdom of God. The preparation came to its completion in John, who straddled both eras and had the unique task of assisting Jesus in sowing the seed of the kingdom, while Jesus himself sent his disciples out to begin the work of harvest. Strictly speaking, the figure of sowing belongs to the beginning of the ministry of Jesus, the initiation of his "mission" from the Father, while the continuity in his work of establishing the kingdom may be characterized as "growth." That becomes apparent in the four parables of the Growing Seed, the Mustard Seed (with which the parable of the Leaven is linked), the Sower, and the Wheat and Tares. These we shall now consider.[48]

i. The Growing Seed: Mark 4:26–29

This brief parable is found in Mark only. Its interest is focused on the farmer who sows, the seed which is sown, and the earth with its power to make seed grow. Emphasis has been placed by interpreters on each of these three elements. The *Gospel of Thomas,* by its increased abbreviation, lays stress on the farmer:

> Let there be among you a man of understanding; when the fruit ripened, he came quickly with his sickle in his hand, he reaped it. (21)

The name commonly given to the parable, "The Seed Growing Secretly," emphasizes the second element. In recent times, however, the third element is seen to be particularly significant, namely the extraordinary power of the earth to make what is sown in it to grow.

> The earth produces of itself, first the stalk, then the head, then the full grain in the head.

The Greek term rendered "of itself" is *automatē;* it has come into our language in such words as "automatic," "automatically," but

---

[47] So Otto, *Kingdom of God and Son of Man,* 109; A. N. Wilder, *Eschatology and Ethics in the Teaching of Jesus* (rev. ed.; New York: Harper, 1950) 149.

[48] On the relation of the mission of the Son to that of the disciples in John 4:35–38, see C. H. Talbert, *Reading John* (New York: Crossroad, 1992) 116–17.

in Greek literature, notably in Jewish writings, it has various related meanings such as "without visible cause" (Job 24:24, Septuagint), "incomprehensibly" (Philo), and even "worked by God," which is its meaning in the only other passage in the New Testament where the term occurs, Acts 12:10 (the prison gate opened to Peter "of its own accord," i.e., miraculously). Rainer Stuhlmann, who in his article on the parable drew attention to this significance of *automatē,* also compares its appearance in Joshua 6:5 with a very similar meaning:

> At the blast of the rams' horns, when you hear the trumpet sound, the whole army must raise a great shout, the city wall will collapse.

The Septuagint renders the last clause, "the city wall will fall *automata,*" i.e., as in Acts 12:10, by the power of God.

The use of this term in our parable has a closer parallel in the observance of the year of Jubilee as commanded in Leviticus 25:11f.:

> The fiftieth year shall be a jubilee year for you; do not sow, and do not reap what grows of itself. . . . Eat only what is taken directly from the fields.

Once more the Septuagint renders in this context the phrase "of itself" as *automata.* Stuhlmann maintains that the word when used for "what comes up of itself" is a technical term for "plants which (in the Sabbath year, Leviticus 25) grow without sowing." Accordingly the parable is not really concerned with the contrast between activity and passivity (of the farmer, who sows, and then leaves the seed), but with the activity of God in nature. The contrast then lies in the opposition between the incomprehensible growth of the seed and its powerful end in the harvest.[49]

Self-evidently the parable moves to its climax in the harvest, as typically in prophetic and apocalyptic literature. But the distinguishing feature of the parable is its representation that a sowing has taken place with which the almighty working of God is joined *and continues,* and which therefore will certainly issue in the final harvest of the judgment and kingdom of God. The sowing relates above all to God's sovereign action in Jesus. That was something questioned not only by his opponents, but

---

[49] R. Stuhlmann, "Beobachtungen und Überlegungen zum Markus iv. 26–29," *NTS* 19 (1973) 154–57.

by some who listened to him with wonder and admiration, and yet with a certain hesitation as to whether it could possibly be true. Accordingly the parable is addressed to these, perhaps especially to the latter. Such was the conviction of A. M. Ambrozic, who wrote:

> Jesus is not merely affirming that the kingdom is coming; no one in his audience had doubts about that. What Jesus is affirming is that his coming and activity are intimately linked with the glorious manifestation of the kingdom in the future, that his ministry is the first step of its arrival.[50]

The purpose of this parable, therefore, is to encourage confidence in the authenticity of the mission of Jesus in relation to the kingdom of God. As surely as God's people know that God is behind the order of harvest after sowing, so truly is he at work in him whom he sent to initiate his kingdom, and no power in heaven or earth or hell can prevent its completion.

ii. *The Mustard Seed and the Leaven: Mark 4:30–32; Matthew 13:31–33; Luke 13:18–21*

A preliminary question is whether these two parables originally belonged together. They are linked in the Q tradition of the sayings of Jesus, but Mark has the Mustard Seed parable alone and apparently did not know that of the Leaven. The *Gospel of Thomas* reproduces both parables but separately. It is evident that the two parables circulated in the early church both together and alone, but when one contemplates the many hours that Jesus will have preached and taught in various areas, it seems possible that he may have uttered them both together and separately. In any case it is clear that the two parables set forth under two quite different figures an identical lesson, namely the small beginning and great ending of the kingdom of God initiated in the work of Jesus.

The Mustard Seed parable is the only one reproduced in all three Synoptic Gospels that explicitly compares the kingdom of God to a situation or process. In this case it is likened to a mustard seed in its tiny form, which, planted in the earth, grows to become a "tree." The description of the seed as "the smallest of all seeds on earth" is in harmony with popular thought, for the smallness of the black mustard seed was proverbial. In some Jewish rules of

---

[50] Ambrozic, *The Hidden Kingdom*, 119.

cleanness it is said that the slightest quantity defiles, "even as little as a grain of mustard seed" (*m. Nid.* 5:2). Even today there is an Arab proverb, "No mustard seed slips from the hands of a miser."[51] That in its full growth it should be described as a "tree" was held by Jeremias as unrealistic, and due to the influence of Daniel 4:17,[52] but that is not necessarily so. Mark himself says that it becomes the greatest of all *herbs,* Luke that it becomes *a tree,* Matthew combines both and writes that it grows greater than all herbs and becomes a tree! In fact Hunzinger points out that Theophrastus, in his classification of plants, coins the double word "tree-herb" *(dendrolachanon),* and he further mentions that to this day in the vicinity of Gennesaret the mustard grows to a height of two-and-one-half to three meters.[53]

Without doubt the feature of birds of the air nesting beneath the tree's branches is an echo of Ezekiel 17:23; 31:6; and Daniel 4:10–12. Each of these passages uses the figure of a great tree beneath which beasts find shelter and in whose branches birds nest, to describe a kingdom which rules over many nations.[54] However, while Ezekiel 31 and Daniel 4 have in view heathen empires, Ezekiel 17:22–24 is a prophecy of the messianic kingdom. Moreover the latter explicitly speaks of the planting of a *small* shoot which grows to become a great tree, thus:

> The Lord God says:
> I, too, shall take a slip from the lofty crown of the cedar
> and set it in the soil;
> I shall pluck a tender shoot from the topmost branch
> and plant it on a high and lofty mountain,
> the highest mountain in Israel.
> It will put out branches, bear its fruit,
> and become a noble cedar.
> Birds of every kind will roost under it,
> perching in the shelter of its boughs. (REB)

---

[51] Cited by C. H. Hunzinger, "σίναπι," *TDNT* 7.288.

[52] Jeremias, *Parables of Jesus,* 31.

[53] Hunzinger, *TDNT* 7.288–89.

[54] Crossan rejects linking the parable with these O.T. passages. He notes that they relate to a great tree, not a bush, and that they all have the parallelism of resting beasts and nesting birds. He therefore holds that the parable has in view Psalm 104:12, which has nothing apocalyptic about it but expresses God's care for nature, *In Parables,* 47–51. The suggestion is not convincing. Psalm 104:12 has much less in common with the parable than Ezekiel 17; 31; and Daniel 4.

Although Ezekiel is here writing of Israel's restoration, it is a restoration under the divine sovereignty, and therefore an allegory of the kingdom of God. The parallel with the basic comparison of a seed that becomes a "tree" to represent the kingdom of God needs no further demonstration, but the picture is more vivid when the seed is a mustard seed—"a midget of a seed among seeds," which grows to become "a veritable tree among herbs."[55]

Some interpreters have hesitated to accept this interpretation of Jesus' parable because the prophecy of Nebuchadnezzar's humiliation in Daniel 4 is much better known than Ezekiel 17. The parable of the Leaven is even more startling as a figure of the kingdom of God, since it is manifestly a symbol of evil in the Bible. Dispensationalists have therefore viewed the two parables as representing the growth of apostasy in the church,[56] a notion surely alien to the teaching of Jesus; it led C. H. Spurgeon, in whose day this interpretation arose, to observe that the two parables liken the growth of the seed and the penetration of leaven to the kingdom of *God,* not the kingdom of the *devil!* Nevertheless scholars have raised the question whether Jesus may have deliberately chosen images in these parables to counter the charge of Pharisees that he and his followers were worldly and unclean, and therefore could not be associated with the kingdom of God.[57]

The latter suggestion is perfectly possible, but it is by no means necessary, for despite the traditional Jewish view of leaven as a symbol of evil, notably as seen in the Passover ritual (Exodus 12:15, 19; 13:3, 7), other Jewish sources employ leaven to illustrate the highest good. David Flusser called attention to the comparison by Chiya bar Abba (c. A.D. 280) of the influence of the study of the Torah to the action of leaven. Chiya said that even if the children of Israel abandon God and yet continue to occupy themselves with the study of the Torah, the leaven of the Torah will bring the people back to God. Equally remarkably

---

[55] C. W. F. Smith, *The Jesus of the Parables* (rev. ed.; Philadelphia: 1975) 53.

[56] See the C. I. Scofield edition of the Bible ad loc.

[57] E. Schweizer asked, "Is this meant to alert the listener through its alienating effect, using unheard-of, iconoclastic images for the kingdom of God? Was Jesus perhaps even thinking of his own band of disciples, the tax collectors and ignorant fishermen who were worldly and unclean by Pharisaic standards?" *The Good News according to Matthew* (Atlanta: John Knox, 1975) 306–7.

R. Joshua ben Levi is said to have compared the effect of peace with that of leaven:

> Great is peace, for as peace is to the land so is leaven to the dough. Had the Holy One, blessed be he, not given peace to the land, the sword and the beast would have devastated it.[58]

Admittedly these two examples come from a later time than that of Jesus, but when one recalls that in Jewish thought the Torah is the essence of the divine revelation and that peace is the comprehensive term for the salvation of the kingdom of God, it is remarkable that rabbinic scholars of any time in the formative period of Judaism were able to conceive of the effect of God's law and his gift of peace in terms of leaven. How much more comprehensible is it that Jesus should do the like in one of his many comparisons of the kingdom of God.

We need have no hesitation, therefore, in acknowledging with the majority of scholars that the parables of the Mustard Seed and Leaven are contrast parables of the beginning and the end of the kingdom of God brought by Jesus. Indeed we may go further, for these parables have a related significance with that of the Growing Seed, which emphasizes the powerful action of God in the presence and growth of the saving sovereignty, and so assures its triumphant conclusion. W. Lütgert was right in his affirmation that the contrast in the two parables is not simply between beginning and end, but also between cause and effect: the cause is God active in and through Jesus, the effect is the powerful initiation of the divine sovereignty.[59] With that we thoroughly agree. These parables, no less than others that Jesus spoke, have a dual function: they reveal God's action in Jesus whereby God's kingdom of salvation is truly initiated; and at the same time they issue a call to respond to the new opportunity and experience the power of the saving sovereignty.

iii. The Sower: Mark 4:1–9 (13–20); Matthew 13:1–9 (18–23); Luke 8:4–8 (11–15)

By placing this parable at the head of his collection of parables of growth and adding related material to the whole, Mark has made this section the longest "discourse" of Jesus in his

---

[58] Cited by Young, *Jesus and His Jewish Parables*, 211–12.
[59] W. Lütgert, *Das Reich Gottes nach den synoptischen Evangelien: Eine Untersuchung zur neutestamentlichen Theologie* (Gütersloh: C. Bertelsmann, 1895) 99.

Gospel, other than that of chapter 13. Moreover the fact that he has added an interpretation to the parable, and prefaced and concluded the parable with words of Jesus, "*Listen!* . . . Let anyone who has ears to hear *listen!*," indicates the prime importance that it had for Mark—and for the Lord. "The command to listen," remarked Schweizer, "is a summons to awaken to a manner of listening which leads to involvement and decision."[60]

Despite the general recognition of its importance, scholars have differed to an unusual degree as to where the emphasis of the parable lies. Stress has been laid on the sower himself, the seed, the soils, and the harvest.

Most commonly the parable has been called that of *the Sower,* and it is so named by Matthew (13:18). Without doubt the figure of the sower is important, for despite the non-mention of his name after the opening sentence the parable throughout its length describes his action, and it is comprehensible that through the years he has been viewed as representing Jesus. Strictly speaking the sower should be taken as a generic figure for anyone who labors in the service of God's kingdom, and so can apply to the disciples in their mission with Jesus, and those who perform such service in the time of the church (hence the importance of the interpretation in vv. 13–20). Nevertheless it is difficult not to see in the Sower in the first instance a depiction of Jesus in his service of the kingdom of God, but described in terms of a farm laborer engaged in the task of sowing with a view to producing a harvest.

In this respect Jeremias called attention to the curious procedure of the sower in scattering seed on (or beside) the path, and among thorns, and on rocky ground. He explained, "This is easily understood when we remember that in Palestine sowing precedes plowing."[61] For this custom he quoted G. Dalman, who read in the Talmud, "In Palestine plowing comes after sowing" (*b. Shabb.* 73b), and affirmed, "This is still done today."[62] Jeremias also cites W. G. Essame, who found an example of this in the *Book of Jubilees* (11:11), thought to be written about the second century B.C.:

---

[60] E. Schweizer, *The Good News according to Mark,* 90.

[61] Jeremias, *Parables of Jesus,* 11.

[62] G. Dalman, "Vierlei Acker," *Palästina-Jahrbuch* 22 (1926) 120–32, and idem, *Arbeit und Sitte in Palästina* (Gütersloh: C. Bertelsmann, 1932) 2.179ff.

> Prince Mastema (= Satan) sent ravens and birds to devour the seed
> which was sown in the earth . . . before they could plow in the seed
> the ravens plucked it from the surface of the ground.[63]

It seems reasonably clear that such a custom did exist and continued in Palestine, and it is generally accepted by recent commentators on the parable. K. W. White, however, contested the view in
light of "normal Palestinian practice."[64] The evidence cited by
White is dubious, but some Old Testament texts indicate that the
practice of sowing first and then plowing was not universal in
Palestine. Jeremiah 4:3 reads:

> Thus says the Lord to the people of Judah and to the inhabitants of
> Jerusalem:
> Break up your fallow ground,
> and do not sow among thorns. (NRSV)

A similar appeal occurs in Hosea 10:11–12:

> Ephraim was a trained heifer
> that loved to thresh,
> and I spared her fair neck;
> but I will make Ephraim break the ground;
> Judah must plow;
> Jacob must harrow for himself.
> Sow for yourselves righteousness;
> reap steadfast love;
> break up your fallow ground;
> for it is time to seek the Lord,
> that he may come and rain righteousness upon you. (NRSV)

In the light of such evidence it would appear that the custom of
sowing before plowing was not universal, but it seems to have
been in view in our parable.

Other scholars have been impressed by the statement in
Mark's interpretation of the parable, "The seed is the word" (v. 14;
Matthew has "the word of the kingdom," 13:19; Luke "the word
of God," 8:11). That accords with the frequency with which the
seed is mentioned in the parable, and in particular with the way
that Mark differentiates between seed in the singular in vv. 4, 5, 7
("a seed . . . another seed . . . another seed . . . "), and in v. 8 the
plural, ("other seeds fell on the good earth"). If the point of the
parable is the destiny of the word of the kingdom proclaimed by

---

[63] W. G. Essame, "Sowing and Ploughing," *ExpT* 72 (1960–61) 546.

[64] See K. W. White, "The Parable of the Sower," *JTS* n.s. 15 (1964)
300–307, and the reply of Jeremias, *NTS* 13 (1966–67) 48–53.

Jesus, the loss of the word is more than compensated for by its great fruitfulness.

But that recalls the most popular interpretation of earlier times: since the fate of the word is dependent on the varying soils on which it falls, the parable should be called "The Parable of the Four Soils," or "The Parable of the Fourfold Field." That approach is in harmony with the interpretation added by Mark in vv. 13–20, but it has led to a strong tendency to emphasize the lack of success depicted in the parable. J. Schniewind, for example, drew from the parable the conclusion, "The normal result of God's word is failure."[65] In a similar vein R. Guardini spoke of the parable as setting forth "the unspeakable tragedy of almighty truth and creative love doomed, for the most part, to sterility."[66] The exposition of the parable by Helmut Thielicke is uncharacteristically depressing. He wrote:

> The parable is really pointing out how frequently the divine seed is destroyed—destroyed in stony hearts, by the heat of the sun, by choking thorns and predatory birds—this is why there is in this parable a deep sense of grief and sorrow. And all this is seen and proclaimed while outwardly the people are coming in droves, inspired with festive enthusiasm, and the hucksters are rubbing their hands with delight over this "colossal" attraction and raving about this great new "star" who is able to draw such crowds. Is it so surprising that the Saviour should be sad when he sees the fate of the Word of God?[67]

This emphasis on the "fate" of the seed, the unproductive soil, and the sadness of the Savior is exaggerated. Admittedly the hardness of the path and the shallowness of the soil on rocky places are mentioned, but the hindrances and elements of opposition that prevent full growth of the seed—the birds of the air, the thorns, and the scorching sun—are yet more serious. Further, the detailed description of the areas in which the seed is sown can give the impression that the seed is sown equally on the path, among the thorns, on the rocky ground, and on the rest of the field, so that three-quarters of the seed is wasted and only one quarter is productive. Such is often stated, but a little thought should suffice to dispel that mistake. For example, the path is not a highway running through the midst of the field!

---

[65] Schniewind, *Das Evangelium nach Markus,* 74.

[66] R. Guardini, *The Lord* (London: Longmans, Green, 1956) 175.

[67] H. Thielicke, *The Waiting Father* (London: James Clarke, 1960) 53.

In reality the point of emphasis in the parable is the harvest, as in the other parables of growth. J. D. Crossan has pointed out that the detailed account of the threefold lack of productivity of the seed sown is balanced by the declaration of a threefold growth of seed more briefly stated in v. 8, with its thirtyfold, sixtyfold, and hundredfold increase.[68] The work of a farm laborer in sowing and plowing a field and enduring the vicissitudes of an uncertain climate may be tough, but it is rewarded in the production of an abundant harvest. Jeremias accordingly saw in the Sower a contrast between the frustrations of a sower's toil and its end in the harvest field; hence he commented:

> Jesus is full of joyful confidence. . . . In spite of every failure and opposition, from hopeless beginnings, God brings forth the triumphant end which he had promised.[69]

This is entirely in harmony with the Gospel records of the ministry of Jesus. But is there anything in those records to correspond with the negative and positive elements within the parable—its depiction of frustration and opposition on the one hand and of joyful hope on the other? Decidedly, yes. Mark has narrated in 2:1–3:5 five incidents of opposition to Jesus by Pharisees and teachers of the law, culminating in a conspiracy of the former with the Herodians to destroy him (3:6). That could have been an important factor in the decision of Jesus to pursue his ministry mainly outside the synagogues, in the open country and in the homes of the people. When he did preach in the synagogue of his own town he was met with rank unbelief and rejection (6:22ff., cf. Luke 4:23–30). We also read of teachers of the law coming down from Jerusalem, alleging that his exorcisms showed that he was an agent of the devil, with the unexpressed implication that the people should keep clear of him (3:22ff.). That probably contributed to the attempt of his family to take him home and make him cease his ministry (3:20f., 31ff.). These events were but forerunners of the increasing opposition to Jesus as his ministry continued, leading him at length to prepare his disciples for the end of this antagonism in his death (8:31), and to call on them to share in his sufferings (8:34ff.). We cannot plot precisely the timing and progress of this opposition, but it clearly began early on in his public ministry and advanced in its intensity as it

---

[68] Crossan, *In Parables,* 41.

[69] Jeremias, *Parables of Jesus,* 150.

proceeded. In contrast to all this, every stream of the Gospel traditions reveals the consciousness of Jesus that the powers of the kingdom of God were operative in and through him, together with their profound effects in the lives of many of his hearers (e.g., Mark 1:27–28; 2:18f.; 3:27; Matthew 12:28; 11:5, 12; Luke 10:17–20; 17:20–21).

Taking these facts into account, it is understandable that Jesus should compare the service of the kingdom of God with that of a laborer sowing seed in anticipation of a harvest. The arduousness of the task is compounded by the obstacles provided by nature, but they are endured precisely because in the end nature itself is on the sower's side. The parable accordingly may be said to depict the action of the representative of God's kingdom as he goes out in God's name to make known by word and deed the good news of the inauguration of God's saving sovereignty. More precisely, it sets forth *the mission of God, acting in sovereign grace toward men through the one whom he sent to initiate his kingdom.*[70] In the Bible the world of nature and the world of humankind are one world under God. The earth produces thorns and thistles and birds that eat seed that is sown—and harvests of grain and fruits. Human beings likewise manifest sin and disobedience to God, but are also capable of faith that works by love. That is the context of the mission of the kingdom—a fallen world into which the saving sovereignty of God is brought by one in whom sovereign grace was perfectly manifested and through whom it is mediated.

In the other parables of growth, harvest is a figure for the goal to which the saving sovereignty moves. The same applies to the parable of the Sower, but the differentiation of harvest growth in terms of thirtyfold, sixtyfold, one hundredfold is not to be pressed; in the parable its function is to indicate the extraordinary multiplication of the seeds in the harvest. So also its relevance for the ministry of Jesus is primarily to illustrate the reality of the beginning of the saving sovereignty in the mission of Jesus despite all opposition. The motive for telling this parable, as of the other parables of growth referred to, is on the one hand to encourage the followers of Jesus in their faith that in him the kingdom of promise has truly begun and is destined to triumph by the power

---

[70]The sending of Jesus is rarely mentioned in the Synoptic Gospels—it is found, e.g., in Mark 9:37; Matthew 15:24; 23:37f.; but no less than thirty-eight times in the Gospel of John. Cf. Bultmann, *Gospel of John,* 249 n. 2, and my work, *Gospel of Life* (Peabody, Mass.: Hendrickson, 1991) 15–33.

of God; on the other hand it is to challenge hearers who have not responded to his message to recognize that in him the kingdom of salvation is present among them, to repent and thus to open themselves to its saving grace.

The authenticity of the interpretation of the parable given in Mark 4:13–20 and parallels has long been debated and is frequently denied by critical scholars, though not always on adequate grounds. It is objected that the parable has been allegorized in the interpretation; but the distinction between parable and allegory can no longer be rigidly maintained. The language is said to be Markan, and characteristic of the church rather than of Jesus; even if this were true (it is disputed) its significance is not great, since some important terms are used both by Jesus and the church, and Markan language can express Jesus' thought. Some maintain that parables of Jesus did not require interpretation; but in the Old Testament, interpretations are given to parables, and in Judaism it became standard practice among the rabbis. The parable is eschatological in intention, while it is said that the interpretation stresses psychological aspects; but the interpretation emphasizes also the eschatological elements. The one major difficulty in the relation of parable and interpretation is the clear statement in the latter (v. 14) that the seed is the word, exactly as in the parable, but it is followed by the apparent identification in vv. 15–20 of "those sown" as both the seed of the word and those who receive the word. This is puzzling, yet is constant in the interpretation. It further causes an obscuring of the balance in the parable between the three unfruitful sowings and the three fruitful ones—the former are emphasized separately, the latter are presented as one.

Nevertheless recent scholars are increasingly concerned to acknowledge the close relation of the interpretation with the parable; as, e.g., R. Guelich, who affirmed that the difference between the two is "descriptive rather than prescriptive,"[71] P. Bonnard, who states that the parable and interpretation bring us "very precise echoes" of our Lord's teaching,[72] E. E. Ellis, who speaks of the interpretation as giving "the mind of Jesus,"[73] and R. Schnackenburg, who affirms that the interpretation shows "a freedom of

---

[71] Guelich, *Mark 1–8:26*, 224.

[72] P. Bonnard, *L'Evangile selon Saint Matthieu*, 196.

[73] E. Ellis, *Gospel of Luke* (New Century Bible Commentaries; Grand Rapids: Eerdmans, 1981) 129.

applied instructions" which is conscious of "its original meaning and presupposes it."[74] I. H. Marshall stated, "Once the vital equation, 'The seed is the word of God' has been made, the essential lesson follows inescapably"; this he sees present in both the parable and the interpretation, but just as Luke shows signs of editing Mark's account and adapts it in the light of his own situation, so it is possible that Mark has done the same, and that the detailed form of the explanation may represent a development of hints given by Jesus.[75] That is a not unreasonable solution to the problem.

iv. The Darnel and the Field: Matthew 13:24–30 (36–43)

The above title given to this parable, reproduced only by Matthew, is that given to it by the disciples of Jesus in the interpretation that follows in Matthew 13:36–43. The parable is now most frequently known as "The Wheat and the Weeds," but the Greek term *zizania* (a loan word from Semitic languages) actually denotes darnel, defined by the Oxford English Dictionary as "a deleterious grass which in some countries grows as a weed among corn." It used to be common in Britain when seed corn was largely imported from Mediterranean countries, where darnel abounded. It is closely related to bearded wheat, and in early stages of growth it is hard to distinguish from it. In Palestine, darnel seeds were often grown for feeding poultry; their similarity to ordinary wheat caused them sometimes to be mixed accidentally with wheat grains, and if such should be sown with wheat it was not difficult to remove the plants in the early stages of growth. In the parable, however, so much darnel appeared in the time of growth, it was realized that this was no accident: "An enemy has done this," was the farmer's conclusion. The workers understandably wished to pluck up the darnel at once, but they were forbidden by the farmer to do it, lest the genuine wheat be thereby destroyed. "Let both grow together till the harvest" was his decision. Then the wheat could be gathered for the barn, and the darnel could be bound into bundles as fuel.

Curiously, a number of interpreters have responded to the parable by suggesting that the events narrated are so far from

---

[74] R. Schnackenburg, *God's Rule and Kingdom* (New York: Herder & Herder, 1963) 152.

[75] Marshall, *Commentary on Luke*, 323–24.

reality, they must have been constructed for the sake of the message in the parable. That is quite mistaken. The story all too well reflects the malice of which men have at all times been capable in agricultural areas. To sow obnoxious weeds in a freshly plowed field is a way of getting revenge or of giving vent to hate. Two German scholars traveling in Palestine early in this century encountered an interesting example of the situation described in the parable. They were entertained by a hospitable Arab in his home, who told them of a time when he and his neighbor had a violent quarrel. Shortly afterwards he found by a stream a mass of kusseb (reeds) in seed, and so he gathered the seeds in the skirt of his robe. He recounted to his guests:

> I went to Abu Jassin's kitchen garden. It was freshly ploughed. There I scattered the kusseb seeds. The new year had scarcely come before the garden was thick with kusseb. From that day to this—it is now some twenty years—he could not plow a single furrow in it for the mass of kusseb. The olive trees withered away.[76]

According to C. A. Bugge this was a criminal act dealt with in Roman law in the *Digests* of the *corpus juris civilis*.[77]

It is universally agreed that the two statements "An enemy has done this," and "Let both grow together till the harvest," provide the clues to the intention of the story. But what exactly is in mind? Through the Christian centuries it has been commonly believed that the "enemy action" carried out by Satan (see the interpretation, v. 39) has been to plant false members in the church to compromise its teaching and weaken its witness in the world; the natural impulse of its leaders to root out the pseudo-members is forbidden by the Lord, on account of the obvious danger of expelling from the church genuine Christians also, for only God can truly read aright the human heart.

This interpretation was established by Augustine in his controversy with the Donatists in his diocese. By his time the Roman emperors had capitulated to the lordship of Christ and the empire was nominally Christian, hence it had now become plain that the church was a *corpus mixtum* of true and false believers. The Donatists believed that this was a denial of the true church; they

---

[76] H. Schmidt and P. Kahle, *Volkserzählungen aus Palästina* (Göttingen: Vandenhoeck & Ruprecht, 1918) 1.31.

[77] Lib. ix., tit. 2, lex 27, 14 (ad legem Aquiliam, cited in *Die Haupt-Parabeln Jesu* (Giessen: J. Ricker'sche, 1903) 130.

wrote to Augustine, pointing out that since holiness was an essential mark of the church, its unholy members should be excommunicated. To this Augustine replied that the holiness of the church was guaranteed by the presence of the Holy Spirit; the demand of the Donatists was contrary to the Lord's command not to separate the wheat from the weeds before the harvest, when God himself will carry out the judgment. Thereupon the Donatists wrote back and said, "By Christ's own showing 'the field' is not the church, but the world; the parable, therefore, does not bear on the dispute between us and you." On this R. C. Trench, in his account of the controversy, commented:

> It must be evident to every one not warped by a previous dogmatic interest that the parable is, as the Lord announces, concerning *"the kingdom of heaven,"* or the Church.[78]

This notion that the kingdom of God is the church, again cherished through the centuries by most theologians until recent times, has led Christians astray in more ways than one, not least from perceiving the point of this parable. Curiously enough, Matthew is the only Gospel writer to use the term "church" (in 16:15 and 18:15–20); he could easily have introduced the term into the interpretation if he had intended the parable to be applied to the church. Moreover it is plain from the latter passage that the church of Matthew practiced excommunication. As W. D. Davies and D. C. Allison remarked, "The community pulled up Christian weeds when it was necessary. It did not wait for the eschaton to sort the good from the bad."[79] Furthermore it is mistaken to understand "The field is the world" as having special application to the church; on the contrary, as E. Lohmeyer observed:

> As the field belongs to the farmer, so the world—not the community, or the nation—belongs to the Son of Man; he is its sole Lord.[80]

For the right interpretation of this parable it is important to recall that the parables of growth, which we have examined, indicate that the sowing featured in all of them reflects the inauguration of the kingdom of God in and through the ministry of Jesus. Indeed, the parable of the Sower makes much of the

---

[78] R. C. Trench, *Notes on the Parables of Our Lord* (London: Kegan Paul, 1898) 92.

[79] Davies and Allison, *Gospel according to St. Matthew*, 2.409.

[80] E. Lohmeyer and W. Schmauch, *Das Evangelium des Matthäus* (KEK; 3d ed.; Göttingen: Vandenhoeck & Ruprecht, 1962) 223.

obstacles in the way of the seed sown issuing in the harvest of the kingdom, but the parable of the Wheat and Darnel highlights a more serious opposition to the kingdom of God. Whereas in the interpretation of the Sower the birds are viewed as representing the devil's work of annulling the word of the kingdom, in the Wheat and Darnel another sowing takes place, representing a countermovement to the kingdom of God in the world. Davies and Allison draw attention to this:

> Note that in 13:25 the devil does what the Son of Man does: *he sows.* Thus the devil is made out to be an imitator, a maker of counterfeits. The result is that just as there are wolves in the midst of sheep (7:15), so too there are weeds in the midst of wheat.[81]

This "sowing," however, is represented as taking place in the world. It is in opposition to what God is doing in the Christ for the salvation of humankind. Bonnard saw this clearly when he pointed out that the work of the enemy is not simply sowing evil in general, or causing Christians to suffer, or planting sinners in the church: *"The world is the theater of two opposed sowings."* [82]

What then is to be done about this situation? Assuredly not organizing an opposition to the opposition, an equivalent in life of rooting out the darnel. This was the solution of the Qumran volunteers, who prepared themselves to fight against the sons of darkness whenever the Messiah(s) should appear, and of the Zealots, who wanted to declare all-out war against the Roman overlords of Palestine (and did, to the ruin of their nation). Even John the Baptist became impatient with Jesus as he languished in prison, wondering when Jesus was going to begin the real messianic task of judging the human race—in his own imagery, winnowing the grain on the threshing floor, gathering the wheat into the barn and burning the chaff with inextinguishable fire (Matthew 3:12; 11:2–3). How many others in Israel harbored such thoughts as they listened to Jesus teach and witnessed (or heard about) his works of power? To all who looked for him to obliterate the opponents of the kingdom of God in a universal judgment he offered a wholly different solution.

First, the sowing of the kingdom of God was no merely human operation, "of the flesh" as the Jews would say, partaking

---

[81] Davies and Allison, *Gospel according to St. Matthew,* 2.412.
[82] Bonnard, *L'Evangile selon saint Matthieu,* 199.

of the weakness of humanity and thereby helpless before the powers of evil; it was God himself, working through Jesus, who began the establishment of the saving sovereignty in the world and continues its operation, hence no evil power in the universe can prevent the harvest of the kingdom and the destruction of the opposition to it. Secondly, a corollary of the initiation of the kingdom of God in the world is that "the coming of the kingdom is itself a process of sifting, a judgment."[83] That is inevitable, in so far as the hearing the word of the kingdom creates positive and negative reactions, i.e., of faith or rejection; accordingly the verdict of the judgment at the end of the age is already being enacted by the hearers of the gospel (cf. the very similar thought in John 3:19–21). From that point of view the present time is as truly eschatological as the end time, for it is kingdom time. Disciples of the Lord therefore need not attempt action in anticipation of the final judgment; on the one hand their understanding is too limited to pass judgment on the lives of people, on the other hand the hearers of the word of the kingdom are already doing it for themselves.

A third deduction from the parable is the implied emphasis on a positive rather than negative attitude to opponents of the kingdom. Daniel Patte pointed out the purely negative response of the servants to evil action in the parable:

> For the servants, as soon as one discovers a manifestation of evil, it is self-evident that it should be removed; one's will, one's vocation, is to react against what is evil so as to condemn it and destroy it. *The presence of evil demands active judgmental interventions against it.* But the householder's response shows that this view is totally wrong: one's will or vocation should be established in terms of the manifestations of good, that is, in terms of what is good to do vis-à-vis the wheat. . . . The disciple's vocation is to be established in terms of the kingdom as the ultimate good—by repenting, by turning oneself toward the kingdom. In other words, one cannot become a disciple—and have the proper vocation—as long as one thinks that one's vocation should primarily be negative, judgmental, a vocation to fight evil.[84]

The relevance of this concept to Jesus is seen in his concentration on the service of the kingdom in the totality of his ministry. He was sent to be the mediator of the saving sovereignty of God, not

---

[83] Dodd, *Parables of the Kingdom,* 185.

[84] D. Patte, *The Gospel according to Matthew: A Structural Commentary on Matthew's Faith* (Philadelphia: Fortress, 1987) 194.

of judgment. The time for the latter is in the Father's hands, and it will certainly take place. Meanwhile his mission is to reveal the compassion of God towards all to whom he has been sent, and to call on his followers to do the same, that the unbelievers of their nation—and subsequently of all nations—may be led to repentance, and so experience the salvation of the kingdom of God. "Let both grow together till the harvest" thus signifies a rejection of the impatience characteristic of God's people and a call to cherish instead the patience of God.

The interpretation of the parable supplied by the evangelist in Matthew 13:36–43, even more than that of the parable of the Sower in Mark 4:13–20, bears the stamp of the evangelist with respect to vocabulary and style.[85] Nevertheless it is foundational in Gospel research that knowledge handed on from others can be reproduced in one's own language. For example, the expression "explain to us the parable," Matthew 13:36, appears in Matthew 15:15, while Mark has the reasonable equivalent ". . . they asked him about the parable"; "the sons of the kingdom," v. 38, occurs also in 8:12 ("the sons of the kingdom will be thrown outside"), whereas Luke 7:28 has the abbreviated equivalent, "*you* (will be thrown outside)"; "the consummation of the age," v. 39, occurs in 24:3, where Matthew has expanded the parallels in Mark 13:4 and Luke 21:7 because he has conjoined with the Markan discourse the Q apocalypse reproduced by Luke in 17:20–37. The interpretation of the parable actually begins with an identification of the figures within the parable (vv. 37–39), as though the evangelist assumed that to provide such is the key for understanding the parable. What follows concentrates on the separation that will happen in the harvest, when "the Son of Man will send his angels, who will gather out of his kingdom every cause of sin, and all whose deeds are evil," which assumes that his kingdom will be worldwide. J. Schniewind affirmed:

> The interpretation sharpens the truth proclaimed in the parable, just as in the parable of the Sower: the judgment will bring the separation of good and evil. That the evil ripens like the good is a foundational truth of New Testament proclamation. . . . The evil will be taken away from the realm of his sovereignty, his "kingdom"; then (cf. 1 Corinthians 15:24) God's sovereignty will appear in power (v. 43) . . . and the righteous belong to it.[86]

---

[85] See especially Jeremias, *Parables of Jesus,* 82–85.
[86] Schniewind, *Das Evangelium nach Matthäus,* 172.

Many would agree with Michaelis that "The parable and its interpretation are well attuned to one another."[87] But the citation from Schniewind indicates how well the interpretation is "attuned" also to the teaching of the early church. The least therefore that one can say regarding the authenticity of the interpretation is, in the words of David Hill: "The evangelist may be editing (and applying to his own time) earlier genuine material, rather than creating a wholly allegorical interpretation."[88] That "earlier genuine material" most plausibly will have come from the one who originally told the parable.

3. Parables of Judgment

i. The Rich Man and Lazarus: Luke 16:19–31

A single motif binds together the two parables of Luke 16 and the separate sayings that occur between them, namely the responsible use of wealth. The chapter begins with the parable of the Dishonest Manager (vv. 1–8), and it is followed by sayings that Luke must have regarded as applications of that parable, to which he has added others related in part to the same theme. Then follows the parable of the Rich Man and Lazarus, with its contrast between one man who lived in luxury and a beggar at his gate who was poverty-stricken, hungry, and ill. In Luke's Gospel it is addressed to Pharisees, whom he describes as avaricious, for they had ridiculed Jesus' teaching. According to Luke the last statement which they had heard from Jesus was the assertion, "You cannot serve God and money" (16:13).

It must be made clear at the outset is that this is a *parable,* not a literal description of what happened to two particular men after their death. It has two quite different themes: the first relates to God's judgment on people, according to their attitude to God and their fellow humans in need; the second, the unlikelihood that a resurrection would lead to repentance people who refuse God's revelation in the law and the prophets. It will be seen that the emphasis in the parable falls on the second theme.

It is possible to read the parable as a crude contrast between the destinies of the wealthy and the poor: in the life to come their circumstances are reversed; the former become wretched and

---

[87] W. Michaelis, *Die Gleichnisse Jesu: Eine Einführung* (UB 23; 8th ed.; Hamburg: Furche, 1956) 51.
[88] Hill, *The Gospel of Matthew,* 235.

suffer torment, for no other reason than their possession of riches during their life on earth; the latter are in the company of the blessed, simply because they knew hardship and misery in their period of earthly living (see vv. 22–23, 25). This would be a simplistic interpretation, but the features in the parable in all probability are due to the use of a story well known in ancient Egypt, which was adapted in various forms by the Jews; it appears to have been taken up by Jesus and given a unique application. The story is known from a papyrus manuscript, written on the back of two Greek business documents, now in the British Museum, and runs as follows:

> Once upon a time the magicians of Egypt were challenged by a mighty sorcerer from Ethiopia, but no Egyptian was a match for him. So an Egyptian in Amnte (land of the West, the abode of the dead) prayed to Osiris, the Ruler of Amnte, "Let me go forth to the world again." Osiris gave command that he go forth to the world. The man, though dead for centuries, awoke in Memphis, where he was reincarnated as the miraculous offspring of a childless couple and given the name Si–Osiris (Son of Osiris). When the boy was twelve years old he dealt quite adequately with the foreign sorcerer, and vanished from the earth.
>
> But at a still more tender age the boy took his father on a tour of Amnte. This he had to do because of a remark he made one day about two funerals. First a rich man was borne out to the mountain, shrouded in fine linen, loudly lamented, abundantly honoured; then a poor man, wrapped in a mean straw mat, unaccompanied, unmourned, was taken out to the necropolis of Memphis. The father exclaimed he would rather have the lot of the rich man than that of the pauper. But little Si–Osiris impertinently contradicted his father's wish with an opposite one: "May it be done to you in Amnte as it is done in Amnte to this pauper, and not as it is done to this rich man in Amnte!"
>
> Si–Osiris leads his father through the seven classified halls of Amnte, where the dead lead their new life in the halls appropriate to the merits and demerits each has earned on earth. In the fifth hall they see a man in torment, the pivot of the door being fixed in his right eye-socket, because of which he prays and grievously laments. In the seventh they see Osiris enthroned, the great god, Ruler of Amnte, and near him a man clad in fine linen and evidently of very high rank. Si–Osiris identifies the latter to his father as the miserably buried pauper of Memphis and the tormented one as the sumptuously buried rich man. Belatedly he now adds the theodicy: at his judgment the good deeds of the pauper had outweighed the bad, but with the rich man it had been the reverse. The boy also adds that Osiris had ordered the rich burial-linen of the magnate to be given to the former pauper to wear in Amnte. Then he reminds his father of his really

filial wish spoken at Memphis. The father is completely placated and congratulates himself that when his time comes he in Amnte can claim such a son as this.[89]

This story became known to the rabbis in Israel, doubtless on account of the large settlement of Jews in Alexandria; it became current among them in no less than seven different forms. The oldest is that preserved in the Palestinian Talmud, where the rich man is a tax-gatherer and the poor man is a student of the law. It runs as follows:

> Two godly men lived in Ashkelon. They ate together, drank together, and studied the law together. One of them died and kindness was not shown to him (i.e., nobody attended his funeral). The son of Mayan, a tax-gatherer, died, and the whole city stopped work to show him kindness. The (surviving) pious man began to complain; he said: "Alas that no evil comes upon the haters of Israel!" In a dream he saw a vision; and one said to him: "Do not despise the children of your Lord. The one (the pious) had committed one sin and departed (this life) in it (i.e., his mean funeral cancelled it); and the other (the wealthy publican) had performed one good deed and departed (this life) in it" (i.e., his splendid funeral cancelled it). . . .

> After some days that godly man saw the godly one his (former) companion walking in gardens and parks beside springs of water (in Paradise). And he saw the son of Mayan, the publican, stretching out his tongue on the edge of a river; he was seeking to reach the water, and he could not.[90]

The points of similarity and dissimilarity between the two quoted stories and that of Jesus are striking. All three concern the contrast between the destinies of a wealthy man deficient in good deeds and a poor man rich therein. The Egyptian story ends with the statement:

> He who has been good on earth will be blessed in the kingdom of the dead, and he who has been evil on earth will suffer in the kingdom of the dead.

In the Jewish adaptation the mere fact that the son of Mayan was a publican was enough to warrant his description as "a hater of

---

[89] H. Gressmann called the attention of scholars to the Egyptian demotic narrative in his article, "Vom reichen Mann und armen Lazarus," *Abhandlungen der kaiserlichen preussischen Akademie der Wissenschaften* (1918) no. 7. The account reproduced is that of K. Grobel, slightly abbreviated, in "Whose Name was Neves," *NTS* 10 (1964) 376–78.

[90] *Y. Ḥag.* 2.77d, cited, with explanatory comments, by Manson, *Sayings of Jesus,* 297.

Israel," therefore evil, but the student of the law is said to be "godly"; the narrative, however, has a rigid reckoning of works of merit and demerit. In the parable of Jesus the characters of the rich man and poor man are more indirectly referred to than in the Egyptian and Jewish parallels, perhaps because Jesus knows that the story is familiar to his hearers. The sheer luxury of the rich man's living, without any care for the poor creature at his gate, is a condemnation of him, increased by the vain desire of the beggar to eat the bread that was thrown from the table to the ground, and which the dogs reached first: the rich man evidently couldn't care less about the beggar's hunger.[91] That Lazarus "lies" at the gate suggests that he is a cripple, unable to walk. While no "works" of his are mentioned, his name hints of his character: Lazarus is an abbreviated Greek equivalent of Eleazar, meaning "(the man whom) God helps"; he has indeed no other helper to whom he may look.[92]

All three accounts of the state of the departed give the impression that the deceased enter upon their "recompense" at once—in each case the formerly wealthy individuals are in torment, and the previously poor are in a blessed place, apparently the equivalent of paradise.[93] That raises a difficulty for the Lazarus story, for the teaching of Jesus and of the rest of the New Testament writers links the judgment with the coming of the Lord at the end of the age. The parable actually states that the rich man is in *Hades*, i.e., the realm of the dead, not *Gehenna*," i.e., hell; but the KJV renders *Hades* here as "hell" (v. 23), presumably because the text says that the man is "in torment." Scholars differ as to whether the parable identifies *Hades* with hell. It may be purely a

---

[91] According to Jeremias "That which fell from the rich man's table" was not crumbs, but pieces of bread which the guests dipped in the dish, used to wipe their hands with and then threw under the table. In *t. Ber.* 5.8 it is written, "One should not bite a piece of bread (which has been dipped in the dish) and then dip it in again on account of danger to life," *Parables of Jesus*, 184 n. 53.

[92] That Lazarus is the only person named in a parable of Jesus, that he died and was the subject of discussion as to whether he should rise from the dead, has provoked debate on the relation of the parable and the narrative of the raising of Lazarus in John 11. Some argue that the parable led to the creation of the miracle story, others that the reverse happened (the narrative gave birth to the parable). Neither suggestion is plausible. R. Schnackenburg suggested that the original parable about a rich man and a beggar may have had the name Lazarus introduced from the account in John 11, *Gospel according to John*, 2.342.

[93] In *1 Enoch* 22 the righteous are depicted as beside "a spring of water with light upon it" (v. 9) and the evil are in great pain (v. 11).

reflection of the original story—recall that this is a parabolic picture, not a statement of doctrine. On the other hand Jewish apocalyptic can reconcile the two representations: the dead in *Hades* are separated, awaiting the judgment of the last day. Both Jesus and the apostles refer to an immediate passage on death to the presence of the Lord (Luke 23:42–43; 2 Corinthians 5:6–8; Philippians 1:21–23); but the author to the Hebrews in a single sentence speaks of man "appointed once to die and after that judgment," and the coming of the Lord for the salvation of those awaiting him (Hebrews 9:27–28). It could be that we have here in picture language the old representation of the certainty of "recompense" for all, without distinctions of time. The details all have parallels in Jewish apocalyptic and other literature.[94]

In vv. 27–28 the parable enters upon a second part: a plea is made that Lazarus be sent to the rich man's five brothers, that he may "bear solemn witness" to them about the terrible place to which their deceased brother has gone, and so save them from the same fate. To this Abraham replies, "They have Moses and the prophets," i.e., the testimony to God's will and purpose in the books of the law and the prophets, the latter including the historical books of the Old Testament; these are read every Sabbath in the synagogue for all Jews to hear, so let the brothers listen to *them!* But the rich man knows his five brothers, who presumably no more listen to Moses and the prophets than he did! He therefore persists in his plea: "No, father Abraham, but if someone goes to them from the dead they will repent." Abraham replies: "If they do not listen to Moses and the prophets, neither will they be persuaded (to change their ways) even if someone rises from the dead."

That last sentence is the climax of the parable and declares its message. The message is the urgent importance of giving heed to the word of God; every element in the parable is subordinate to that. For this reason Jeremias preferred to call the parable not "The Rich Man and Lazarus," but "The Parable of the Six Brothers." He commented:

---

[94] For Lazarus going to Abraham cf. 4 Maccabees 13:17: "After our death in this fashion (i.e., with the same courage as the seven martyr brothers) Abraham, Isaac, and Jacob will receive us, and all our forefathers will praise us." The "chasm" which none can cross appears to be described in *1 Enoch* 18:11–12, "a desolate and terrible place." 1 Peter 3:18–22 and 4:6 seems to entail a different understanding of Hades.

They had their counterpart in the men of the Flood generation, living a careless life, heedless of the rumble of the approaching flood (Matthew 24:37–39), living in selfish luxury, deaf to God's word, in the belief that death ends all (v. 28).[95]

The "word of God" is certainly stated plainly in "Moses and the prophets," as Jesus made abundantly clear on many occasions, above all in his messianic exposition of the law in Matthew 5. His mission was to bring the Old Testament revelation to its completion and to fulfill its promise of life in the saving sovereignty of God.

It is noteworthy that what the deceased brother asked for was that Lazarus should be sent to warn his five brothers (v. 27), presumably in a dream or vision; when the request was denied, he renewed it and asked that Lazarus should *go from the dead to them* (v. 30). Abraham's objection that rejecters of the word of God will not believe though one "rises" from the dead is to be understood in that sense—a visitation from the realm of the dead is meant. Certainly that would have been an impressive sign, but insufficient to bring about authentic repentance. The Christian believer, when reading those words, cannot resist thinking of Easter and the resurrection of Jesus. That was no mere visitation from the world beyond; it was nothing less than God's vindication of Jesus as the Messiah-Redeemer (so e.g., Acts 2:36; Philippians 2:9–11; 1 Timothy 3:16) and the beginning of the new creation in him (2 Corinthians 5:17). The effect of that event in world history has been staggering, as its first proclamation by a Christian preacher on the day of Pentecost illustrates, and in the history of the church ever since.

Again, however, one cannot but recognize that not all who heard the earliest preaching of the gospel of Christ crucified and risen for the redemption of the world received it and believed it. The response of the Jewish high priests to Peter's proclamation of the gospel was anger, first that he preached in the person of Jesus resurrection from the dead (Acts 4:2—the priests were Sadducees, who rejected the doctrine of resurrection), secondly that Peter and the other preachers were blaming them for the death of Jesus (Acts 5:28; cf. 2:23–24). The mixed reception that the gospel received among the Jews was repeated among the nations in the first century, but whereas the time came when the Jewish people

---

[95] Jeremias, *Parables of Jesus,* 186.

generally rejected it, the Gentile nations increasingly accepted it, until it became (nominally, at least) the religion of the west.

In modern times the preacher of the gospel this side of the first Easter can claim one thing: the resurrection of Jesus showed that Moses and the prophets were right! So Luke in his resurrection narratives records Jesus as saying (Luke 24:27, 44-45, 46-47). That, too, we may declare in our proclamation of the gospel, but one thing we must not fail to do: we should repeat the dictum of Father Abraham at the close of the parable, lest modern hearers come under the same condemnation as the six brothers.

ii. The Wicked Tenant Farmers: Mark 12:1-12; Matthew 21:33-46; Luke 20:9-19

Discussion of this parable of Jesus, perhaps more than any other of his parables, has been dominated by the issue of whether it is a genuine parable or an allegory representing the dealings of God with his people. The opening sentence of Mark 12:1 recalls Isaiah's "love song of my beloved's vineyard" (Isaiah 5); therein God is the owner who prepared it, and the vineyard is Israel, who yielded to God wild grapes instead of authentic fruit. On this basis it was natural for Mark to set out from the same fundamental presupposition: God is the owner, the vineyard the nation, the slaves sent to collect the fruit the prophets sent by God to recall the people to repentance and obedience, and the owner's son is Jesus; the rejection and ill-treatment of the prophets through Israel's history culminated in the rejection and murder of the Son of God and the consequent judgment of God upon the nation. The violence of the tenant farmers in the parable is consistent with the interpretation of the fruit offered by Israel to God at the end of Isaiah's song:

> He expected justice, but saw bloodshed;
> righteousness, but heard a cry! (5:7, NRSV)

Mark concludes the parable with a citation of Psalm 118:22-23:

> The stone which the builders rejected
> has become the cornerstone;
> this was the Lord's doing,
> and it is amazing in our eyes.

In Mark's eyes (as of the church generally) the rejected stone is clearly Jesus, who has been vindicated by God. This identification has its counterpart in the description of the owner's son as his "beloved son" (v. 6); the expression is used by the voice from heaven addressed to Jesus at his baptism (1:11), and to the disciples, referring to Jesus, at his transfiguration (9:7); moreover it occurs in the Septuagint of Genesis 22:2, 12 regarding Isaac as Abraham's "only" son, in a story entailing a typology deeply embedded in the consciousness of the early church (cf. Romans 8:32); accordingly this element in the parable is often viewed as Mark's "christological" addition.

Matthew and Luke appear not only to have shared Mark's view of the parable as fundamentally allegorical, but to have carried further the same mode of interpretation. Mark tells of a single slave sent each time by the owner to the tenant farmers, the last being killed by them; he then adds in v. 5, "and many others; some they beat and some they killed," prior to the sending and murder of the son, evidently having the prophets in view. Matthew groups those sent into two companies. Of the first company, the tenants "beat one, killed another, and stoned another" (21:35); and when the owner sent another group they did similarly to them (v. 36). This would appear to represent the early and later prophets of Israel, but in following their sending with the mission of the "beloved son" Matthew has retained the threefold structure which is common in parables. He concludes the parable in v. 43 with the observation, ". . . the kingdom of God will be taken from you and given to a nation that produces its fruits," thereby giving the impression that the vineyard represents the kingdom of God and the church replaces Israel as its heir. Luke's version is closer to Mark's, but clearly continues the allegorical understanding of the parable. He follows the citation of Psalm 118 regarding the rejected stone with a reminiscence of Daniel 2:34–35, 44–45:

> Everyone who falls on that stone will be broken to pieces; and it will crush anyone on whom it falls. (Luke 20:18, NRSV)

It was noted by Rabbi Simeon ben Jose ben Laqonia that while in the scriptures the Israelites are compared with the rocks and the stones, the nations are compared with potsherds; he commented: "If the stone falls on the pot, woe to the pot! If the pot falls on the stone, woe to the pot! In either case, woe to the pot!"[96] Luke would have made a different application of that observation; for

---

[96] *Midrash Esther* 3, 6 (94b), cited in Strack-Billerbeck, *Kommentar zum NT,* 1.877.

the "stone cut without hands" was hurled to break the power of pagan rulers of this world, and Jewish rulers who reject the Messiah sent to them would suffer a similar fate.

The recognition of these allegorizing features in the parable led Jülicher to view it as a product of early Christian theology, and so a creation of the church.[97] At first many critical scholars agreed with him in this judgment, but there has been an increasing reaction to it. C. H. Dodd protested at the wholesale rejection of the authenticity of the parable. He maintained that the essential story in the parable was characteristic of the situation in Palestine, and especially Galilee, in the time of Jesus. Large estates in that period were owned by foreigners, who let out their lands to tenant farmers, but these grudged handing over the produce annually demanded. After the revolt of Judas the Gaulonite the whole area was disaffected and nationalist feeling ran high; the conditions therefore were present under which the refusal of rent could be the prelude to murder and forcible seizure of land by the peasantry. It is the logic of the story which caused the owner to send his son, and the tenants to stoop to his murder. The parable therefore stands on its own feet as a dramatic story, inviting a judgment from the hearers, and the application of the judgment is clear enough without any allegorizing of the details.[98]

When Dodd wrote that he assumed that the parable earlier circulated in a simpler form. Since then an example of what it may have been has come to light, namely the version in the *Gospel of Thomas*. It reads as follows:

> A good man had a vineyard. He gave it to husbandmen so that they would work it and that he would receive its fruit from them. He sent his servant so that the husbandmen would give him the fruit of the vineyard. They seized his servant, they beat him; a little longer and they would have killed him. The servant came, he told his master. His master said, "Perhaps he did not know them." He sent another servant; the husbandmen beat him as well. Then the owner sent his son. He said, "Perhaps they will respect my son." Since those husbandmen knew that he was the heir of the vineyard, they seized him, they killed him. Whoever has ears let him hear. Jesus said: Show me the stone which the builders have rejected; it is the corner-stone.[99]

---

[97] Jülicher, *Die Gleichnisreden Jesu*, 2.385–406.

[98] See Dodd, *Parables of the Kingdom*, 125–32.

[99] *Gospel of Thomas*, 65–66, translated by A. Guillaumont et al. in *The Gospel according to Thomas* (Leiden: Brill, 1959) 39.

It is noteworthy that this version does not have the allegorical elements seen in the parable in the Synoptic Gospels, and it retains the threefold structure typical of parables, as Matthew also does. It should not be assumed, however, that this was the original form of the parable. The last sentence is witness to a citation of Psalm 118:22, which the author of Thomas has omitted; he could as well have omitted the beginning of the parable which plainly echoes the Song of the Vineyard in Isaiah 5. And the penultimate sentence ("Whoever has ears . . . ") is probably imported from elsewhere (e.g., Mark 4:9). Nevertheless the opening sentence of Mark's version is an invitation to read the parable with an allegorical implication, particularly in light of the context in which it is set. Howard Marshall concludes his discussion of the origin of the parable thus:

> It seems possible, therefore, indeed probable, that we have here an authentic parable of Jesus which has obvious allegorical possibilities; these were developed in the tradition, but in such a way that the genuine latent thrust of the parable was expressed more clearly for a Christian audience.[100]

This solution of the problem commands the assent of a considerable number of contemporary scholars.[101]

The most important question raised by the parable is its intention. The answer to that depends on the identity of the addressees. Mark introduces the parable, "He began to say to them," (12:1), which harks back to 11:27ff. There representatives of the Sanhedrin ask Jesus what authority he possesses to do "these things," i.e., clearing the temple of its traders, and who gave him that authority. Mark follows the parable with the statement, "They sought to seize him . . . for they knew that the parable was addressed to them"; that confirms that the same questioners are in view, hence that the parable is bound up with the issue of his authority. Jesus did not, in fact, give a direct answer to the Jewish leaders' question. Instead he put to them one of his own: "The baptism of John, was it from heaven (i.e., commanded by God) or from men (i.e., John's own idea)?" The leaders' dilemma was

---

[100] Marshall, *Commentary on Luke*, 727.

[101] Note, e.g., the statement of Bonnard: "In a parable like this the whole text is at the same time tradition and commentary on sayings of Jesus," *Matthieu*, 317. See further Jeremias, *Parables of Jesus*, 70; H. Montefiore and H. E. W. Turner, *Thomas and the Evangelists* (SBT 35; London: SCM, 1962) 63–64; Crossan, *In Parables*, 91–95; Fitzmyer, *Gospel according to Luke*, 2.1280.

patent. John's baptism embodied his call to the nation to repent in light of the Messiah's impending coming for judgment, and they had neither repented nor received his baptism. Clearly they had not regarded John's baptism as "from heaven," but this they did not dare to say publicly because the people looked on John as a prophet; i.e., they believed that he had been sent from God. The Sanhedrin representatives therefore lamely replied that they did not know the answer to Jesus' question. Jesus then replied that he would not answer their question about his own authority. Mark follows this episode at once by the parable of the Wicked Tenants.

An extraordinary deduction has been drawn from this ordering of the two paragraphs. Two recent writers, motivated by quite different concerns, D. Stern[102] and A. M. Lowe,[103] have set forth the view that Jesus told the parable to condemn the Jewish leaders for their rejection of John the Baptist, leading to his subsequent death. Stern asserts, "If the wicked husbandmen are the Jewish leaders, then the figure of the son most clearly symbolizes John the Baptist."[104] Lowe sees in the cleansing of the temple, the question on the authority of Jesus, and the parables of the Two Sons, the Marriage Feast, and the Wicked Tenants a "Baptist sequence," wherein John the Baptist is the (obedient) son and the stone rejected by the builders.[105] This identification of the Son with John the Baptist is a curiosity of exegesis. The question of Jesus concerning the authority of John the Baptist surely had a simple rationale behind it: the ministries of John and Jesus were closely related, so that to acknowledge John's baptizing ministry as authorized by God carries with it the recognition of Jesus' ministry also; the refusal of the Jewish leaders to recognize *both* as sent by God demonstrated their guilt in rejecting God's message through them to his people.

The parable of the Wicked Tenants goes further. On the one hand it sets the guilt of Israel's leaders in rejecting the word of God

---

[102] D. Stern, "Jesus' Parables from the Perspective of Jewish Literature: The Example of the Wicked Husbandmen," in *Parable and Story in Judaism: Studies in Judaism and Christianity* (ed. C. Thoma and M. W. Wyschogrod; New York: Paulist, 1989) 42–80.

[103] "From the Parable of the Vineyard to a Pre-Synoptic Source," *NTS* 28 (1982) 257–63.

[104] Ibid., 65–66.

[105] "From the Parable of the Vineyard," especially 257–58. As to this view of Lowe, see Fitzmyer's comment in *Gospel according to Luke*, 2.1278.

in the context of Israel's history of rejecting the word through the prophets; on the other hand not only is the official leadership of Israel (the Sanhedrin) guilty, but also the contemporary spiritual leaders of the people who prided themselves on being experts in the law and custodians of the truth of God, the so-called scribes and Pharisees. Most of these were one in their conviction that Jesus led the people astray and in their determination that he must die according to the law's prescription (Deuteronomy 13:1–6; for such decisions see Mark 3:6; John 11:53).[106] This intention Jesus perceived with all clarity, and declared that the judgment of God would fall on these leaders for their iniquity, and that their role as spiritual leaders of the people would be given to "others" (Mark 12:9).

The question arises: Who are these "others"? Who but the leaders of those Jews who accepted the message from God that Jesus brought, i.e., in the first place the apostles appointed by him as his associates in his mission to Israel, and whom he would later commission for the wider mission to Israel and the nations?

If that is a startling thought it is not without parallel in the Gospels. The saying in Matthew 19:28/Luke 22:30b has obvious relevance here. But Matthew 21:43 has an expansion of Mark 12:9: "The kingdom of God will be taken from you and given to a nation that produces its fruits." Matthew sees that Israel will not only have new and renewed leaders, but that the people of God will be renewed as a whole in the church, which in his time consisted of Jews and Gentiles. If it is called new Israel, let it be remembered that it is Israel made new in the remnant, taking into itself followers of Jesus among the Gentile nations. Matthew has gone further in defining the new Israel as the heir of the kingdom of God. Does that mean that he has defined the vineyard as the kingdom of God? That is doubtful. He is making it plain that the kingdom of God is no longer exclusively Jewish but for all the Messiah's people.

Precisely that is the message of Matthew 8:11–12/Luke 13:28–29, where Jesus speaks of many coming from all parts of the world and joining Abraham, Isaac, and Jacob for the feast of the kingdom of God, whereas "the sons of the kingdom" will be

---

[106] On John 11:53 see E. Bammel, "Ex illa itaque die consilium fecerunt . . . (John 11:53)" in *The Trial of Jesus*, ed. E. Bammel (Festschrift C. F. D. Moule; SBT 2d series; London: SCM, 1971) 35, and the discussion in my commentary on John, 196–99.

excluded from it. That is a solemn warning to his fellow Jews to ensure that they do not miss the inheritance for which they were created. Similarly we may also see in the parable of the Wicked Tenants an unspoken call for repentance, even on the part of Israel's spiritual leaders. That would entail, as E. Schweizer saw, a fresh weighing up whether it is to be a Yes or a No to Jesus:

> Which it is depends upon whether a man thinks he has a special place in God's favor and can make special demands upon God; or whether he, like the Gentiles, waits for the grace of God with empty hands (cf. 7:24–30).[107]

And that is a challenge which the parable of the Wicked Tenant Farmers poses to every reader.

B. PARABLES OF ACTION IN RELATION TO THE KINGDOM OF GOD

1. Action Commensurate with the Presence of the Kingdom of God

i. The Good Samaritan: Luke 10:25–37

This famous parable of Jesus is reported only by Luke in the New Testament Gospels, and it has an interesting context. A lawyer "tests" Jesus with a question concerning what he must do to inherit eternal life (i.e., life in the future kingdom of God; the question is identical with that put to Jesus by a rich young man, Mark 10:17/Luke 18:18). While the term "test" can have the meaning of "tempt," there is no indication that in asking the question the teacher of the law has any hostile intention. "It is the supreme religious question," observed T. W. Manson, "and so the supreme test of a religious teacher. By their answers to just this question all religions are judged."[108] Instead of answering it, however, Jesus puts the ball into the questioner's court: "What is written in the law?" he asks, "How do you read it?" The lawyer replies by citing the double command of love, first from Deuteronomy 6:5, "You must love the Lord your God with all your heart, and with all your soul, and with all your strength, and with all your mind," and then Leviticus 19:18, but as a continuation of his

---

[107] Schweizer, *Good News according to Mark*, 242.
[108] Manson, *Sayings of Jesus*, 280.

sentence: ". . . and your neighbor as yourself." Jesus responds, "Right! Keep on doing this and you will have life in the kingdom of God."

This has a remarkable parallel in Mark 12:28–34. A scribe (another name for a lawyer) asks Jesus which is the greatest commandment of all. That is a natural question for a Jewish Bible teacher to ask, since to a Jew the Bible is the law (the Pentateuch) plus explanation in the rest of the books of the Old Testament. But the scribe knew perfectly well that a number of rabbis would have answered, "There is *no* greatest commandment, for *all* are important." So the question was really twofold: "Is there a greatest commandment? If so, what is it?" Like the other lawyer, he was testing Jesus! Jesus answered by setting together the two commandments of Deuteronomy 6:5 and Leviticus 19:18. The scribe applauded him for it, and Jesus said, "You're not far from the kingdom of God" (Mark 12:34).

The moot question that scholars ask is, Are these different events, or are they variant reports of one occasion? My own conviction is that they are different, and that Luke omitted Mark's account because he has such a good illustration of the commandment. The occasions are different because (i) the parable of the Good Samaritan is a notable answer to the lawyer's question, who in self-defense had asked, "Who is my neighbor?" (ii) It is not impossible that the lawyer himself could have cited the double commandment. On the one hand T. W. Manson urged that the conjunction of the two commands was so important that Jesus would have said it over and over again: "Great teachers constantly repeat themselves"; and the lawyer would have known that Jesus taught the double command.[109] On the other hand there is a Jewish work of uncertain date, *The Testaments of the Twelve Patriarchs,* that repeats three times in various ways the double command, "Love the Lord and your neighbor" (*Testament of Issachar* 5:2; 7:6; *Testament of Dan* 5:3). The difficulty about this is that this work has a number of Christian insertions (Christians liked the book!), and whereas various sections of it are among the Dead Sea scrolls, the Testaments of Dan and Issachar are not there, so we cannot use them as evidence that Jews in the time of Jesus did link the two commands in this manner. But the issue is not of first importance. When someone pointed out to Julius Wellhausen

---

[109] Ibid.

that nearly all the teaching of Jesus is contained in the Talmud he replied, "Yes, and a great deal more!" Thereby he indicated that Jesus concentrated on and wonderfully illuminated the primary issues of the Old Testament revelation. Certainly the double commandment dominated the life and teaching of Jesus, and it became central to his followers in the post-Pentecost church. It is an instance of Jesus' own assertion, "I came not to destroy, but to fulfill."

The lawyer's question, "Who is my neighbor?" is by no means superfluous, even if it was asked because he felt he looked silly. It could be viewed as a further test for Jesus, in view of the rabbinic discussions about it. In Leviticus 19:18 the command "Love your neighbor as yourself" relates not to the family next door, but to one's fellow Jew (check the passage, 19:13–18). In reality it embodies a great ideal: God's people should love all the members of their nation as truly as they love themselves; when the command is conjoined to Deuteronomy 6:5, they are to love one another with the same wholehearted devotion as they love the Lord. In practice, of course, that's difficult, and in Judaism distinctions came to be made in accordance with the ambiguity of the Hebrew word for "neighbor," *re'a.* It comes from the verb *ra'ah,* "to associate with," and has various descending meanings: (i) friend, companion, (ii) fellow-citizen, (iii) another person with whom one stands in reciprocal relations, (iv) other (as in "one another"), which can become weakest of all (see, e.g., 2 Kings 3:23). In Leviticus 19:33–34 the command to love the neighbor is extended to the alien who lives among the Jews in Palestine, but the rabbis applied that only to proselytes who fully identified themselves with Jews. Aliens who did not become proselytes within a year were viewed as heathen, and were excepted from commands relating to Israel's neighbors. For example, with regard to the biblical provision, "If someone willfully attacks and kills another (Hebrew: "his neighbor") by treachery, you shall take the killer from my altar for execution"; *Mekilta* on Exodus 21:14 (*Pisha* 86b) comments, " 'Against his neighbor,' that excludes the 'others' " (i.e., non-Israelites, for killing one of whom the Jew does not die). On Leviticus 20:10, "If a man commits adultery with the wife of his neighbor, both the adulterer and the adulteress shall be put to death," on which the same comment is made: "that shall exclude the wife of the 'other' " (non-Israelite). Deuteronomy 15:1–2 commands a remission of debts every seventh year, hence a creditor must not exact a debt from "a neighbor and his brother"; *Sipre Deut.* §112 comments on "neighbor," "excepted are the 'others' "; on "brother," "excepted is the foreigner" (who has not become a proselyte).[110]

One can see from these examples what a slippery concept "neighbor" had become in Judaism, and how it was that the lawyer posed his question to Jesus. The answer of Jesus, however, was not a definition of the term but a story. And what an amazing story it was in its setting!

A man "goes down" from Jerusalem to Jericho (so the Greek, literally). Apart from the Jews' habit of referring to "going down" from Jerusalem to anywhere in the country, Jericho was seventeen miles from Jerusalem via a rocky, winding road, infested by robbers, and that descended more than three thousand feet. Not surprisingly the traveler in the parable was mugged, and left half dead. A priest on his way home (many priests lived in Jericho), perhaps after performing duties in the temple, saw the victim and kept his distance—how could one know whether the robbers were watching? A Levite followed, one of those responsible for temple liturgy and for policing the temple; he did a little better than the priest: He "went up close" to see the victim properly, but decided not to attempt to help him. Did the priest and Levite think the man was dead and refrain from touching him to avoid defilement from a corpse? No mention is made of that; in any case regulations regarding touching corpses were in the Samaritan Pentateuch also, and did not prevent a Samaritan from going to the man's aid. Alas, these men's religion seems to have increased their heartlessness rather than overcome it.

The astonishing feature of the story is that the person who showed love in action towards the wounded Jew was a Samaritan, a member of a little nation whose relations with Israel were characterized by mutual hate. The Jews despised the Samaritans as half-heathen, descended from a remnant of Jews left in the land after the deportation of 722 B.C. and pagans brought in by the Assyrians; and heretics, because the Samaritans would not worship in the Jerusalem temple. The Samaritan temple on Gerizim was burned by the Jews in 128 B.C. The Samaritans in revenge strewed dead men's bones in the Jerusalem temple during a Passover between A.D. 6 and 9. But here was a Samaritan who

---

[110]These examples are cited from Strack-Billerbeck, *Kommentar zum NT,* 1.353–54.

overcame the traditional antipathy in the presence of a Jew in desperate need. He went to the limit in so doing, presumably using some of his own clothing for bandages, pouring in olive oil and wine to soften and disinfect the wounds, set the man on his own donkey, looked after him in the inn, paid for his continuing care by the innkeeper (two denarii—a day's board cost one twelfth of a denarius) and promised to pay for additional care if needed. That is *love in action* indeed!

Jesus follows the parable by a question addressed to the lawyer: "Which of the three do you think proved to be a neighbor of the one who fell into the hands of robbers?" Every preacher knows that Jesus' question was not the same as the lawyer's: the latter had asked, "Who is my neighbor?" Jesus in effect asked, "To whom am I a neighbor?" The parable supplies the answer to both questions.

This needs to be recognized, for some have maintained that Jesus' question concentrates attention not on the Samaritan but on the wounded man. R. Funk pointed out that Jews listening to Jesus will have been horrified to hear of a Samaritan helping a Jew; *they wouldn't want help from such a man!* He added:

> The narrative is not complete until the hearer is drawn into it as participant. . . . Is he willing to allow himself to be the victim, to be served by an enemy? . . . The future which the parable discloses is the future of every hearer who grasps and is grasped by his position in the ditch.[111]

On this view Jesus stands behind the Samaritan as the one from whom they want no help. Yet, Funk affirms, Jesus is declaring who God is, and that he is looking at the in-breaking of a kingdom nobody else sees. The parable is "permission on the part of Jesus to follow him, to launch out into a future that he announces as God's own."[112]

One appreciates that there are people who should be reminded where they are—in a ditch, needing Jesus—but that is not the lesson of the parable. It is provided by Jesus himself in his final words to the lawyer: "Go and do likewise." That is somewhat stronger than "permission" to follow him!

The parable still makes Jews uneasy. My brother-in-law was leading a party of tourists in Israel, and the group was traveling

---

[111] R. Funk, *Language, Hermeneutic, and the Word of God* (New York: Harper & Row, 1966) 214.

[112] Ibid., 215–16.

by coach on the road from Jerusalem to Jericho. They came to a point in the journey where the Israeli guide said to the passengers, "You have all doubtless heard the anti-Semitic story that Jesus told about a Samaritan who went to the aid of a wounded Jew; well, there is the so-called Inn of the Good Samaritan." My brother-in-law had something to say to the guide about that remark! But that man was not alone in his view of the "story." Samuel Sandmel was one of the best-known Jewish scholars of the United States to make himself expert on the Christian faith and the New Testament. He wrote a book, *Anti-Semitism in the New Testament*,[113] in which he admitted that in itself the parable is not anti-Jewish, but "in the total context of Luke it does lend itself to a possible alignment with other anti-Jewish passages." On the contrary, J. A. Fitzmyer, to whom I owe that quotation, observes that Luke's emphasis on the Samaritan is simply in line with his stress on universalism and the unimportant in Palestinian society.[114] A similar effect would be produced today if one were to substitute for "Samaritan" a member of the Hezbollah group who had compassion on an Israeli soldier dying of his wounds on the Golan Heights. It would be out of keeping with everything that one would expect from a member of Hezbollah, but entirely in harmony with the parable, and with the counsel of Jesus, "Go and do likewise." For that is kingdom of God action.

ii. The Unmerciful Servant: Matthew 18:23–35

The parable forms the conclusion of a discourse about relationships among the people of God, a discourse compiled by Matthew from his records of the teaching of Jesus. Immediately preceding the parable Peter addresses a question to Jesus: "How many times am I to forgive my brother when he sins against me? Is it up to seven?" "Not seven," replies Jesus, "but seventy-seven." Or is the number to be reckoned as "seventy *times* seven"? We're not sure. One cannot but recall the song of Lamech in Genesis 4, where he tells his wives:

> I have killed a man for wounding me,
> a young man for striking me.
> If Cain is avenged sevenfold,
> truly Lamech seventy-sevenfold. (Genesis 4:23–24, NRSV)

---

[113] Philadelphia: Fortress, 1978.
[114] *Gospel according to Luke*, 2.885.

A. H. M'Neile, noting the possibility of a recollection of that song in v. 24, remarked, "The unlimited revenge of primitive man has given place to unlimited forgiveness of Christians."[115] The pertinence of that comment indicates the secondary significance of the uncertainty of number in Jesus' answer to Peter. As W. D. Davies and D. C. Allison noted, "One is not commanded to count, but to forgive without counting."[116]

The question and answer on forgiveness is followed by the parable about forgiveness. The emphasis in the two passages is not the same, inasmuch as the issue in the former relates to forgiveness of repeated offense, whereas in the parable the immensity of God's forgiveness strongly contrasts with the trifling nature of the human offenses which we are called on to forgive. But the saying of Jesus and the parable have in common the thought of limitless forgiveness: on the one hand, the infinite compassion of God toward his children, which encourages them to forgive others; on the other hand, the readiness constantly to forgive those who offend us.

The parable begins with the comparison of the kingdom of heaven with a king who calls for a reckoning of accounts held by his "servants." "In the Bible and in the East 'the king's servants' is the term for his higher officials," said Jeremias. He pointed out that the magnitude of the sum involved shows that the "servant" must have been a governor of a province; in Ptolemaic Egypt a treasury official was personally responsible for the revenue from his province.[117] In the process of reckoning a governor was brought before the king who owed no less than ten thousand talents. That was a fantastic sum of money. A talent was worth six thousand denarii; ten thousand talents therefore amounted to six million denarii.[118] It is difficult to translate meaningfully a figure from the ancient world into modern currency. A denarius was the standard wage for a day's work in the lifetime of Jesus (Matthew 20:2), so six million

[115] A. H. M'Neile, *Gospel according to St. Matthew* (London: Macmillan, 1938) 268. The number is ambiguous, as in Genesis 4:24, where the Hebrew reads seventy-seven but the Septuagint seventy times seven. The same uncertainty is seen in the versions, with a tendency to read seventy times seven.

[116] Davies and Allison, *Gospel according to St. Matthew*, 2.793.

[117] Jeremias, *Parables of Jesus*, 210.

[118] See the article "Weights and Measures" by M. A. Powell in the *Anchor Bible Dictionary* (6 vols.; ed. D. N. Freedman et al.; New York: Doubleday, 1992) 6.907–8.

denarii, taking account of Sabbaths and holy seasons, represent the payment for twenty-two thousand years of work. That would have beggared the mind of any Palestinian peasant. The accused governor, accordingly, must be envisaged as having misused or misappropriated funds or failed to control subordinates on a huge scale, and as having been unable to recover the debt he had incurred. The king commanded therefore that he, his family, and his property be sold, not to recover the debt, for the proceeds of the sale would come nowhere near doing that, but to punish the offense. The governor, overwhelmed at the sentence, prostrated himself before the king and pleaded for time to repay what he owed (an impossible accomplishment to achieve!). The king, however, responded with unheard-of generosity: he took pity on him and canceled the entire debt.

One would have expected the miscreant governor to walk out on air from the king's presence. On the contrary, he found a lesser colleague who owed him a hundred denarii. If he "found" him, he first looked for him. His treatment of the man was as astounding as his own cancellation of debt, but in a reverse manner: he took him by the throat and choked him, and demanded instant repayment of what he was owed. The debtor then repeated precisely what the fellow who had him by the throat had done: he cast himself before his creditor and pleaded for time to gather the money; but the governor refused, and had him thrown into jail until he paid what he owed. The other officials who had witnessed what happened were aghast; they reported to the king what had happened. The king was furious and sent for the governor: "You scoundrel!" he said; "I cancelled all that debt when you appealed to me; weren't you bound to show mercy to your fellow servant as I showed mercy to you?" The king handed him over to the torturers till he paid everything that he owed. That he could never have done. So the man who showed no mercy to his fellow servant was condemned to be at the mercy of torturers for the rest of his days.

The extravagant proportions of this story have led some to believe that they have been exaggerated. It is recalled that in the parable of the Great Banquet the man who provided it was described by Luke as "a certain man," whereas in Matthew he was a king who arranged a banquet for his son's wedding (22:10–11). Ten thousand talents is so vast as a personal debt, it is suggested that the original sum must have been inflated; perhaps it was ten talents,[119] or ten thousand denarii.[120] When the story is scaled down in that manner the situation becomes more comprehensible: the "king" will have been a master *(kyrios)* with slaves (he is referred to five times in the parable as *kyrios,* but as king only once, v. 23). The cancellation of the debt of the steward (as he will have been) remains very generous, and should have led him to show similar generosity to his fellow servant who owed him so small a sum. The master's wrath in deciding in the first instance to have the steward put in prison till he repaid his debt, and later in handing him over to the torturers for the same purpose, again is comprehensible and within the bounds of possibility.[121]

The argument in favor of so scaling down the parable is plausible, but unconvincing. There is no parallel report of the story in the other Gospels with which to compare it. Many Jewish parables center on a king and his servants. Whereas the figures of the debts are astronomical, stories of such wealth in Gentile lands were not unknown in Palestine. Most important of all, we are not examining a report of an alleged historical event, but a parable that compares the infinite mercy of God to his erring creatures and the effect that it should have on their mutual relations. A debt is a familiar picture for sin—it occurs in the Lord's Prayer (Matthew 6:12/Luke 11:4). The gigantic debt of the governor to the king is a deliberate foil to the trifling debt owed by a colleague to the forgiven man—six hundred thousand times less than his own debt that had been remitted![122] The unwillingness of human beings to forgive others is thereby unforgettably caricatured. It is so utterly unreasonable. The king's wrath becomes reflected in our own reactions as we see therein a horrible reflection of experience that is all too common: it is scandalous, shocking, despicable, disgusting, contemptible, repulsive—words fail one to describe the attitude of the unforgiving man in the parable to his fellow servant, the more so as we take into account that he is typical of too many of us Christians. Eduard Schweizer acknowledges that the exaggeration manifest in this parable, like that of the Wheat

---

[119] So Manson, *Sayings of Jesus,* 213.

[120] See M. C. de Boer, "Ten Thousand Talents? Matthew's Interpretation and Redaction of the Parable of the Unforgiving Servant," *CBQ* 50 (1988) 214–32.

[121] Such is the interpretation of Davies and Allison, *Gospel according to St. Matthew,* 2.795–97.

[122] Correcting Eduard Schweizer, who made it five hundred thousand times less (*Good News according to Matthew,* 378).

and Darnel, shows our inability to define the kingdom of God in human images:

> God's inconceivable act of mercy, which contradicts all human notions of justice, is so displayed that the listener can only stand in awe and amazement. So incomprehensibly great is God's goodness toward man, his strange righteousness that restores instead of destroying. When God's goodness comes alive in Jesus' preaching and ministry, transforming the world, only creation itself is comparable.[123]

The primary purpose of the parable, then, is to illustrate the illimitable nature of God's forgiveness in such a manner as to inspire forgiveness in his children. B. T. D. Smith expressed it very simply: "Matthew 6:14–15 gives the moral of the story."[124] That passage reads thus:

> If you forgive others their trespasses, your heavenly Father will also forgive you; but if you do not forgive others, neither will your Father forgive your trespasses. (NRSV)

Daniel Patte, on the basis of that saying, declares that disciples should forgive those who have wronged them before asking for God's forgiveness. Asking whether forgiveness of others is a condition for receiving forgiveness from God, he replies, "The text does not allow us to give any other answer than a positive one." He adds:

> Clearly, this radical attitude of forgiveness is made possible by God's prior intervention, but so far in the Gospel, this prior intervention has not been described as God's forgiveness.[125]

In accordance with this Patte does not believe that the parable teaches that people are under obligation to forgive others because they have been forgiven by God: that, he claims, would contradict all that Matthew said concerning the internalizing of God's will (Matthew 5:21–28). It is the relationship of a tightly bound community, embracing the king and his people, that makes people forgive "from the heart" (18:35). The unforgiving servant sees no value in such a community, hence for him forgiving people is pointless.[126]

---

[123] Ibid., 378–79.

[124] B. T. D. Smith, *Parables of the Synoptic Gospels* (Cambridge: Cambridge University Press, 1937) 219.

[125] Patte, *Gospel according to Matthew*, 89.

[126] Ibid., 256–57.

No Christian with understanding would wish to diminish the importance of the church as the reconciled family of God, which wants to maintain its unity in love to one another. But the church is what it is because of the redeeming and recreative work of God in Christ. The Sermon on the Mount was not preached in full at the beginning of Jesus' ministry as a kind of manifesto of things to come. It is a summary of the life in the kingdom of God which was initiated through God's action in Jesus, declared in his preaching, revealed in his deeds of power, and climaxed in his death and resurrection. The Sermon presupposes all that. Matthew along with Mark and Luke tells of the healing of the paralytic, to whom Jesus spoke the assuring word, "Your sins are forgiven." When scribes present objected to such a declaration as blasphemous Jesus said, "That you may know that the Son of Man has authority on earth to forgive sins"—he said to the paralyzed man, "Stand up, take your bed, and go home," and he did so (Matthew 9:2–8). The renewal that the saving sovereignty of God effects is manifest in the healing of the paralyzed man in Capernaum; that enables a follower of Jesus to say the Lord's Prayer as *a forgiven person who wishes to continue in the fellowship of the forgiven, and so must forgive in order to remain forgiven;* and that same kingdom of God renewal lies behind the parable of the Unforgiving Servant.

Not the least remarkable feature of the parable is that the servant's experience of the king's munificent forgiveness appears to have made no effect on his character. He had not grasped its significance, hence he lost it. Matthew 6:14–15 attests the possibility of believers' being in the same position. I have personally known the anger of some Christians on declaring to them the plain meaning of Matthew 6:14–15, when their consciences smote them. Accordingly, as in all the parables of Jesus, there is an unspoken, yet unmistakable appeal for hearers and readers to repent, and gain—and regain—the full blessing of life in the kingdom of God, and live in accord with the gift that has been bestowed.

2. Action in the Light of the Future of the Kingdom of God

i. The Dishonest Estate Manager: Luke 16:1–8

As the title implies, the parable centers on the manager of the estate of a wealthy man. The owner does not appear to live on his estate, for he receives an accusation about the administrator, and asks him, "What is this that I am hearing about your squandering my property?" The manager can hardly have been doing that if the owner had been on the spot; presumably the latter had been living in another property, whether in the same country or abroad.

Among the Jews an estate manager was not infrequently a slave born in the house and trained to occupy so responsible a position. In the parable, however, this person would have been a freeman, since when faced with the prospect of being relieved of his work he did not know where he would go, or what he would do for a living. A manager of an estate certainly had an authoritative position. He was appointed as an agent of the owner, and on the basis of the Jewish maxim, "A man's agent is as himself," he had full authority to act with the legal capacity of his master.[127] Such a position was one of trust, and it is evident that this manager had abused the trust placed in him. For this reason he was summoned by his master and told that he must give up his position at once, and that he must render a statement of his "management," i.e., provide an inventory of the estate, a list of his transactions, of debtors and what they owe.[128] No protestations of innocence are recorded (contrast the merciless governor of Matthew 18); we are given the impression of a man who was stunned, in total uncertainty as to what he should do and where he should go.

There followed a flash of insight: "I've got it! I know what I'll do!" He sent for the debtors and reduced their liability one by one. A couple of examples are given as to his procedure. One man owed a hundred "baths" of olive oil. A "bath" (a Hebrew measure) appears to be about nine gallons, so this person (who would surely have been a merchant) owed the cost of about nine hundred gallons, worth about one thousand denarii. He was given his bill and told to write a fresh one for five hundred denarii (it needed to be in his own handwriting). Another owed payment on a hundred "kors" of wheat, i.e., somewhat over a hundred bushels; the value of that would have been about twenty-five hundred denarii. This man was told to write a bill for eighty bushels, a deduction of a fifth of the price. It so happens that the cash saving on the two bills cited was about the same, since oil was dearer

---

[127] J. D. M. Derrett, "Fresh Light on Luke XVI," *NTS* 7 (1960–61) 198–219.
[128] So Fitzmyer, *Gospel according to Luke*, 2.1100.

than wheat.[129] The question arises on what basis the manager made the reductions of debt, for these are mere examples of his actions. Therein lies a much discussed problem.

Traditionally it has been assumed that the manager simply falsified the accounts in order to win friends among the many debtors of his master; that will have been in line with the accusation that he squandered the owner's property: he was continuing his accustomed dishonesty in a blatant fashion. It is certainly true that his motive in reducing the debts was to win friends on whose hospitality he could live for a long time (v. 4). There is, however, a difficulty about this solution: in v. 8 it is stated that the "master" praised his dishonest manager for acting so prudently, when he was robbing him of yet more money! Admittedly there is some uncertainty about that, for the term *kyrios* is ambiguous; twice in the parable it denotes "master" (i.e., of the estate, vv. 3, 5), and outside the parable again in v. 13 ("No man can serve two masters"); yet Luke in his Gospel frequently uses *kyrios* for "Lord," i.e., Jesus. If Jesus were in mind here that would compound the difficulty, for then it would be Jesus who praised the dishonest manager for his criminal actions; that has led some non-Christians to criticize Jesus for adopting a double ethical standard. Most modern exegetes consider that the *kyrios* in v. 8 refers to the master in the parable, since in v. 9 Luke makes a fresh start ("And I say to you . . ."), thereby apparently distinguishing Jesus from the estate owner. The one way of easing this difficulty of praising criminal action would be that of T. W. Manson, who said:

> Whether it is the employer or Jesus that speaks, we must take the purport of the speech to be: "This is a fraud; but it is a most ingenious fraud. The steward is a rascal; but he is a wonderfully clever rascal!"[130]

A totally different solution to the problem of the manager's action that wins the approbation of his employer is possible: the reduction of the debts exemplified in the parable is not in the least criminal but the very opposite; in each case it is *an elimination of interest*, so that the sum written down by the debtors was the actual sum they owed.

---

[129] For information on these quantities and prices see Jeremias, *Parables of Jesus*, 181, and the commentaries on Luke of I. H. Marshall and J. A. Fitzmyer ad loc.

[130] Manson, *Sayings of Jesus*, 292.

This suggestion came from J. D. M. Derrett, who has much expertise in oriental law. The chief point is that in the Old Testament it is unlawful for Jews to charge interest on loans to fellow Jews, an enactment of which Judaism continued to be very aware. But Jews who were tempted to venture into the field of money-lending, like Moslems who have a similar law, were always finding ways of evading that law. One of the major ways was to liquidate debts and restate them in terms of natural products, a practice which appealed to the Pharisees. They argued that when people had a product like oil, for example, to "borrow" more of the same at a price was not strictly charging interest. Every debtor will have had enough oil to light a lamp and enough wheat to make a loaf, so loans were translated into the prices of wheat and oil, and charges made accordingly. On this practice Derrett stated:

> The Pharisees had thus been scrupulous; their scrupulosity had not amended the court-law; and it had been vitiated by an enormous loophole. The reason why that loophole was there is stated indirectly by Luke: they were lovers of money, and piety and good business ought not to be incompatible.[131]

Needless to say, interest on the loans will have been charged by the manager as part of the remit by the estate owner, and it will have been heavy: 25 percent in the case of the wheat (the usual interest rate) and 50 percent in the case of the oil (reminiscent of the astronomical figures of the parable of the Merciless Governor in Matthew 18!). The delight of the debtors will have known no bounds. But what about the estate owner, who lost the interest? All the debtors will have assumed that he was the one responsible for canceling it, and in so doing he was acting in obedience to the law of God. What a godly man he was! Yes, indeed, but how could he possibly deny that it had anything to do with him? He was wearing a halo such as he never had before, and he felt good! The manager had hit on an extraordinary scheme for securing gratitude from the debtors and approbation from his master, which, according to the parable, he ungrudgingly gave ("he *praised* the dishonest manager for acting prudently!").

There is a third suggestion, made by J. A. Fitzmyer. He points out that when an agent lent his master's property out to others the promissory notes included charges plus commission or interest, without separate mention of the latter. In this case when

---

[131] Derrett, "Fresh Light on Luke XVI," 208.

the dishonest manager requested the debtors to make out fresh promissory notes, they were to do so minus the interest, for *that was his commission which he was foregoing.* That explains the exceptionally cheerful attitude of his employer. "The master praises the manager for his prudence, because he realizes that the manager has eliminated his own commission from the original usurious bonds."[132]

Fitzmyer freely admits that such reduction of sums is not attested elsewhere, as far as he knows. The same, presumably, would apply to the manager's actions on Derrett's interpretation. It would, indeed be possible to link the two interpretations together—the technical avoidance of interest as Derrett has expounded, and the manager's giving up his commission as Fitzmyer suggests. One must admit, however, that the latter would be out of keeping with the manager's accustomed way of life, there is no hint that he is giving up anything to accomplish his ends, and the owner of the estate comes off scot free. While the issue can be left open there is one aspect of the story that may affect our decision, namely Dan Via's suggestion that the parable has the flavor of a picaresque comedy. That is a technical expression for a story which centers on "a successful rogue who makes conventional society look foolish but without establishing any positive alternative. . . . Shallowness and not criminality is the key to his character. He secures and plays on his victim's consent and has a rudimentary rather than a distorted soul."[133] Robin Hood, with his constant getting the better of the sheriff of Nottingham, is the most famous example of this kind of character. So the manager in the parable "in one way or another won the approval of his victimized employer. It is this element of success which belongs to the picaresque mode."[134] That would favor Derrett's interpretation of the story.

So now we must ask, What is the lesson of the parable? Let us note that although Luke states that the parable is addressed to the disciples (v. 1) the immediately preceding parables of chapter 15 are said to have been directed to the Pharisees (15:1–3), and they are represented as still present in the background (16:14–15). Luke, or his source, apparently sees the purpose of the parable in v. 9, to which he has added vv. 10–15:

---

[132] Fitzmyer, *Gospel according to Luke,* 2.1098.
[133] Via, *The Parables,* 159–60.
[134] Ibid., 161.

Use your worldly wealth to win friends for yourselves, so that when money is a thing of the past you may be received into an eternal home. (REB)

This rendering of REB avoids the idea that money can win friends who will welcome us in heaven when we come to die. The third person plural ("they may welcome . . . ") is a common way of expressing a passive (as in v. 4); in Jewish writings it is often a way of referring to an action of God, and in that case it would mean "that God may welcome you." That expresses an eschatological lesson, namely, taking steps to prepare for life with God in his eternal kingdom; generous giving of alms can be a way of showing love to God and man.

But the parable depicts an urgency in the manager's situation, for he was in a crisis with which he had to come to terms immediately. That reminds us of the central message of Jesus to his people, summarized in Mark 1:15: "Repent, for the kingdom of God is upon you." That message Jesus continued to preach, but more and more emphasizing the necessity for the people to repent, for on the whole they had not done so, and the danger of their reaping what they were sowing was increasing (cf. Luke 13:1–5, 6–9, 22–30, 34–35; 19:41–44; 23:27–31). Accordingly in this parable Jesus appeals to hearers who had not responded to the message of the kingdom of God to turn to God *now,* and thereby avert judgment and gain the kingdom.

ii. The Judge and the Widow: Luke 18:1–8

Luke has placed this parable immediately following a series of sayings in the source common to him and to Matthew which speak of "the day when the Son of Man is revealed" (17:22–37). As Matthew does not reproduce the parable, it will have come from the source available to Luke alone, so he has linked it with related teaching. Of it C. E. B. Cranfield affirmed: "The passage expresses what I take to be the characteristic eschatology of the New Testament as a whole."[135] Needless to say, it is just as truly characteristic of Jesus.

Luke introduces that parable with what amounts to an interpretation of it: "He told them a parable about the need to pray continually and never lose heart." That sounds as though

---

[135] C. E. B. Cranfield, "The Parable of the Unjust Judge: The Eschatology of Luke–Acts," *SJT* 16 (1963) 300.

Jesus was giving a purely general exhortation to pray, whereas the parable encourages persistent prayer for the deliverance of God's people when his kingdom comes in power. It may be viewed as a stimulus to continue seriously to pray, "Thy kingdom come." Interestingly, Luke immediately follows his version of the Lord's Prayer with a parable closely related in intent, namely, the Friend at Midnight (11:5–8); it is as though he recognizes that if God is prepared to answer prayer for the coming of the kingdom, we should not hesitate to bring our lesser needs to him.

The parable is recounted in two parts, vv. 2–5, telling of an unscrupulous judge and a widow who pestered him to come to her aid, and an interpretation in vv. 6–8a, plus a challenging question at its close (v. 8b). The judge is introduced first as one who had "no fear of God or respect for man." Jewish trials were held in synagogues; how is it that a man who boasted that he had no fear of God or respect for man came to be a judge in Israel? J. D. M. Derrett informs us that at this time a secular system existed alongside the usual Jewish system of courts; it was open to any Jew to resort to the former, though the Torah forbade the people to do so. Perhaps because of fear that her case might be settled by arbitration or compromise, which was not unknown in Jewish courts, the widow went straight to the administrative judge and asked him, "Take up my case against my opponent" (not, as in KJV, "Avenge me of my adversary"). She wanted justice, not revenge, but had little hope of it unless one like this independent judge sorted it out.[136]

The judge wouldn't listen to the woman at first, but neither would she take no for an answer; she "kept on coming" with the same request (v. 3). At length the judge gave way, and that for a significant reason: "Even though I have no fear of God or respect for man . . . I will take up this woman's case *to stop her from disgracing me*" (vv. 4–5). The word rendered "disgrace" is a paraphrase for *hypōpiazō*; it originated in boxing, and means "to give a black eye." The thought of the judge dreading the widow doing that to him is not a little comical, and so through the years the word has been paraphrased rather weakly by "lest she wear me out." Derrett pointed out that in many cultures throughout the Orient the term signifies "blacken," i.e. to disgrace. "This very

---

[136] J. D. M. Derrett, "Law in the New Testament: The Parable of the Unjust Judge" *NTS* 18 (1972), especially 185–87.

ancient Asian idea goes back to a time when the words for the colours were few; the sallow skin turned ashen gray at the moment of realization of disgrace."[137] So the man who had no respect for men fears that a widow woman could defame and disgrace him! We are to assume that the judge did what the woman wanted.

Now what has that to do with prayer? Jesus gives the answer:

> Listen to what the unjust judge says.
> Surely God will bring about justice for his elect
> who cry to him day and night, won't he?
> And he will be patient with them, won't he?

It is almost universally assumed that Jesus is here contrasting the unjust judge with God, as though to say, "If a judge like that would give way to the pleas of a helpless widow and see that justice is done for her, how much more will God listen to the prayers of his people and bring about their deliverance!" That is a perfectly acceptable interpretation, but Derrett has put forward another possibility. The judge's action on behalf of the widow was prompted by one consideration: *he did not want his name to be disgraced.* God also has a name to be maintained, a name for faithfulness to his covenant and promises to his people.[138] This is often referred to in the Old Testament, but nowhere so strikingly as in Ezekiel 36:16–32, the heart of which is in vv. 20–22:

> Whenever they (the Jews) came among the nations, they caused my holy name to be profaned. It was said of them, "These are the Lord's people, and it is from his land they have gone into exile." So I spared them for the sake of my holy name which the Israelites had profaned among the nations to whom they had gone. Therefore tell the Israelites that the Lord God says: It is not for the sake of you Israelites that I am acting, but *for the sake of my holy name.* (REB)[139]

This interpretation, that God as well as the unrighteous judge is concerned for his name, appears to me preferable to the usual

---

[137] Derrett adds: "To the European (= Westerner) this is difficult to understand, since disgrace does not have the tragic and paralysing connotations it has in the East, where people will lose everything, even their lives, rather than lose their prestige, and where an enemy wishes nothing so much as that his enemy's prestige should suffer" (ibid., 190).

[138] Ibid., 191.

[139] We have already drawn attention to this passage to illustrate the petition in the Lord's Prayer, "Hallowed be thy name"; it must have been of special importance to Jesus.

one, not least in that the second part of the parable is then continuous with the first, and makes the parable a unity.

A further issue of interest is the relationship of this parable to a passage in Sirach 35. It reads as follows:

> The Lord is a judge who knows no partiality.
> He has no favourites at the poor man's expense,
> but listens to his prayer when he is wronged.
> He never ignores the appeal of the orphan,
> or the widow when she pours out her complaint.
> How the tears run down the widow's cheeks,
> and her cries accuse the man who caused them!
> . . . The prayer of the humble pierces the clouds,
> but he is not consoled until it reaches its destination.
> He does not desist until the Most High intervenes,
> gives the just their rights, and sees justice done.
> The Lord will not be slow,
> neither will he be patient with the wicked,
> until he crushes the sinews of the merciless
> and sends retribution on the heathen. . . . (vv. 12–15, 17–18, NEB)

The likeness of the above to the parable of Jesus is remarkable, not only the emphasis on prayer for God's intervention on behalf of the righteous, which is answered, but also the couplet,

> *The Lord will not be slow,*
> *neither will he be patient with the wicked.*

Most scholars hold that the question of Jesus in v. 7 echoes that statement, but with a significant modification: Ecclesiasticus says that the Lord in answer to his people's cry will not be patient with the wicked but will destroy them. Jesus says that God *is* patient (the same unusual verb), but *patient with his people who cry to him for deliverance,* which will certainly come, though they may have to wait for it.[140]

If it be asked, "What has Jesus to do with Sirach?" we would point out that it was a favorite book of the Qumran community; its members prepared themselves to be the instruments through whom the (two) Messiahs would achieve the annihilation of the wicked. Jesus implies that that is not the task of the priests of Qumran, the Zealots, or anyone else in Israel. Their mission is to receive the word of the kingdom and spread it

---

[140] On the interpretation of *makrothymei ep' autois,* which we have interpreted as "(God) is patient over them," see Marshall, *Commentary on Luke,* 674–75.

through the nation, and withal to pray that the Lord who brought it will himself complete it.

And that leads to the unexpected conclusion to the parable: "When the Son of Man comes, will he find (the) faith on the earth?" This question does not suggest a fear on Jesus' part that faith will have disappeared from the earth when he returns. His service of the kingdom, his teaching on it, his forming a people to be its instrument, and his anticipation of his death and resurrection for it, all rule out any thought of pessimism. The question he asked is to be weighed by every hearer of the parable.

Clearly the disciples must face it. They have heard Jesus warn of difficulties ahead through their association with him; will they have the faith that endures the opposition they will meet and fearlessly go on, in confidence that God will keep his word? Will they persist in prayer for the kingdom, foreshadowed by the widow in the parable, certain that God will fulfill his will for his people and for the world?

We know that when Jesus addressed his disciples others were often listening too, uncommitted to him, yet fascinated by his teaching, for they were among those who, like Simeon, were looking for the consolation of Israel (Luke 2:25). They heard his message of the kingdom, and sometimes saw it in action through his deeds of power. The faith of which Jesus speaks in Luke 18:8 includes acknowledgment of him as the Son of Man, which determines entry into the awaited kingdom (Luke 12:8f.). Will the Son of Man find that faith in them? Each one has to answer the question for himself or herself.

The conclusion of Luke's version of the eschatological discourse of Jesus is very close to the conclusion of the parable we have been considering:

> Be on the alert, praying at all times for strength to pass safely through all that is coming and to stand in the presence of the Son of Man. (21:36, REB).

They who respond positively to that appeal of Jesus will be amongst those in whom the Son of Man will find the faith for which he looks.

iii. Ten Young Women and a Wedding: Matthew 25:1–13

The picture of Palestinian wedding customs given in the parable before us presupposes considerable differences from those of a modern Western wedding. In the Anglo-Saxon tradition the central figure is the bride, plus her bridesmaids in their beautiful dresses, and the bridegroom waits for the bride to arrive for the marriage service. In the old Jewish tradition that is reversed; the bridegroom may keep his bride waiting a very long time! The extraordinary feature of this description of a Jewish wedding (the ceremony itself is not described) is that there is no mention at all of the bride! At least, that is true of the great majority of manuscripts of Matthew. There are some very reliable manuscripts which in the opening sentence read that the ten young women went out with their lamps "to meet the bridegroom *and the bride.*" It is the conviction of most scholars that the reference to the bride is a later insertion by copyists, who did not notice that the mention of the bride would disturb the interpretation of the parable. In view of the theme of the parable attention is quite deliberately fastened on the coming of the bridegroom.

Western weddings are normally held in the morning or afternoon; that depicted in the parable has not begun by midnight. The bridegroom with his friends are welcomed by a group carrying lamps or torches; the lights are cheerful, and are needed for the bridegroom and his friends to see the way. The wedding feast (in Britain always called "wedding breakfast"!) in the west is a single meal, though increasingly the meal is followed by further entertainment; in the east, when the bride is a virgin, the celebrations last for a week.

Strictly speaking, the parable describes no more than the preliminaries to the actual wedding, but to illustrate more fully what the parable presupposes, it may be of interest to cite the report by the father of Joachim Jeremias of a Jerusalem wedding which took place early in the twentieth century:

> In the late evening the guests were entertained in the bride's house. After hours of waiting for the bridegroom, whose coming was repeatedly announced by messengers, at last he came, half an hour before midnight, to fetch the bride; he was accompanied by his friends, floodlit by burning candles, and received by the guests who had come out to meet him. The wedding assembly then moved off, again in a flood of light, in festal procession to the house of the bridegroom's father, where the marriage ceremony and fresh entertainment took place.[141]

Jeremias added that the reception of the bridegroom with lights and the hours-long waiting for the bridegroom's arrival are often

---

[141] Jeremias, *Parables of Jesus,* 173.

mentioned in reports of Arab weddings in Palestine. The usual reason for the delay is inability to agree about the presents due to the relatives of the bride—both for the bridegroom to show proper regard for them, and on the other hand for the bride's relatives to compliment the bridegroom by showing reluctance in giving the bride to him.

This is one of the instances where the old issue arises of whether we have here a true parable or an allegory. No little heat has been expended in settling it, in part due to varied interpretations of the passage. Matthew has linked the parable with the discourse of chapter 24, in which he has brought together Mark's discourse on the tribulation of Israel and the coming of Christ in chapter 13, plus the eschatological teaching of Jesus in the source he has in common with Luke (12:35–46; 17:26–27); with the three parables of chapter 25 it is the longest section in the Gospels on the climax of the age. Plainly Matthew sees in the parable the coming of Christ the bridegroom for his bride the church. Not a few scholars hold that Matthew has presented a post-Easter view, chiefly on the grounds that (i) the parable reflects the church's experience of the delay of Christ's coming;[142] (ii) the belief that the representation of the Messiah as a bridegroom is foreign to the Old Testament and the literature of early Judaism;[143] (iii) the conviction that the original parable had in view not the coming of the Lord, but the eschatological crisis precipitated by the ministry of Jesus, which the Jews were ignoring.[144] None of these viewpoints is really plausible.

(i) The emphasis in the parable on the delay of the bridegroom's arrival is integral to the picture of an oriental wedding, and as we have seen, it applies to this very day. It is unreasonable for it to be made a ground for attributing the parable to the later church. (ii) It is rare for Jeremias to nod, like Homer, over a datum of early Jewish literature, but he has done so here. Max Meinertz has pointed out that the Targum on the Wedding Psalm, 45:3, comments: "Your beauty, O King Messiah, is more excellent than that of the rest of the children of men"; Meinertz states that that

---

[142] So G. Bornkamm, "Die Verzögerung der Parusie," *In Memoriam E. Lohmeyer* (ed. W. Schmauch; Stuttgart: Evangelisches Verlagswerk, 1951) 123–25.

[143] So Jeremias, *Parables of Jesus*, 52.

[144] Thus Dodd, *Parables of the Kingdom*, 172. Whereas Dodd stressed the ministry of Jesus as constituting the eschatological crisis, Jeremias believed it to be the imminent end of the age (*Parables of Jesus*, 53).

psalm was taken into the canon because it was understood as a messianic psalm.[145] Jeremias himself later alluded to *Pesiq.* 149a, in which the bridegroom of Isaiah 61:10 is interpreted of the Messiah.[146] In any case Jesus in Mark 2:19 refers to himself as the messianic bridegroom, adapting the concept of the feast of the kingdom to that of celebrating with his friends the "marriage" festival of the Bridegroom-Messiah. (iii) The belief that the parable of the Young Women has in view the developing eschatological crisis precipitated by Jesus is linked both by Dodd and Jeremias with other parables which they believe to have the same meaning, namely the Burglar (Matthew 24:42–44) and the Faithful Servant (24:45–51). On this issue W. G. Kümmel points out that this interpretation not only waters down these parables but gives no explanation why in all of them the *coming* of the master, the bridegroom, the thief is constantly mentioned. "It follows also," wrote Kümmel, "from all these exhortations to be on the alert and to be prepared that Jesus describes the coming of the Son of Man, and therewith the entry of the kingdom of God, as possibly very imminent . . . although its actual date was completely unknown."[147]

This brief review of arguments that the parable is an allegory would be unnecessary were it not for the insistence of some that the allegorical features are the marks of a late misunderstanding of the teaching of a (possibly) original parable. These positions we have seen reason to believe are false. We have further noted that parables frequently have within them allegorical elements, so that such elements are of themselves insufficient grounds for denying their integrity.

The purpose of the parable of the Young Women is not difficult to elucidate: it is the necessity to be on the alert for the coming of the Lord. In light of Palestinian wedding customs the opening sentence makes this evident: "The kingdom of heaven is like the situation of ten young women who took their lamps and went out to meet the bridegroom." These girls are not to be understood as friends of the bride but as servant girls who are charged with the task of escorting the bridegroom to the bride's house, and afterwards to his own or his parents' house. Since they

---

[145] M. Meinertz, "Die Tragweite des Gleichnisses von den zehn Jungfrauen," *Synoptische Studien* (A. Wikenhauser; Munich: K. Zink, 1953) 100.

[146] Jeremias, *Parables of Jesus*, 52 n. 12.

[147] Kümmel, *Promise and Fulfillment*, 58–59.

are said at the outset to have gone out to meet the bridegroom we are to assume that they had all lit their lamps and begun their vigil. The difference between the wise and foolish girls consists of one thing: since all had to ensure that their lamps remained alight when the bridegroom arrived, and since it was impossible to know when that would be, it was imperative for them to take an additional supply of oil; a jug full was enough, but the wise took the precaution and the foolish did not.

Time went by, but the bridegroom did not appear and the girls all nodded off. Their lamps continued to burn, and the oil was becoming low. Then came the cry at midnight: "Look, the bridegroom! Go out to meet him!" The sensible young women poured the extra oil in their lamps, trimmed the wicks, and were ready to go. The foolish ones saw that their lamps were going out, and they asked the others to give them some of their oil. They refused, for they couldn't be sure how much they would need for the bridegroom, so they told them to go and buy their own. While they were gone the bridegroom came, and the door was shut. When the foolish young women came back and appealed to the bridegroom to be allowed in, his reply was, "I don't know you." That is a Jewish idiom meaning, "I want nothing to do with you." In this context it is the equivalent of last judgment.

The parable closes with a saying that may have been independent or its true conclusion: "Keep on the alert, then, for you do not know the day or the hour," i.e., of the coming of the Lord. Naturally, it's not a call to remain awake literally (all the young women in the parable slept); it's a call to be vigilant, for it is possible to find the door of the kingdom shut. P. Bonnard asked how we are to do that, i.e., to live in a state of preparedness for that day. He found the clue in the two parables that follow this one: to accomplish faithfully the mission received (vv. 14–30), and to go to the aid of the least of the brothers and sisters of the Son of Man (vv. 31–46).[148]

iv. The Talents and the Pounds: Matthew 25:14–30; Luke 19:11–27

Formerly it was assumed that these two parables, which have a very similar plot, were spoken by Jesus on different occasions. In more recent times scholars have concluded that the similarities are so close, the differences are due mainly to vari-

---

[148] Bonnard, *Evangile selon St. Matthieu*, 358.

ations within the gospel tradition as it handed on a single parable of Jesus, and in measure to the evangelists themselves. The two versions reproduce an identical story: a man hands over to his servants sums of money for trading and goes away; on returning home he interrogates them as to how they fared in their transactions; two report that they have made profits and are rewarded; one admits to having been afraid to do anything with the money, criticizes the master for being harsh, and hands back the sum given to him; the master rebukes this third man for his laziness and for not putting the money to use in a bank; he then gives the sum to the one who has made the most profit.

Luke's version sets the story in a special situation: the man who gives his servants sums of money is a nobleman who goes abroad to claim for himself a kingdom; his citizens object, and send a delegation to declare, "We don't want this man as our king"; but he is appointed, and on his return, after dealing with his servants, he has his opponents slaughtered in his presence. This story is so similar to an event contemporary with the boyhood of Jesus that most believe it to be based on it.[149] After the death of Herod the Great his son Archelaus went to Rome, hoping that the emperor would confirm him as king in succession to Herod. A delegation of fifty Jews also went to oppose his appointment as king and to ask that the nation be joined to Syria and ruled by a governor. The emperor decided to give Archelaus half the kingdom, but disallowed him the title of king till he should prove his worth; the rest of the land he distributed among his brothers. We have no record of Archelaus slaughtering his opponents on returning home, but it is in harmony with the brutality of his rule; ten years after his accession citizens of Judea and Samaria, "not being able to bear his barbarous and tyrannical usage of them," accused him of misrule before the emperor.[150] It is very possible that Jesus told a parable based on the Archelaus incident and that Luke, seeing a parallel between that episode and the Jewish rejection of Jesus, combined it with the better known parable of the "pounds."

What of the variation in the sums of money given to the servants? In Matthew the man handed over to them his cash, or at least a substantial portion of it, for trading, and varied the

---

[149]The event is recorded in detail by Josephus in *Antiquities* 17.299–320 and *Jewish War* 2.80–100.

[150]Josephus, *Antiquities* 17.342.

amounts according to their abilities: five talents to one, two to another, and one to the last—in all cases very large sums of money. In Luke there are ten servants and each receives ten "minas," i.e., a thousand denarii. In reality Luke's record of the ruler checking the results of the servants' trading mentions only three (the first gained ten more minas, the second five, the third put his mina in a sweat cloth, vv. 16, 18, 20). What did the original parable say? Most scholars favor Luke's record in this respect: the nobleman wished to test his men and gave them the identical number of minas. That leads to an extraordinary consequence, however: on his return he rewarded the man who gained ten minas with the rule of ten cities—plus one mina! The man who gained five minas was given the charge of five cities. This must be due to the coalition of the two original parables known to Luke. Matthew's account is intended to show serious trading on a large scale, which involved a real risk; professional investors were usually employed for such trading, not servants. In ancient Babylonia merchants used to trade with the capital of kings and temples, and Hammurabi formulated laws governing such transactions.[151] The larger sum is in harmony with the object of the parable, namely the gift of the kingdom of God, which is inadequately conveyed by comparison with mere minas.[152]

The purpose of the parable is to no small degree bound up with the behavior and fate of the third servant, on whom attention is concentrated. First, let it be clearly recognized that he was entrusted with a very large sum of money, far beyond what a servant could hope to possess. People should never refer to themselves disparagingly as, "I'm only a one-talent person," which I have often heard; the man in the parable is portrayed as being afraid through not knowing what to do with such a huge amount of money, aware that his master would have considerable expectations of gain from his use of it. Dan Via well portrayed the servant's feelings:

> In the fear of the one-talent man we see the anxiety of one who will not step into the unknown. . . . The servant's breach of trust in failing to do business with his master's goods is grounded in his existential flaw. He started as a free man, but he refused to be responsible. The

---

[151] J. D. M. Derrett, "Law in the New Testament: The Parable of the Talents and 2 Logia," *ZNW* 56 (1965) 184–95.

[152] With this A. Weiser agrees; see his meticulous study, *Die Knechtsgleichnisse der Synoptischen Evangelien* (Munich: Kösel, 1971) 263.

servant was paralyzed, not because he was in a victimizing context, but he chose to understand himself as a victim. By that time, however, it was too late to act differently, because the talent was to be taken from him. We see the following connected movement: from the refusal to take a risk, through repressed guilt which is projected on to someone else, to the loss of the opportunity for meaningful existence.[153]

That is a perceptive analysis of the situation of the third servant. If we are right, however, in seeing this parable in the context of the ministry of Jesus and as related to the kingdom of God there is an even more serious issue at stake. Adolf Schlatter saw this clearly and affirmed:

> Because Jesus does not allow any of his servants to live only for themselves, and misinterpret their position merely as their own transference into life, he links the lovelessness which refuses work and is satisfied with keeping what has been received with the man who has been given only the one talent. . . . For from a small amount of power the impulse arises to renounce action, and leave it to those who are equipped with large means. The parable establishes that wherever the gift of Jesus is received, the purpose of life extends beyond one's own concerns.[154]

Whom does this man represent? The answers given by scholars are varied. Dibelius saw in him the Jewish people, who do not know how to use the heritage entrusted to them;[155] Dodd, more especially the Pharisee, who seeks security in the meticulous observance of the law;[156] Jeremias, the scribes, the teachers of the law.[157] Since it is unlikely that the parable was directed to any single group of people, not even to the disciples exclusively, A. Weiser is surely nearer the mark in seeing this man as potentially representing any person who hears the kingdom-proclamation of Jesus. It is true that Jesus created a crisis for Israel, but it was a crisis which personally involved all who were confronted by the reality of the kingdom in his teaching, his action, his person. When such an experience takes place (and one deliberately passes to the present tense) the question has to be faced whether one's life corresponds to "the goodness and the compassion of God as they have come near in Jesus and his word."[158] But to be faced

---

[153] Via, *The Parables*, 118–19.

[154] Schlatter, *Der Evangelist Matthäus*, 721–22.

[155] Dibelius, *From Tradition to Gospel*, 225.

[156] Dodd, *Parables of the Kingdom*, 151.

[157] Jeremias, *Parables of Jesus*, 61–62.

[158] Weiser, *Die Knechtsgleichnisse*, 266.

with the challenge of the kingdom of God revealed in Jesus is not simply an experience of a moment; the acceptance of the word of the kingdom is intended to issue in a life of service of the kingdom. For the kingdom of God is a gift inseparably linked with responsibility to serve it and show it in the kind of action seen in Jesus. He initiated the kingdom not alone by words but by deeds, and they who receive it must continue in the Jesus way. The third servant is a warning of what not to do with the message of the kingdom.

That ties up with another issue that has been vigorously debated: is this a parousia parable, i.e., a story which has at its heart the expectation of the coming of Christ at the end of the age? Exegetes acknowledge that the two evangelists who have passed it on saw it in that light. Luke prefaced the parable with the observation that Jesus told it because the people thought, as they were approaching Jerusalem, that the kingdom of God was about to come (19:11); that indicates that Luke believed that the parable posits a long period of time (cf. v. 12) before the kingdom of glory and its king were to come. Matthew underscores the same conviction, in that the master returns from his journey "after a long time" (v. 19); his congratulation of the two servants who had doubled their money include the words, "Enter the joy of your master," an expression which is claimed to denote the "feast of joy," i.e., the banquet of the kingdom of God;[159] and the master commands that the unprofitable servant be thrown into the outer darkness, i.e., outside the kingdom of God. Clearly these things envisage that the Lord has come, and with him the judgment and the kingdom of God. All that is admitted by scholars generally, but many of them hold that this reflects an allegorizing of the original parable that took place in the church, a process completed by the evangelists. That may very well be so, but there were certain essentials in the parable that led to the allegorizing, namely (i) the fundamental presupposition that the gift of the kingdom demands responsible action, and (ii) the period between the departure of the "master" and his return, during which the responsible action takes place. The absence of the master is a key to the plot of the parable. On this Weiser asserted, "Within the parable as a whole the departure of the master has only the

---

[159] So Dalman, *Words of Jesus*, 116; Strack-Billerbeck, *Kommentar zum NT,* 1.972–73; Schlatter, *Der Evangelist Matthäus*, 722; Jeremias, *Parables of Jesus*, 60.

function of creating for the servants free room for their action."[160]
If then the absence of the master and his return for an assessment
of accounts is imperative for a meaningful present an important
conclusion is to be drawn: "*The picture of the parable is not possible
at all apart from a certain parousia expectation.*"[161] So affirmed A.
Polag, who further pointed out that if the reckoning alone was in
view, the master's departure would have been needless, as we see
in the parables of the Unforgiving Servant (Matthew 18:23–35)
and the Dishonest Manager (Luke 16:1–9). We conclude therefore
that the parable is essentially concerned with the future coming
of the Lord, and its treatment by the evangelists in making this
plain is in harmony with the intention of Jesus when he first
uttered it.

v. A Parabolic Vision of the Last Judgment: Matthew 25:31–46

A comment is desirable as to the title of the final parable
we are to discuss in this book. Whereas it has been universally
known as the parable of the Sheep and Goats, there is a consensus
among scholars that it is not a parable, since the parabolic element in the passage is confined to the opening sentence:

> When the Son of Man comes in his glory, and all the angels with him,
> then he will sit on the throne of his glory. All the nations will be
> gathered before him, and he will separate people one from another
> as a shepherd separates the sheep from the goats, and he will put the
> sheep at his right hand and the goats at the left. (vv. 31–33, NRSV)

The rest of the passage consists of words of the king to the
multitude before him as he pronounces judgment on them. Theo
Preiss, in an illuminating essay on this description of the last
judgment, wrote about the difficulty of giving it a literary classification. It is not an ordinary parable, allegory, novel, legend, etc.;
it is more like an apocalyptic vision, but this last has no traditional form, whereas the passage before us has a clear structure
(in fact it's almost mathematical, which makes it easy to remember). Moreover, Preiss acknowledges that in contrast to apocalyptic visions it has "a sobriety of feature and colour, a reserve, a
bareness" that he can ascribe to no other than Jesus.[162]

---

[160] Weiser, *Die Knechtsgleichnisse*, 264.

[161] A. Polag, *Die Christologie der Logienquelle* (Neukirchen-Vluyn: Neukirchener, 1977) 165.

[162] T. Preiss, *Life in Christ* (SBT 13; London: SCM, 1954) 46.

One appreciates what Preiss was saying. For him it is all part of the uniqueness of the revelation here given, but he surely has overlooked the breadth of the *mashal* concept. *Mashal* is not only a parable in the accepted sense, but a proverb, byword, riddle, fable, allegory, and is extended to include prophetic oracle (cf. the "parables of Balaam," Numbers 23–24). Indeed, some of the Old Testament prophets relate unusual parables and allegories, notably Ezekiel, and engage in parabolic actions to great effect; we think above all of Hosea in his marriage to an immoral woman, enabling him to make his relations with her a parable of God's relations with Israel. In Matthew 25:31–46, then, we have a description of the last judgment which we could justly term a "parable of the last judgment," but it would be misunderstood. A "vision of the last judgment" would convey a more acceptable impression, but its parabolic quality is then unmentioned, and it is certainly not an apocalyptic vision. We have therefore called it a "parabolic vision of the last judgment," for thereby its aspects as parable and vision are expressed. Its nature as a parable is not confined to its introductory sentence, for it includes the whole—the central dialogue as well as the conclusion. It is further a reminder that the judgment scene employs analogies in pictorial language; they convey realities of ultimate importance that transcend the grasp of human thought, yet they have a thrust that is clear and that pierces the conscience like the sharpest blade.

The vision commences with the statement that the Son of Man "comes" and sits on his "glorious throne."[163] The nations are gathered before him, and he separates them as a shepherd separates his flock. The oriental flavor of the scene is already evident, for the flock consists of sheep and goats, which remain together in the day and are separated in the evening (goats don't have woolen coats, and so feel the cold at night!). The very term "gathered" is part of a picture, for gathering assumes scattering; they are familiar terms in the Old Testament for the "scattering" of the Jewish flock by oppressive powers and for their being "gathered" from the nations for the kingdom of God (cf. John

---

[163] Whether there is an echo here of *1 Enoch* 62:22–23 is uncertain; reference to the Son of Man sitting on his glorious throne is already made in Matthew 19:28. It is conceivable that Matthew knew the Parables of Enoch and used its language here, but if so he will have been aware of how totally opposed the judgment scene in *1 Enoch* 62 is to that which he reports from Jesus in the parable.

10:16).[164] It is assumed that the multitude is not of one generation but of all, therefore resurrection has taken place. The pictorial nature of the description is already apparent.

Two elements in this portrayal of the judgment make it unique: first, the criteria used in judging, secondly the relation of the criteria to the King. The former have parallels in other nations of the orient. The oldest example is in the *Egyptian Book of the Dead,* a document existing fourteen hundred years before Jesus. After an inordinately long list of sins which the deceased is to declare that he has not committed he recites:

> I have done that which men praise
> and that whereof the gods rejoice,
> I have satisfied God through that which he loves:
> I have given bread to the hungry
> and water to the thirsty
> and clothes to the naked
> and a ferry to those without ships.[165]

Of many comparable passages that can be cited from rabbinical texts most instructive is the *Midrash* on Psalm 118:

> Ps. 118:19: Open to me the gates of righteousness: In the future world it will be said to men, "What has your work been?" If he then says, "I have fed the hungry!" it will be said to him, "That is the gate of Yahweh, Ps 118:20; you who have fed the hungry, enter in the same!" If he says, "I have given the thirsty to drink!" it will be said to him, "That is the gate of Yahweh; you who have given the thirsty to drink, enter in the same!" If he says, "I have clothed the naked!" it will be said, "That is the gate of Yahweh; you who have clothed the naked, enter in the same!" And similarly he who has brought up the orphans, and he who has given alms, and he who has practiced works of love. And David said, "I have done everything, everything should be opened to me!" Therefore it is said, "Open to me the gates of righteousness (compassion); I will go into them. I will praise Yah."[166]

This last illustrates Jewish tradition that may well have been current in Jesus' day, but the Gospels show that he drew directly from the Old Testament. Matthew 23:23 shows him citing Micah 6:8 as summing up "the weightier matters of the law,

---

[164] So J. Jeremias, *Jesus' Promise to the Nations* (SBT 24; London: SCM, 1958) 64.

[165] Chapter 125. See H. Gressmann, *Altorientalische Texte und Bilder zum Alten Testament* (Berlin: W. de Gruyter, 1926) 188.

[166] Strack-Billerbeck, *Kommentar zum NT,* 4.1.561.

'justice, mercy, and faith.' " Similarly in Matthew 9:13 and 12:7 Jesus quotes Hosea 6:6, "I desire mercy and not sacrifice." In citing that saying Rabbi Johanan ben Zakkai rendered the word "mercy" by "acts of love."[167] The messianic expositions of the law in Matthew 5 conclude with the demand, "Be *perfect,* as your heavenly Father is perfect" (5:48); Luke 6:36 reproduces that saying as, "Be *merciful,* just as your Father is merciful"; Luke's version is likely to be correct, since the perfection of God is seen in his great mercy. It is evident that Jesus set the greatest store on mercy. Most significant of all in relation to Matthew 25, Jesus uttered the beatitude, "Happy are the merciful, for they will receive mercy," i.e., they will receive it in the judgment. That is precisely the criterion of judgment applied in the vision, vv. 35–36, 42–43. In the sight of the King the crucial issue is whether one shows mercy to the hungry, the thirsty, the foreigner, the ill-clad, those who are ill, and those in prison. In singling out these elementary works of mercy Jesus is at one with the Jewish teachers of the law, but his way of stating them is nowhere found in their works of exposition: "*I was hungry* and you gave me something to eat; *I was thirsty* and you gave me a drink; *I was a foreigner . . . I was naked . . . I was ill . . . I was in prison. . . .* " The startling implication of those words is that Jesus identifies himself with those whom he has named. When he represents the "righteous" (= the merciful) as astonished, and asking when they saw him in such need, he replies, "In so far as you did it to one of these my brothers, the least, you did it to me" (v. 40).

We must inquire, Who are these "least brothers" of the King with whom he identifies himself? T. W. Manson proposed that they are disciples of Jesus; the scene depicts the King and his brothers in the center, who together form the Son of Man, as in Daniel 7:13, the good Gentiles on the right, and the wicked Gentiles on the left; the Gentiles are distinguished as good or evil according as they help or ignore (or even oppose) the disciples of Jesus when engaged on their mission.[168] An increasing number are attracted to this interpretation, even to postulating that Matthew will have viewed the "brothers of the King" as the leaders of the church. But this understanding of the passage fails to do justice to the universality of the scene—all nations of all times are

---

[167] Ibid., 4.1.500.
[168] Manson, *Sayings of Jesus,* 249–51.

being judged; and this view of the Son of Man is hardly reconcilable with our Lord's teaching on the Son of Man.

Rightly to understand the vision of the judgment it is of crucial importance to recall the concept of the Son of Man in the Gospels. We have seen that even in his ministry Jesus is, as Son of Man, the representative of the kingdom of God and its mediator (cf. Mark 2:10, 28; Matthew 11:16–19, in agreement with such sayings as Matthew 11:5–6, 12–13; 12:28; Mark 2:27; Luke 17:20–21); that his role in respect of the kingdom reaches its apex in his death and resurrection (so Mark 8:31; 9:31; cf. 14:22–24; Luke 12:49f.; 22:15–20, 29–30); as Son of Man he will consummate the coming of the kingdom of God (Mark 14:62) and be arbiter of entry into the kingdom (Luke 12:8–9). This role is possible on the one hand by reason of his relation to the Father, who commissions him to be the representative and mediator of the saving sovereignty, and on the other hand by his relation to the whole of humankind, alike in his life of service and in his death and resurrection. In all this service of the kingdom of God *Jesus the Son of Man is in solidarity with all humanity.*

The astonishing feature of this parabolic vision of judgment is that this same solidarity of Jesus with the human race is its fundamental presupposition, and it is dominated by the criterion of mercy. Somehow this has been missed by most Christians through the centuries of the church's history. Michelangelo's awe-inspiring picture of the Last Judgment, based on this parable, is actually a caricature of it. It is dominated by the mighty Christ banishing the wicked into hell, whereas the keynote of the parable is, in the words of the brother of Jesus, "Mercy triumphs over judgment" (James 2:13). The surprise of the "righteous" (= merciful) to learn that they had ministered to the Son of Man has in view people outside as well as inside the church, and equally the unpleasant surprise of those who learned that they had not ministered to the Son of Man has in view people inside as well as outside the church.

Let me emphasize the basis of this by citing Jeremias' masterly exposition of the parable. He viewed it as answering the question, "By what criterion will the heathen who have never known you be judged?" In thinking that the "heathen" are exclusively in view I believe that he was mistaken, but he went on to affirm:

> The gist of Jesus' reply is: "The heathen have met me in my brethren. . . . He who has shown love to them has shown it to me, the Saviour of the poor. Therefore at the Last Judgment the heathen will be

examined concerning the acts of love which they have shown to me in the form of the afflicted, and they will be granted the grace of a share in the kingdom if they have fulfilled Messiah's law (James 2:8), the duty of love." Thus for them justification is available on the ground of love, *since for them also the ransom has been paid* (Mark 10:45).[169]

Now Jeremias was a devotee of Adolf Schlatter. The latter wrote a formidable commentary on Matthew, unusual for its combination of linguistic expertise, extensive knowledge of Jewish sources, and profound theology. On this parable he commented:

> By the fact that Jesus speaks with men not of their sins but only of their good works, he reveals himself as *the one who has procured forgiveness for all.* On this the statement is founded which leads those also, who did not know him, into his kingdom.[170]

This, I am inclined to think, provided the inspiration for Jeremias' comment cited above. That the Parable concludes by recounting the banishment of people from the kingdom of God has the same basis as the possibility of the welcome of the merciful into the kingdom: the Lord has brought about a ransom for all, and that is the supreme factor in anyone's being able to enter the kingdom of God, which after all is more precisely described as "the saving sovereignty of God." But the human response to the God who is over all is also crucially important. There are those who receive what they understand of the revelation of God and act in accordance with the divine mercy, and those who reject the revelation and act in accordance with their rejection, and therein lies the difference of destiny. That theology is not confined to the parabolic vision of Jesus; it runs throughout the entire New Testament, including the remaining teaching of Jesus, the Epistles and the book of Revelation. In particular the apostle of justification by faith is in complete agreement with his Lord. The description in Romans 2:6–16 of "the day of wrath and the revelation of the righteous judgment of God" is in accord with Matthew 25:31–46 (check it!); Paul unambiguously states that all Christians must appear before the judgment seat of Christ, to receive what is due for that which has been done in the body, whether good or bad (2 Corinthians 5:10); and the only thing that counts is "faith *working* through love" (Galatians 5:6).

---

[169] Jeremias, *Parables of Jesus,* 210 (italics those of Jeremias).
[170] Schlatter, *Der Evangelist Matthäus,* 726 (italics mine).

The purpose of the parable is not only illumination but to challenge the followers of Christ. I confess that there is no passage of the scriptures which makes me feel quite so uneasy as this one. Without doubt it inspires wonder, but to measure oneself with its standards makes one uncomfortable. We know that the last command of Jesus before his death was that his people should love one another as he has loved them, i.e., love all in the family (John 13:34). In the parable he calls us to love all in the world as he has loved the world, and he gave us concrete illustrations of that way of loving. They are, of course, only examples. There are many, many other ways in which love in action can be expressed. Our great consolation is to realize that the saving sovereignty of God is grace; we have experienced it, we anticipate its consummation in resurrection to the kingdom of glory, and we live by it in the time between. Our calling, as those who know the will of God for his creatures, is to fulfill it before the world as Jesus did. By the grace of God in Christ through the Spirit *we can and we must do it!*

POSTSCRIPT

I bring to an end these reflections on the parables of Jesus, and the book itself, by citing conclusions that Eduard Schweizer draws from the parables of Jesus, particularly with respect to their Christological significance. Professor Schweizer had been persuaded to write a short book summarizing life of Jesus research in the twentieth century. The book was published in 1994 under the title *Jesus the Parable of God*.[1] In this work he devoted a chapter to a consideration of the parables of Jesus and the light they throw on Jesus the Parable-Teller. The chapter concluded with five affirmations on this theme. I am grateful to Dr. Schweizer for permission to cite them, which I now do.

We may conclude by stating that, in some way, Jesus is *the* Parable of God.

1. He is the only one who can tell these parables. He claims that in him the kingdom of God—and this is to say: God as the living God—comes to the hearers of his parables.

---

[1]E. Schweizer, *Jesus the Parable of God: What Do We Really Know About Jesus?* (Princeton Theological Monograph Series 37; ed. Dikran Y. Hadidian; Allison Park, Penn.: Pickwick, 1994). The citations that follow are from pages 32–34.

When in the parables of Jesus the kingdom of God (the active rule of God) approaches the hearers, because the parables become the rule in Jesus' life, death and resurrection, then he himself is *the* parable of God, in which God becomes alive among us.

2. If we want to understand Jesus, we cannot watch him from a distance. . . . He comes directly into our world and opens himself only to those who dare to get engaged in an encounter with him that might change their lives. . . . But just as a parable cannot be understood if we do not let ourselves be dragged into it, and even as love among human beings never becomes true if we only want to look at it from the outside, so Jesus and his stories come to life as *the* parable of God only when we start to live and listen from inside them.

3. Jesus is *the* parable of God, because all the amazing traits which appear in the center of his stories become true in his ministry.

4. Jesus is *the* parable of God, not only because the amazing traits of the stories of Jesus that are glorious and welcome manifestations of God's grace and love and of his final victory became true in his life, but also because of the hiddenness of that grace and love and victory. Where could it be better hidden than in the weakness of this Jesus, rejected more and more and finally disposed of on the cross? And the mystery of the power of God in and through this weakness, the resurrection of the crucified one, the "folly of the word of the cross" that becomes the "power of God" is to be found in Jesus, because he who has been raised and preached to the world became "our wisdom, our righteousness and sanctification and redemption" (1 Cor 1:18, 30). Therefore all his parables will live on and speak again and again in different ways and into different situations.

5. Jesus is *the* parable of God, because he is the guarantor for the kingdom of God, which became present in his ministry and will be fulfilled finally. Without him there is no hope. But all his ministry, all his words and all his deeds, his dying and his rising were always open towards the future of God who will vindicate him and his words and deeds. Jesus is the living "principle of hope" for and in our world.

BIBLIOGRAPHY

This bibliography supplements the titles mentioned in the footnotes.

Ambrozic, A. M. *The Hidden Kingdom. A Redaction-Critical Study of the References to the Kingdom of God in Mark's Gospel.* CBQ Monograph Series 2. Washington: Catholic Biblical Association of America, 1972.

Anderson, C. C. *Critical Quests of Jesus.* Grand Rapids: Eerdmans, 1969.

Barrett, C. K. *The Holy Spirit and the Gospel Tradition.* London: SPCK, 1966.

Berkey, R. F. "EGGIZEIN, PHTHANEIN and Realised Eschatology." *JBL* 82 (1963) 177–87.

Blomberg, C. L. *Interpreting the Parables.* Downers Grove: InterVarsity, 1990.

Borg, M. J. *Conflict, Holiness and Politics in the Teaching of Jesus.* New York: E. Mellen Press, 1984.

_____. *Jesus: A New Vision.* San Francisco: Harper & Row, 1987.

_____. "A Temperate Case for a Non-Eschatological Jesus," *Forum* 2 (1986) 81–102.

Bornkamm, G. *Jesus of Nazareth.* New York: Harper, 1960.

Borsch, F. H. *The Christian and Gnostic Son of Man.* SBT, 2d series, 14. London: SCM, 1970.

Bowker, J. A. "The Son of Man." *JTS* 28 (1977) 19–48.

Bowman, T. J. *Which Jesus?* Philadelphia: Westminster, 1970.

Brown, C. *Jesus in European Protestant Thought.* 2d ed. Grand Rapids: Baker, 1988.

Brown, R. E. *The Gospel According to John.* Anchor Bible. 2 vols. New York: Doubleday, 1966–70.

————. *New Testament Essays.* Milwaukee: Bruce Publishing Company, 1965; New York: Doubleday, 1968.

Buber, M. *Kingship of God.* New York: Harper & Row, 1967.

Bultmann, R. *Jesus and the Word.* London: Ivor, Nicholson & Watson, 1935.

Carlston, C. E. *Parables of the Triple Tradition.* Philadelphia: Fortress, 1975.

Catchpole, D. R. *The Trial of Jesus.* Leiden: Brill, 1972.

Chilton, B., ed. *The Kingdom of God in the Teaching of Jesus.* Philadelphia: Fortress, 1984.

Conzelmann, H. *Jesus.* ET. Philadephia: Fortress, 1973.

Crossan, J. D. *In Parables: The Challenge of the Historical Jesus.* New York: Harper & Row, 1984.

Dahl, N. A. "The Parables of Growth." *ST* 5 (1951) 132–66.

Dalman, G. *The Words of Jesus.* Edinburgh: T. & T. Clark, 1902.

Derrett, J. D. M. *Law in the New Testament.* London: Darton, Longman & Todd, 1970.

Dodd, C. H. *According to the Scriptures.* London: Nisbet, 1952.

————. *The Founder of Christianity.* London: Collins, 1971.

Donahue, J. R. *Are You the Christ? The Trial Narrative in the Gospel of Mark.* SBL Dissertation Series 10. Cambridge, Mass., 1973.

————. "Jesus as the Parable of God in the Gospel of Mark." *Interpretation* 32 (1978) 369–86.

Dupont, J. "La Parabole du maître qui rentre dans la nuit." In *Mélanges Bibliques en hommage au R. P. Beda Rigaux.* Ed. by A. Descamps and A. de Halleux. Gembloux: Dugulot, 1970.

Eckardt, H. R. *Reclaiming the Jesus of History: Christology Today.* Minneapolis: Fortress, 1992.

Evans, C. A. *Life of Jesus Research. An Annotated Bibliography.* N.T. Tools and Studies XIII. Leiden: Brill, 1989.

Fison, J. E. *The Christian Hope. The Presence and the Parousia.* London: Longmans, 1989.

Flusser, F. D. *Jesus.* New York: Herder & Herder, 1969.

Fuchs, E. *Studies of the Historical Jesus.* SBT 42. London: SCM, 1964.

Fuller, R. H. *The Foundations of New Testament Christology.* New York: Scribners, 1965.

Gerhardsson, B. "The Parable of the Sower and Its Interpretation." *NTS* 14 (1968) 165–93.

Glasson, T. F. "The Reply to Caiaphas (Mark 14:62)." *NTS* 7 (1960) 88–93.

―――. *The Second Advent. The Origin of the New Testament Doctrine.* 3d ed. London: Epworth, 1963.

Goppelt, L. "Zum Problem des Menschensohnes: Das Verhältnis von Leidens- und Parusieankündigung." In *Christologie und Ethik.* Pages 66–78. Göttingen: Vandenhoeck & Ruprecht, 1968.

Hahn, F. *The Titles of Jesus in Christology.* London: Lutterworth, 1969.

Hartman, L. *Prophecy Interpreted. The Formation of Some Jewish Apocalyptic Texts and of the Eschatological Discourse of Mark 13 Par.* Coniectanea Biblica, N.T. Series 1. Lund: Gleerup, 1966.

Hengel, M. *The Son of God. The Origin of Christology and the History of Jewish-Hellenistic Religion.* London: SCM and Philadelphia: Fortress, 1976.

Hill, D. "On the Evidence for the Creative Role of Christian Prophets." *NTS* 20 (1974) 262–74.

Hooker, M. D. *The Son of Man in Mark.* London: SPCK, 1967.

Jaubert, A. *The Date of the Last Supper.* ET. New York: Alba House, 1965.

Jeremias, J. *New Testament Theology.* Vol. 1, *The Proclamation of Jesus.* London: SCM, 1971.

―――. *The Prayers of Jesus.* SBT, 2d series, 6. London: SCM, 1967.

Jeremias, Jörg. *Theophanie: Die Geschichte einer alttestamentlichen Gattung:* Neukirchener Verlag, 1965.

Jones, P. R. "The Seed Parables of Mark." *RevExp* 75 (1978) 519–38.

Kähler, M. *The So-Called Historical Jesus and the Historic, Biblical Christ.* ET. Philadelphia: Fortress, 1964.

Käsemann, E. *Essays on New Testament Themes.* SBT 41. London: SCM, 1969.

―――. *New Testament Questions of Today.* Philadelphia: Fortress, 1969.

Kissinger, W. S. *The Lives of Jesus.* New York & London: Garland, 1985.

―――. *The Parables of Jesus. A History of Interpretation and Bibliography.* Methuen, N. J.: Scarecrow Press, 1979.

Koch, D. A. "Zum Verhältnis von Christologie und Eschatologie im Markus-Evangelium." In *Jesus Christus in Historie und Theologie*. Festschrift for H. Conzelmann. Ed. by G. Strecker. Tübingen: Mohr, 1975.

Koch, K. *The Growth of the Biblical Tradition: The Form Critical Method*. New York: Scribners, 1969.

_____. *The Rediscovery of Apocalyptic*. London: SCM, 1972.

Kümmel, W. G. *Dreissig Jahre Jesusforschung (1950–1980)*. Bonn: Hanstein, 1985.

_____. "Eschatological Expectation in the Proclamation of Jesus." In *The Future of Our Religious Past. Essays in Honour of R. Bultmann*. Ed. by J. M. Robinson. Pages 29–48. New York: Harper & Row, 1971.

Ladd, G. E. *The Presence of the Future*. Grand Rapids: Eerdmans, 1974.

_____. *A Theology of the New Testament*. Grand Rapids: Eerdmans, 1974.

Lindars, B. *Jesus Son of Man: A Fresh Examination of the Son of Man Sayings in the Gospels in the Light of Recent Research*. London: SPCK, 1983.

Mack, B. L. "The Kingdom Sayings in Mark." *Forum* 3 (1987) 3–47.

_____. *A Myth of Innocence: Mark and Christian Origins*. Philadelphia: Fortress, 1988.

Mackey, J. P. *Jesus, the Man and the Myth*. New York: Paulist, 1979.

Marshall, I. H. *I Believe in the Historical Jesus*. London: Hodder & Stoughton; Grand Rapids: Eerdmans, 1977.

_____. *Last Supper and Lord's Supper*. Carlisle: Paternoster, 1980.

_____. "The Synoptic Son of Man Sayings in Recent Discussion." *NTS* 12 (1966) 327–51.

Meier, J. P. *A Marginal Jew. Rethinking the Historical Jesus*. Vol. 1, *The Roots of the Problem and the Person*. Vol. 2, *Mentor Message, and Miracles*. New York: Doubleday, 1991–94.

Meyer, B. F. *The Aims of Jesus*. London: SCM, 1979.

Michaels, J. R. "Apostolic Hardship and Righteous Gentiles: A Study of Matthew 25:31–46." *JBL* 84 (1965) 27–37.

Moltmann, J. *The Way of Jesus Christ: Christology in Messianic Dimensions*. San Francisco: Harper, 1990.

Moore, A. J. *The Parousia in the New Testament*. Supplements to Novum Testamentum 13. Leiden: Brill, 1966.

Muddiman, J. B. "Jesus and Fasting, Mark ii, 18–22" in *Jésus aux origines de la Christologie*. Ed. by J. Dupont. Pages 271–81. Louvain: Leuven University Press, 1975.

Ott, W. *Gebet und Heil: Die Bedeutung der Gebetsparänese in der lukanischen Theologie.* Studien zum Alten und Neuen Testament 12. Munich: Kösel, 1965.

Otto, R. *The Kingdom of God and the Son of Man.* London: Lutterworth Press, 1943.

Palmer, D. "Defining a Vow of Abstinence." *Colloquium* 5 (1973) 38–41.

Pannenberg, W. *Jesus, God and Man.* London: SCM, 1970.

Pelikan, J. *Jesus through the Centuries.* New Haven: Yale University Press, 1985.

Perrin, N. *Jesus and the Language of the Kingdom: Symbol and Metaphor in New Testament Interpretation.* London: SCM, 1976.

––––––. *The Kingdom of God in the Teaching of Jesus.* London: SCM, 1963.

––––––. *A Modern Pilgrimage in New Testament Christology.* Philadelphia: Fortress, 1974.

––––––. *Rediscovering the Teaching of Jesus.* London: SCM, 1967.

Pesch, R. & R. Schnackenberg. *Jesus und der Menschensohn.* Festschrift for A. Vögtle. Freiburg: Herder, 1975.

Polag, A. *Die Christologie der Logienquelle.* WMANT 45. Neukirchen-Vluyn: Neukirchener Verlag, 1977.

Quispel, M. "The Gospel of Thomas and the New Testament." *VC* 11 (1957) 189–207.

––––––. "Some Remarks on the Gospel of Thomas." *NTS* 5 (1959) 276–90.

Rad, G. von. *The Message of the Prophets.* London: SCM; New York: Harper & Row, 1968.

––––––. *Old Testament Theology.* 2 vols. Edinburgh: Oliver & Boyd; New York: Harper & Row, 1962–65.

Rigaux, B. "Bdelygma tes eremoseos (Mc 13, 14; Mt 24, 15)." *Biblica* 40 (1959) 675–83.

––––––. "La seconde venue de Jésus." In *La Venue du Messie: Messianisme et eschatologie.* Ed. by E. Massaux, et al. Recherches Bibliques 6. Paris: Desclée de Brouwer, 1962.

Robinson, J. M. *A New Quest of the Historical Jesus.* SBT 25. London: SCM, 1959.

Sanders, E. P. *Jesus and Judaism.* Philadelphia: Fortress, 1985.

Sanders, J. A. "From Isaiah 61 to Luke 4." In *Christianity, Judaism and other Greco-Roman Cults.* Festschrift for M. Smith. Ed. by J. Neusner. Pages 75–106. Leiden: Brill, 1975.

Schnackenburg, R. "Der eschatologische Abschnitt Lk. 17:20–37." In *Mélanges Bibliques en hommage au R. P. Beda Rigaux*. Ed. by A. Descamps and A. de Halleux. Pages 213–34. Gembloux: Duculot, 1970.

_____. *God's Rule and Kingdom*. London: Nelson; New York: Herder, 1963.

_____. *The Gospel according to St. John*. 3 vols. ET. New York: Crossroad, 1968–82.

Schrage, W. *Das Verhältnis des Thomas-Evangeliums zur synoptischen Tradition und zu den koptischen Evangelienübersetzungen*. Berlin: Topelmann, 1964.

Schulz, S. *Q—Dies Spruchquelle der Evangelisten*. Zurich: Theologischer Verlag, 1972.

Schürmann, H. *Der Paschamahlbericht Lk. 22, (7–14) 15–18*. Münster: Aschendorf, 1953.

_____. *Der Einsetzungsbericht Lk. 22, 19–20*. Münster: Aschendorff, 1955.

_____. *Jesu Abschiedsrede, Lk. 22, 21–38*. Münster: Aschendorff, 1957.

_____. *Jesu ureigener Töd: Exegetische Besinnungen und Ausblick*. Freiburg: Herder, 1975.

Schweitzer, A. *The Quest of the Historical Jesus*. ET. London: Unwin, 1910.

Schweizer, E. *Jesus*. London: SCM; Atlanta: John Knox, 1971.

_____. *Jesus Christ, The Man from Nazareth and the Exalted Lord*. Macon Ga.: Mercer University Press, 1987.

_____. *Jesus the Parable of God*. Allison Park, Pa.: Pickwick Publications, 1994.

_____. "The Son of Man." *JBL* 79 (1960) 119–29.

Sneed, R. "The Kingdom of God is within You (Lk 17:21)." *CBQ* 24 (1962) 363–82.

Strecker, G. *Der Weg der Gerechtigkeit*. FRLANT. Göttingen: Vandenhoeck & Ruprecht, 1971.

Ströbel, A. "In dieser Nacht (Lk. 17, 34)." *ZTK* 58 (1961) 16–29.

Suggs, M. J. "Wisdom of Solomon 2.10–5: A Homily Based on the Fourth Servant Song." *JBL* 76 (1975) 26–33.

Tatum, W. B. *In Quest of Jesus*. Atlanta: John Knox, 1982.

Thoma, C. & M. Wyschogrod, "Literary and Theological Aspects of the Rabbinic Parables." In *Parable and Story in Judaism and Christianity*. New York: Paulist Press, 1989.

Trilling, W. *Christusverkündigung in den synoptischen Evangelien*. Biblische Handbibliothek 4. Munich: Kösel, 1969.

Vermes, G. *Jesus the Jew.* New York: Macmillan, 1973.

Via, D. O. *The Parables. Their Literary and Existential Dimension.* Philadelphia: Fortress, 1967.

Vögtle, A. "Exegetische Erwägungen über das Wissen und Selbatbewusstsein Jesu." In *Gott in der Welt.* Festschrift for K. Rahner, Freiburg: Herder, 1964.

Weiser, A. *Die Knechtsgleichnisse der synoptischen Evangelien.* SANT 29. Munich: Kösel, 1971.

Weiss, J. *Jesus' Proclamation of the Kingdom of God.* Philadelphia: Fortress, 1971.

Wheelwright, P. *Metaphor and Reality.* Bloomington, Ind.: Indiana University Press, 1962.

Yoder, J. *The Politics of Jesus.* Grand Rapids: Eerdmans, 1972.

Young, F. "A Cloud of Witnesses." In *The Myth of God Incarnate.* Ed. by J. Hick. London: SCM and Philadelphia: Westminster, 1977.

Zeller, D. "Das Logion Mt. 8, 11f//Lk 13, 28f und das Motiv der 'Völkerwallfahrt.' " *BZ* 15 (1971) 222–37 and *BZ* 16 (1972) 84–93.

Index of

Modern Authors

Allison, D. C., 193, 209, 210, 231, 233
Althaus, P., 61
Ambrozic, A. M., 121, 197
Arndt, W. F., 85

Bammel, E., 156, 224
Barrett, C. K., 37
Barth, K., 35–36
Bartsch, H. W., 41
Bayer, H. F., 138
Beasley-Murray, G. R., 12, 27, 29, 63, 80, 113, 119, 138, 147, 149, 150, 152, 177, 194, 205, 224
Behm, J., 115
Best, E., 178
Billerbeck, P., 119, 180, 185, 220, 228, 252, 255
Blank, J., 101
Blinzler, J., 156
Bonnard, P., 193, 206, 210, 222, 248
Boobyer, G. H., 50

Booth, W., 44
Borg, M. J., 3, 4
Bornkamm, G., 246
Boucher, M., 176
Bratcher, R. G., 85
Braun, H., 132–33
Brown, C., 67–69, 94
Brown, R. E., 35, 38, 46
Brunner, E., 59–60
Büchsel, n.i., 154
Bugge, C. A., 208
Bultmann, R., 11, 68–69, 75, 92, 96, 128, 205
Bunyan, J., 175
Burkitt, F. C., 165
Burney, C. F., 20–21

Cadbury, H. J., 60, 91, 120
Caird, G. B., 117, 190
Carmignac, J., 132
Catchpole, D. R., 156
Chadwick, H., 7
Clark, N., 61

Clark, R. E. D., 7
Colani, T., 158
Cranfield, C. E. B., 240
Crossan, J. D., 3–4, 188, 198, 204, 222
Cullmann, O., 41, 46

Dalman, G., 114, 158, 201, 252
Davies, W. D., 193, 209, 210, 231, 233
de Boer, M. C., 233
Delling, G., 59
Denney, J., 60–62
Derrett, J. D. M., 236, 238–39, 241–42, 250
Dibelius, M., 9, 11, 128, 251
Dodd, C. H., 11, 12–14, 27–28, 79–80, 106, 110–11, 113, 137, 179, 194, 211, 221, 246–47, 251
Donfried, K. P., 46
Drury, J., 176
Dupont, J., 121–22, 124

Ellis, E., 206
Essame, W. G., 201–2
Every, G., 41

Fitzmyer, J. A., 120, 149, 189, 193, 222, 223, 230, 236–39
Flew, R. N., 163–64
Flusser, D., 133, 173, 199
Foerster, W., 131
Ford, D., 152
Freedman, H., 142
Fuller, R. H., 31, 94
Funk, R., 229

Gerhardsson, R., 19–20
Gingrich, F. W., 85
Glasson, T. F., 158
Gloege, G., 166
Gnilka, J., 139–40
Gressmann, H., 215, 255
Grobel, K., 215
Guardini, R., 203
Guelich, R. A., 111
Guelich, R. E., 43, 85, 113, 178, 206
Guillaumont, A., 221

Haldane, J. B. S., 7
Harnack, A., 163
Hauck, F., 193
Hengel, M., 133
Hermaniuk, M., 174
Hesse, M., 68
Hill, D., 193, 213
Hobbes, T., 113–14
Hooker, M., 145
Hoskyns, E., 56–57
Hume, D., 67, 69–70
Hunzinger, C. H., 198
Huxley, J., 7

Jeremias, J., 23, 43, 88, 128, 130–31, 133–34, 140, 145, 158, 178–80, 185, 189, 192, 198, 201, 202, 204, 212, 216–18, 222, 231, 237, 245–47, 251, 252, 255, 258
Jülicher, A., 176, 179, 221

Kahle, P., 208
Kähler, M., 11
Käsemann, E., 2, 87
Koester, H., 3
Kuhn, K. G., 21, 126
Kümmel, W. G., 179, 247
Künneth, W., 35–36

Lake, K., 60, 77, 91
Lake, S., 77
Lampe, G. W. H., 41
Léon-Dufour, X., 144
Linnemann, E., 183, 188
Locke, J., 69
Lohmeyer, E., 112, 179, 209
Lowe, A. M., 223
Lütgert, W., 200

M'Neile, A. H., 231
Mack, B. L., 3–4
Manson, T. W., 89, 107, 133, 136, 190, 191, 215, 225, 226, 233, 237, 256
Marshall, I. H., 54, 132, 149, 160, 207, 222, 237, 243
Martin, H., 168
Martin, R. P., 32
Marxsen, W., 25

Meier, J. P., 3–5
Meinertz, M., 246–47
Menzies, A., 56
Merezhkovsky, D., 49
Michaelis, W., 213
Michel, O., 160
Moltmann, J., 57–58
Montefiore, H., 98, 222
Muddiman, J. B., 181
Muller, K. H., 158

Newton, I., 67

Otto, R., 120, 146, 195

Pannenberg, W., 61
Patte, D., 211, 234
Percy, E., 92
Perrin, N., 25
Pesch, R., 14
Polag, A., 253
Powell, M. A., 231
Preiss, T., 253–54

Quell, G., 190

Rawlinson, A. E. J., 52
Rengstorf, K. H., 159
Reumann, J., 46
Richardson, A., 71
Riesenfeld, H., 19–20
Roberts, C. H., 120
Robinson, J. H., 2
Robinson, J. A. T., 36, 158
Robinson, J. M., 178
Rohde, J., 25–26
Rowley, H. H., 158
Rustow, A., 120

Sanday, W., 42
Sandmel, S., 230
Schillebeeckx, E., 134
Schlatter, A., 47, 88, 146, 178,
   191–92, 251, 252, 258
Schmauch, W., 209
Schmidt, H., 208
Schnackenburg, R., 206–7, 216

Schniewind, J., 123, 175, 203,
   212–13
Schonfield, H., 90–91
Schürmann, H., 144, 145
Schwartzbaum, n.i., 169
Schweitzer, A., 2, 137
Schweizer, E., 199, 201, 225,
   233–34, 261
Scofield, C. I., 199
Sherwin-White, A. N., 156
Simon, M., 142
Smith, B. T. D., 234
Smith, C. W. F., 199
Spurgeon, C. H., 199
Stern, D., 223
Strack, H. L., 119, 180, 185, 220,
   228, 252, 255
Stuhlmann, R., 196

Talbert, C. H., 195
Taylor, V., 22, 149
Telford, W. R., 77
Thielicke, H., 189, 203
Thoma, C., 172, 223
Traub, H., 130
Trench, R. C., 209
Trilling, W., 46, 158
Turner, H. E. W., 222

van der Loos, H., 85
Vermes, G., 133, 158
Via, D., 173, 239, 250–51

Weiser, A., 250–53
Wellhausen, J., 179, 226–27
Westermann, C., 117, 176
White, K. W., 202
Wilder, A. N., 174, 195
Wimber, J., 95
Wright, G. E., 31

Young, B. H., 169, 170, 173, 184,
   200

Zeller, D., 87
Zmijewski, J., 149, 159

Index of Ancient Sources

Old Testament

Genesis
1:2   94
1:3   94
1:6   94
1:28   43
2:4   37
2:19–20   43
4   230
4:23–24   230
4:24   231
5:1   37
10   89
12:1–3   37, 111
14:18   116
22   41, 49, 139
22:2   41, 220
22:12   41, 220
25:22   100
38:6–26   38
42:17   142

Exodus
4:22–23   132
8:19   178
9:18   153
10:14   153
12:2   172
12:15   199
12:19   199
12:46   51
13:3   199
13:7   199
16:15–18   96
16:31–36   96
19   49
19:4–6   135
24   49
24:8   53, 146
28:41   53
34   49

Leviticus
16:29–31   179
19:13–18   227
19:18   225–27
19:33–34   227
20:10   227
25   80, 196
25:11f.   196

Numbers
9:12   51

23–24   171, 254
23:23   124

Deuteronomy
6:5   44, 225–27
13   73–74
13:1–6   224
15:1–2   227–28
15:19   53
15:21   53
18:15   111, 134
18:18   134
23:3   38
28:37   169

Joshua
2   38
6:5   196
7:19   101

Judges
9:8–15   170
14:14   169

Ruth
3:1–14   38

2 Samuel
1:1–7   170
2   134
7   134
7:12   37
7:14   132
11:3   38
12:25   38

1 Kings
1:5–40   38
9:7   169
18:20ff.   49
19:8ff.   49

2 Kings
3:23   227
14:9   170

1 Chronicles
29:11   126

2 Chronicles
24:21   140

Job
9:8   96
19:26–27   123
24:24   196

Psalms
2   41, 51, 111, 134
2:7   41, 46, 132
7   139
8   111
22   51, 56–57   139
24:4   123
26   139
34:19   51, 139
37   123, 124
37:11   123, 124
41:10   51
42:6   55
43:6   51
44:14   169
45   247
56   139
57   139
58:4   100
59   139
69   51, 57, 139
77:16–19   96
93:3–4   94–95
104:12   198
106   95

106:9   95
110   111
110:1   51, 156
118   220
118:22   138, 222
118:22–23   219
118:25–26   51
118:26   98

Proverbs
13:12   168
24:26   168
25:26   168
26:3   168

Isaiah
2   129
4   129
5   219, 222
5:1–2   171
5:3–7   171
5:7   219
6:9–13   140
7:14   36
8:16   159
9   134
11   129, 134
11:1ff.   36
11:6–9   43
13:10   153
20   171
22:15–25   47
23   76
25   182
25:6–8   123
25:6–9   81, 182, 184
25:6–10   103, 180
25:8   129
26:1–15   129
27:12–13   192
32   129
34   117
34:4   153
35   117
35:5–6   10, 83, 99, 117
40:9   115
40–55   31, 58, 83,
    110, 134
40:1–11   129
40:3–5   42
42   41
42:1   41
42:1–4   36
43:3   83
43:10   96

43:13   96
43:25   96
45:15   83
45:21–22   83–84
49   134
49:3–7   89
49:5–6   37
49:24–25   81–82,
    177–78
50   134
51:17   55–56
51:19–20   56
52:7   10, 115
52:10   115
52:13–15   135, 140, 141
52:13–53:12   37, 41,
    53, 58, 140
53   134, 139, 141, 145
53:3   140
53:3–4   140
53:4–6   140
53:6   139, 140
53:7–8   140
53:7–9   140
53:8   140, 181
53:10   140, 145
53:10f.   145
53:10–11   140
53:10–12   139–41
53:11   140
53:12   40, 145
54:4–10   180
54:5   180
56:7   51, 77
58:6   121
58:7   121
60:1   172
60:19–22   101
61   80, 116–17, 124
61:1   117, 121, 123
61:1ff.   10
61:1–2   116, 121, 124
61:1–2a   116
61:1–3   115, 124
61:3   124
61:6   124
61:7–8   117
61:10   247
61:11   115
62:4–5   180
65:17–25   43

Jeremiah
1:5   53, 100
4:3   202

7:8-15 77
7:11 77, 150
18:2-3 51
24:9 169
24:22 76
26:20-24 140
31:18-20 190-91
31:31 146
31:31-34 53
39:6-15 51
47:4 76
51:33 192

Ezekiel
1:3 178
3:14 178
3:22 178
4 171
8:1 178
9-11 150
14:8 169
14:21-23 151
16 171
16:7-8 180
17 198-99
17:22-24 198-99
17:23 198
18:30-32 115
20:45-49 171
23 171
24:15-24 171
26-28 76
31 198, 199
31:6 198
33:22 178
34 171, 188
36:16-32 128, 242
36:20-22 242
36:22-23 129
36:31-32 129
37:1 178
40:1 178

Daniel
2 174
2:34-35 220
2:44-45 220
2:44-47 174
4 198-99
4:10-12 198
4:17 198
4:25-26 114
7 110, 134, 157, 158
7:13 51, 143, 157,
    158, 256

7:13f. 143
7:13-14 156
7:21-22 158
9 153
9:26-27 152
9:27 152
11:31 152
12:1 151, 153
12:2-3 141
12:6-7 151
12:11 152

Hosea
1-3 171
2:19 180
6 142
6:1-2 142
6:6 256
1:10 123
6:11 192
10:11-12 202

Joel
2:16 181
2:10 153
2:28-32 8, 13
3:13 192
4:15-16 153

Amos
9:1 150
9:5 153

Micah
1:4 153
3:12 150
6:8 255

Nahum
1:5 153

Habakkuk
3:6-11 153

Zechariah
8:19 179, 180
8:20 181
9:9 51
11:12-13 51
12:10 52
13:7 51
14:5-7 101

Malachi
4:5-6 50

APOCRYPHA

Sirach
4:10 133
35:12-15 243
35:17-18 243

1 Maccabees
1:54 152

2 Maccabees
7:37-38 141

Wisdom of Solomon
2:10-5:23 141
2:28 133

NEW TESTAMENT

Matthew
1-2 35
1:18 36
3:8-12 40
3:12 74, 210
4:23 111
4:23-25 80
5 121, 256
5:3 122-23
5:4 122
5:5 122-23
5:6 123, 124-25
5-7 23, 80, 107
5:7 123
5:9 123
5:10 124
5:15-16 22
5:17 109, 110, 173
5:20 111
5:21-28 234
5:21-48 23
5:23-24 132
5:48 256
6:1-18 125-32
6:12 233
6:14-15 132, 234, 235
6:25-34 132
6:33 127
7:1-2 22
7:9-11 135, 187
7:15 210
7:25 22
7:29 22
8-9 80

8:5ff. 86–87
8:11f 87
8:11–12 224
8:12 184, 212
8:13 87, 88
9:1–6 90
9:2–8 235
9:13 256
9:15 179–82
9:37–38 89, 193
10 90
10:5–6 88
10:7–8 89–90
10:12 89
10:13 89
10:15 89
10:17–20 151
10:37 159–60
10:40 164
11:2–3 74, 210
11:4–6 75
11:5 10, 117, 205
11:5–6 72, 257
11:12 12, 205
11:12–13 118, 194,
    257
11:16–19 257
11:20–24 76, 78
11:25 126
11:25–26 164
11:27 135, 164
11:28–30 162, 164
11:29 177–79
12:7 256
12:11f. 187
12:15 160
12:28 72, 82, 92, 113,
    178, 205, 257
13 22
13:1–9 200–207
13:17 72
13:18 201
13:18–23 200
13:19 202
13:24–30 207–13
13:25 210
13:31–33 197–200
13:36 212
13:36–43 207–13
13:37–39 212
13:38 212
13:39 208, 212
13:42 184
13:43 212
13:44–46 184–86
15:15 212

15:23 88
15:24 88, 205
16:15 209
16:17–19 46, 163, 164
16:18 47, 163
16:19 46, 47
16:19b 46
16:21 48
17:9 49
18 236, 238
18:12–13 187
18:12–14 136
18:15–17 162–63
18:15–20 209
18:18 46, 47
18:23 233
18:23–35 132, 136,
    230–35, 253
18:24 231
18:35 234
19:28 146, 224, 254
19:29 146
20:2 231
21:1–9 51
21:33–46 219–25
21:35 220
21:35–36 182
21:36 220
21:43 220, 224
22:1–14 182–84
22:5–6 182
22:10–11 232
22:11–14 183
22:13 184
22:13f. 149
23 191
23:4 110, 162
23:13 47
23:23 255
23:36 154
23:37f. 205
23:37–39 140
23:39 175
24 147, 149, 246
24:3 212
24:27 148
24:28 149
24:31 50
24:37 148
24:37–39 218
24:39 148
24:40 149
24:42–44 155, 247
24:45–51 155, 247
24:51 184
25 155, 246, 256

25:1–13 244–48
25:14–30 155, 248–53
25:19 252
25:30 149, 184
25:31–33 253
25:31–46 248,
    253–59
25:35–36 256
25:40 256
25:42–43 256
26:42 126
26:53 55
26:64 157–58
27:3–10 51
28:11–15 61
28:18 65
28:19 164

Mark
1:4 40
1:10 40–41
1:11 41, 220
1:12–13 178
1:14 115
1:14–15 80, 112–13
1:15 10, 19, 80, 113,
    121, 240
1:16–20 80
1:21–45 16–17, 80
1:22 94
1:27 94
1:27–28 73, 205
2:1–12 17–18, 75
2:1–3:5 204
2:1–3:6 179
2:5–12 131
2:7–12 40
2:10 257
2:13–17 186
2:17 84–85
2:18f. 205
2:18–22 179
2:19 179, 247
2:19–20 179–82
2:19a 179
2:19b 179
2:20 179
2:27 257
2:28 257
3:6 74, 165, 204, 224
3:14 164
3:20f. 204
3:22 73
3:22ff. 204
3:22–30 191

3:23   177
3:27   43, 81, 93,
    177–79, 205
3:31ff.   204
4:1–9   200–207
4:4   202
4:5   202
4:7   202
4:8   202, 204
4:9   222
4:11   174
4:11–12   164, 174–75
4:13–20   200–207, 212
4:14   202, 206
4:15–20   206
4:21–25   22
4:26–29   195–97
4:30–32   197–200
4:35–41   93
4:39   95
5:34   84
6:6–13   89
6:7–13   164
6:20   96
6:22ff.   204
6:22–33   95
6:30–44   93
6:31–44   44
6:45   95
6:45–46   98
6:48   95
6:52   82
7:5–9   73
7:5–13   110
7:24–30   88, 225
7:31–37   83
8:11   78
8:11–12   44
8:12   78
8:14–21   82
8:22–26   82
8:27ff.   14
8:27–33   44
8:30   46
8:31   48, 135, 138,
    204, 257
8:34   48, 136, 160
8:34ff.   204
8:38   133, 134
9:1   50
9:2–8   48–51
9:7   220
9:14–29   91
9:23   164
9:30–32   138

9:31   48, 135, 138,
    139, 257
9:37   205
9:49–50   22
10:13–14   22
10:14   122
10:15   122
10:17   225
10:17–31   102–3
10:27   164
10:29–30   165
10:32   48, 138
10:32ff.   138
10:42–45   136
10:45   56, 135,
    143–45, 258
10:46–52   100
11:11   51
11:12–14   77, 93
11:15–19   51
11:17   77
11:23–24   164
11:25   133, 135
11:27ff.   222
11:27–33   40
12:1   219, 222
12:1–12   219–25
12:5   220
12:6   220
12:9   224
12:17   22
12:28–34   226
12:30   44
12:34   226
12:38–40   191
13   23, 147, 149–55,
    201, 210, 246
13:2   150, 152
13:3   152
13:3–4   150–52
13:4   212
13:5–6   151
13:5–23   151
13:7–8   151, 154
13:9   151
13:9–13   151
13:10   151–52, 164
13:11   151, 178
13:12–13   165
13:14   153
13:14–20   151, 152
13:15f.   148
13:15–16   153
13:17   153
13:17–18   148
13:18   153

13:19   151, 153
13:20   153
13:21   120
13:21–23   151
13:24–27   153, 154
13:26   50
13:28–29   119, 154
13:28–37   154
13:30   50, 154
13:30–32   154
13:32   4, 42, 133, 135,
    155
13:33–37   155
13:34–36   155
14:10   139
14:17–21   51
14:22   53–54, 146
14:22–24   257
14:24   53, 146
14:25   145, 146
14:26–31   51
14:32–42   51
14:33   55
14:34   55
14:36   55, 126, 133
14:41   139
14:43–52   51
14:49   51
14:53–72   51
14:55–64   155
14:58   47
14:62   51, 135,
    155–58, 257
15:1   139
15:4–5   78
15:15   139
15:21   100
15:24   63
15:32   44
15:34   56
15:37   58
15:38   89
15:39   58

Luke
1–2   35
1:1–4   24
1:35   36
2:8–20   39
2:25   244
2:49–50   134
3:22–37   38
4:14–15   80
4:16–21   80, 179
4:21   10

4:23-30   204
4:31ff.   80
5:27-32   186
5:29   187
5:34-35   179-82
6:17   160
6:20-23   121
6:20-49   108
6:36   256
7:10   88
7:21   99
7:28   212
8:4-8   200-207
8:11   202
8:11-15   200-207
9:2   89
9:2-3   89
9:28-29   49
10:1   89
10:2   193
10:2-3   89
10:6   89
10:7   89
10:12   89
10:17-20   89, 205
10:19   164
10:25-37   225-30
11:1-4   125-32
11:2   135
11:2-4   21
11:4   233
11:5-8   187, 241
11:13   40
11:20   32, 92, 94, 117,
   178
11:22   177-79
11:32   9
11:50-51   154
12:8   157
12:8f.   244
12:8-9   157, 164, 257
12:11-12   151, 164,
   178
12:31   127
12:32   164
12:35-38   155
12:35-46   246
12:49f.   257
13:1-5   150, 240
13:6-9   93, 240
13:18-21   197-200
13:22-27   87
13:22-30   240
13:28-29   87, 224
13:31-33   142
13:33   140

13:34-35   150, 240
14:14-24   182-84
14:17   182
14:23   183
14:24   183
14:26   160
15   22, 188, 239
15:1-2   186-87
15:1-3   239
15:1-32   186-92
15:3   187
15:3-7   85, 171
15:8-10   85
15:10   187
15:24   189
15:25-32   85
15:31   181
15:32   189
15:32a   192
16   213
16:1   239
16:1-8   213, 235-40
16:1-9   253
16:3   237
16:4   237, 240
16:5   237
16:8   237
16:9   237, 239
16:10-15   239
16:13   213, 237
16:14-15   239
16:16   118, 194
16:16-18   22
16:19-31   188, 213-19
16:22-23   214
16:23   216
16:25   214
16:27   218
16:27-28   217
16:28   218
16:30   218
17:7-10   187
17:20   119
17:20-21   120, 205,
   257
17:20-37   212
17:21   120
17:21a   120
17:22   148
17:22-37   120,
   147-49, 240
17:23   148
17:24   147, 148
17:25   148
17:26   147
17:26-27   246

17:26-30   148
17:30   147
17:31   148
17:32   148
17:33   148
17:34   149
17:35   149
17:37   149
18:1-8   240-44
18:2-5   241
18:3   241
18:4-5   241
18:6-8a   241
18:7   243
18:8   244
18:8b   241
18:12   180
18:18   225
19:11   48, 252
19:11-27   248-53
19:12   252
19:12-27   155
19:16   250
19:18   250
19:20   250
19:28-38   51
19:37   160
19:41-44   240
19:44   150
20:9-19   219-25
20:18   220
20:49-51   140
21   149
21:7   212
21:15   178
21:36   244
22:15-18   123, 145
22:15-20   257
22:19-20   53, 145
22:20   164
22:27   144
22:28   44
22:28-30   123
22:29   146, 164
22:29-30   146, 257
22:30b   224
22:31-34   46
22:43-44   55
22:69   157-59
23:8-9   78
23:27-31   240
23:28-31   150
23:42-43   217
23:53   136
24:26   148
24:27   219

24:44   148
24:44–45   219
24:46–47   164, 219

John
1:1–18   33
1:29   51
1:33   41
1:51   80
2–12   27
2:1–11   81, 93
2:25   168
3:14–16   135
3:17   102
3:19–21   211
3:29   163
4:35–38   193, 195
4:37–38   194
4:50   104
4:50–53   88
5:17   104
5:19–20   94
5:21   64
5:21–22   104, 105
5:24   64
5:25–26   105
5:25–27   135
5:31–40   194
5:36   71
6   97
6:14–15   97, 98
6:15   44
6:50   97
6:51   104–5
6:60   160
7:5   60
7:49   186
8:46   40
9   100–102
9:39   102
10   171, 188
10:9–10   163
10:11   188
10:11–16   163
10:16   255
11   74, 216
11:25   64
11:25–26   105
11:49–53   74
11:53   224
12:27   55
12:31–32   58, 63, 93, 136
13–14   28
13–17   28

13–21   27–28
13:31–32   50
13:34   259
13:34–35   65
13:36   48
14:10–11   94
14:11   71
14:19   66, 105
14:26   28–29
14:31   28
15–16   28
15–17   28
15:1–10   163
16:16–22   181–82
17   52
17:19   52, 53
17:20–23   130, 163
17:21   65
17:21–23   65
18:1   28
18:15   27
18:28   54
19:9   78
19:11   55
19:14   54
19:29   56–57
19:30   58, 146–47
19:31–37   51, 54
20:21   65, 163, 164
20:23   46
20:28   79
20:30–31   29, 71, 79
20:31   29
21:15–17   46
21:24   26–27

Acts
1–5   59
1:7   155
2:17ff.   13
2:22   71
2:22–24   79
2:23   52
2:23–24   8, 218
2:33   64
2:36   8, 218
3–4   15
3:15   59
4:2   218
4:25–30   51
4:32–35   59
4:33   59
5:28   218
6:11   178
10   14

10:36–43   13
10:38   91, 94
12:10   196
12:25   23

Romans
1:4   72
2:6–16   258
4:25   139
5:12–21   45
6:4   64–65
6:17   19
8:1–2   64
8:4   64
8:14–17   124
8:23–24   124
8:32   139, 220
9–11   165
11:25–29   175
14:9   65

1 Corinthians
1:18   8, 262
1:18–25   9
1:21   8
1:30   262
10:13   132
11:24   53
11:26   104
15   59
15:3–4   13, 60, 137
15:5–8   61
15:7   60
15:12   59
15:12–19   63–64
15:22–26   66
15:24   212
15:44–45   62

2 Corinthians
3:18   50
5:6–8   217
5:10   258
5:14–15   105
5:16   33
5:17   62, 64, 147, 218
5:18f.   58

Galatians
1:18   13
5:6   258
2:11   47
2:14   47

Ephesians
1:14   13
4:18   99
5:14   99
6:12   43

Philippians
1:21–23   217
2:6–11   32
2:9–11   218
3:10   162

Colossians
1:13–14   137
1:15–20   33

1 Thessalonians
4:1–8   19
4:14–17   153
4:15–17   50

2 Thessalonians
3:6   19

1 Timothy
2:5–6   144
2:6   145
3:16   218

2 Timothy
1:10   66
2:1–2   9

Hebrews
2:10   59
2:18   45
9:27–28   217

James
1:1   107
2:2–4   108
2:8   258
2:13   257
4:1–4   108
5:1–6   108
5:8–9   154

1 Peter
1:8   162
1:19–20   52
3:18–22   217
4:6   217
5:13   23

2 Peter
1:16–19   50

Revelation
3:20   162
11:3–12   50
12:10   114
13:8   52
21:9–22:5   147
22:3–5   123

PSEUDEPIGRAPHA

Apocalypse of Elijah
4:27–29   141

1 Enoch
18:11–12   217
22:9   216
22:11   216
62   254
62:22–23   254

Jubilees
11:11   201–2

4 Maccabees
6:28–29   141
6:29   145
13:17   217

Testament of Dan
5:3   226

Testament of Issachar
5:2   226
7:6   226

DEAD SEA SCROLLS

1QS
2:11f.   116
9:10–11   116

1Qsa
2:11ff.   132

4QFlor
1:6–7   132

MISHNAH, TALMUD,
AND RABBINIC
LITERATURE

Baba Qamma
826   190

b. Šabbat
73b   201

b. Sanhedrin
10:3   76
43a   74

m. Niddah
5:2   198

t. Berahot
5.8   216

y. Ḥagigah
2.77d   215–16

ʾAbot de Rabbi Nathan
36   76

Genesis Rabbah
6.3   172

Mekilta
Exod 21:14   227

Midrash Esther
3   220
6 (94b)   220

Midrash Psalm 118
19–20   255

Midrash Rabbah
Genesis 22:4   142
Genesis 42:18   142
Exodus 19:16   142
Joshua 2:16   142
Jonah 2:1   142
Ezra 8:32   142
Hosea 6:2   142
Esther 5:1   142

Pesiqta de Rab Kahana
5.14   172

Pesiqta Rabbati
15   172
149a   247

Sipre Deuteronomy
§112 228

Song of Songs Rabbah
4.12 185

Targum on the
    Wedding Psalm
45:3 246

Yalquṭ Berešit
8 172

Yalquṭ Jesaia
500 172

JOSEPHUS

Antiquities of the Jews
17.299–320 249
17.342 249

Jewish War
2.80–100 249

CHURCH FATHERS

Justin
Dialogue with Trypho
108.2 61

Origen
Contra Celsum
6.34 6–7

OTHER ANCIENT
    WRITINGS

*Egyptian Book of the
    Dead*
ch. 125 255

Gospel of Thomas
21 195
65–66 221–22
76 184
109 184